Wing Wind

The Legacies of Arnan: Book Two

Paige L. Christie

Awen Publishing

Wing Wind originally published April 16, 2018 by Prospective Press; Revised edition published October, 2018 by Prospective Press; Third Edition published by Awen Publishing Company 2024

Publisher's Note

Book Cover by Craig Priestley

First Awen Publishing Company edition 2024

For my brother – Brett L. Christie

Praise for Wing Wind

"Two fast friends, welded by choice and fate to an incompatible dynamic — and a love that will try the depth and scope of their human destinies as never before. A powerful second book for a brand new series."

~ Janny Wurts, author of the *Wars of Light and Shadow* series

"Christie's second novel hums with tension, as Leiel and Cleod rush headlong towards their opposing destinies with heartbreaking inevitability. Christie's intense characterisation and masterful use of atmosphere make Wing Wind a joy to devour. Themes of storytelling and sisterhood are further developed, as are the violent consequences of a rigid gender divide. All serving to highlight, of course, Wing Wind's moments of peace and reflection, which are delivered with hope for a future that may not yet be lost. A truly superb sequel to Draigon Weather."

~ Lucy Holland, author of *Sistersong* and *Song of the Huntress*

Praise for Long Light

"A superbly crafted sequel, Long Light sets the stage on fire for the finale of Paige L. Christie's series — a story that engages and upends the very fabric of myth and stereotype."

~ Janny Wurts, author of the *Wars of Light and Shadow* series

Praise for Storm Forge

*"**Storm Forge** is the last book in the four-book series, Legacies of Arnan, by u/PaigeLChristie. It delivers from start to finish, weaving all of the threads from the first three books into a perfect conclusion while simultaneously elevating the earlier books into something more than they already were with new layers and hidden context."*

~ u/sparkour r/Fantasy

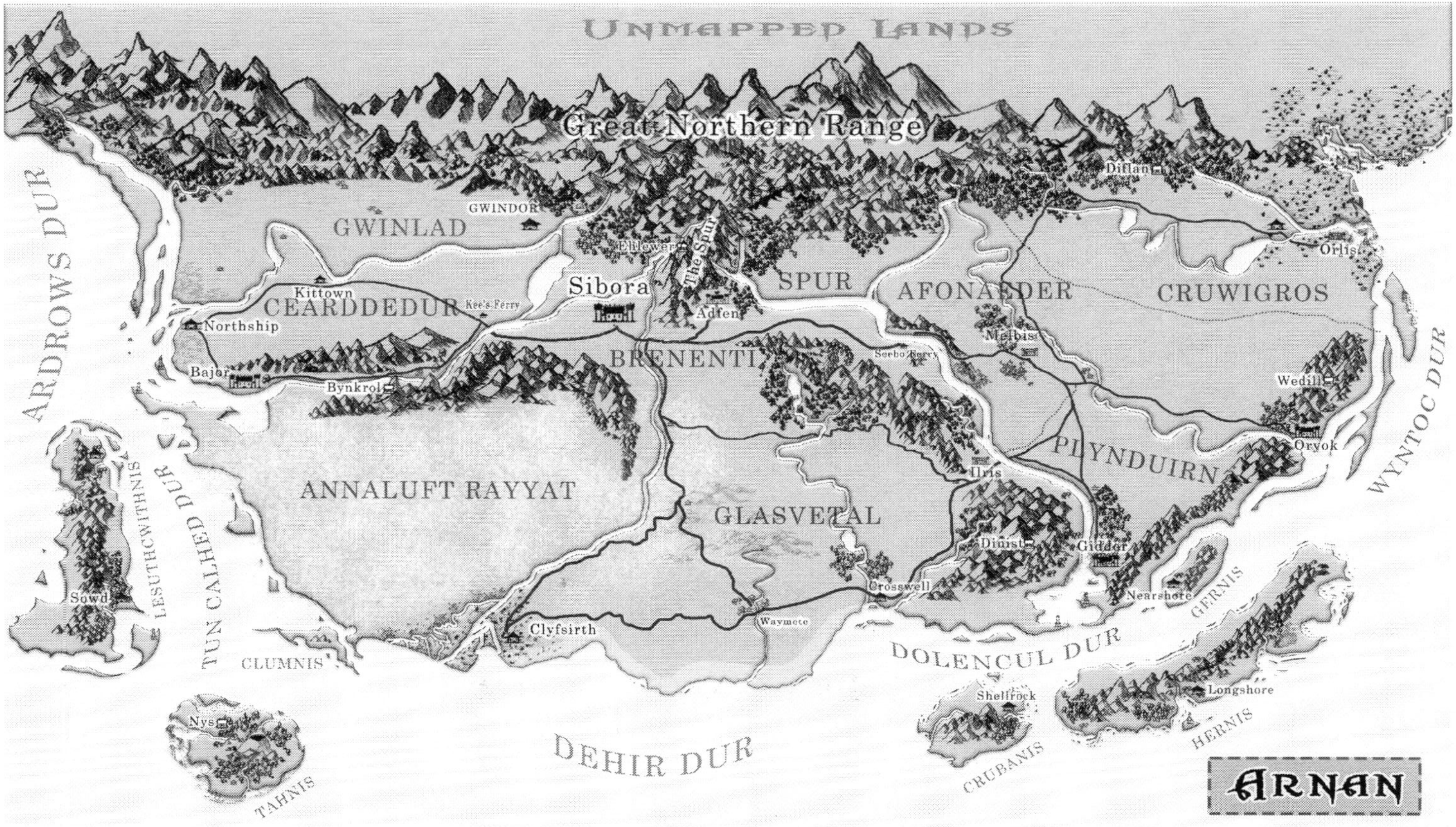

Unmapped Lands
Great Northern Range
Diflan
Orlis
GWINDOR
GWINLAD
Ellewer
The Spur
SPUR
AFONAEDER
CRUWIGROS
Kittown
Sibora
CEARDDEDUR
Kee's Ferry
Adfen
Northship
Melbis
Bajor
BRENENTI
Seebo Ferry
Bynkrol
Wedill
Oryok
PLYNDUIRN
Ilris
ANNALUFT RAYYAT
GLASVETAL
Dinist
Gidder
Crosswell
Nearshore
GERNIS
Sowd
LESUTHCWITHNIS
TUN CALHED DUR
Clyfsirth
Waymete
DOLENCUL DUR
CLUMNIS
Shellrock
Longshore
Nys
DEHIR DUR
CRUBANIS
HERNIS
TAHNIS
ARDROWS DUR
WYNTOC DUR
ARNAN

Only when they spread their wings
are they wakers of a wind.
~ Rainer Maria Rilke

CHAPTER 1

Cleod – 38 years - 1195

Her stare pierced him.

Crouched in a heat-packed circle of bare earth still smoldering from the fires he and Trayor had set to clear it, Cleod draped a forearm over his knees and looked away, staring over the plains toward the setting sun. When he had killed Eirar, the Sacrifice had been frantic with terror. At the Sacrifice on the Spur, Leiel had been eerily calm on the way up the mountain. But today, this woman watched him, stone-eyed. Something about her pressed at his senses. Her gaze encompassed nothing of the landscape, only him—as though she had measured everything about him, and found too much wanting.

Behind him, the scrape of boot leather over earth signaled motion. Cleod glanced over his shoulder at Trayor's stiff-legged approach.

The Draighil stopped, hands on hips. "Nothing. Where is the beast, you Draigon-damned, cefreid traitor?"

Cleod frowned. Should he be bothered by those words? He was all of those things... He shook his head, returned his attention to the horizon. Through the long, sweltering day, the skies had remained clear of any dark silhouette that would mark the arrival of the beast they were here to kill. He imagined the frantic whispers back in Melbis, fear streaming off the Council along with sweat. Had there ever been a day like this in the history of the Sacrifices? A day a Draigon refused to meet the Draighil in battle and claim its prize?

Old knowledge, long relegated to the back of Cleod's mind, circled and flitted behind his eyes: the records of great battles of old, losses and defeats, the histories of the Enclaves. Recalling those, this wait, or perhaps flat refusal, to join in battle, was unprecedented.

When Shaa had come for Leiel, it had been only moments from the time the key turned in her manacles to the time the monster had swept over the Spur. So fast then. Not so this day. Why the delay?

For an instant Cleod's senses shifted, filled with the scent of smoldering leaves and rush of wind over the ridge top, then the shivering dry heat of the plains, dust, and blowing husks of broken grain returned. And still no Draigon.

Trayor swore. Something bumped Cleod's shoulder and he glanced over to see a canteen held in Trayor's gloved hand. "I can't have you falling over."

Another memory stirred—iced water on a Tower balcony. Cleod grinned and took the canteen, even as old laughter echoed through his ears and flipped his stomach. He raised the flagon to his lips and drank. The water was hot, and he smiled. Even being Draighil had only so many advantages. A chill rolled through him with thought of the title. Old. Coveted. New again...

The woman shifted and the chains, trailing from her wrists to the thick post embedded in the earth behind her, clanked. He looked at her. She must be thirsty and afraid. But she asked nothing of them, just sat with her back to the post and watched in silence.

Cleod got to his feet and walked toward her. She met his gaze in the dying light. The long slant of the sun's rays coated her in gold, a prize out of legend. She was purely of Arnan, dark where the Farlan were pale. Her gaze was determined and resigned, and her presence pushed at his mind—tangled and tested his thoughts. In the dimming light, he might have mistaken her for Leiel.

For a moment the horizon tilted before him, spun into color and light, then the weight of the sword on his back settled him, righting the world. Familiar and strange at once, the pressure of the harness across his shoulders was eased by the patched fireleather he wore. Earthy and spiced and drenched in the acidic sweetness of cuila, the Draighil uniform was sweat slick inside, and the long day of waiting had marked his body with heat rash. The once familiar uniform molded every muscle under its weight, focused his awareness as it had so many years ago. Along his hips, the scars ached—scars left by the monster he was here to kill at last.

Cleod smiled at the woman. "Teska Healer," he said. "Would you like water?"

She sat a moment, then pushed to her feet. "Yes." The first word she had spoken all day, despite heat and wind and blazing sun. Her voice was marked by her light Melbin accent, nothing like Leiel's firm, northern tones.

He stepped closer and offered her the canteen. She took it with both hands. Her eyes never left his face as she raised it and drank, the chains rattling with the action. Lowering the container, she wiped the back of a dusty wrist across her mouth.

"Two Draighil," she said, her voice soft. "That's never been the way."

"He's no Draighil." Trayor lifted his voice so it carried loud in the small distance between them.

The woman paid no attention but asked Cleod, "How many times have the two of you done this?"

"Never," Trayor said as he stepped up beside Cleod.

She gave a tug of her wrist, turned away as far as the bindings allowed, and looked over her shoulder at the two of them. "Because the Draigon is Shaa," she said.

Cleod's scalp tightened against his skull.

"Because I can," Trayor said and laughed a little, the arrogance of it so familiar to Cleod's ears. As it had a lifetime ago, the sound both grated and amused.

Cleod looked at Trayor, and then up again to the sky. Not a cloud. Not a sign.

Shaa. Late, this time. Waiting. Making him wait. But the beast would come. It would fill the sky and burn the air and shake the earth until standing and breathing were both near impossibilities. It would bring heat and fury—and it would not be surprised to find two men waiting.

The beast—he frowned, knowledge churning his gut—was not a beast. A shiver crossed his shoulders, and for a moment his vision swam. He inhaled, counted the beat of his pulse in his neck as he held the breath. He let it out and smiled. A challenge. The best kind—of skill and will and a determination that he had nearly forgotten how to call up.

The woman turned back to him and offered the canteen. He took it, and their eyes met again. The same. The same as Leiel's—torn and sad. And pitying. *Books and stories. The feel of a fresh shirt on his bare skin. Leather—supple and shielding.*

The feel of a sword in his grasp—! His belly turned molten and heat streaked up his spine, burst at the base of his skull, and flared through his mind. For a moment, he claimed awareness of every hair on his scalp as the fever seared over his head. His cheeks burned.

He stepped back, ran his fingers back through his hair. The length was wrong, too long for any Draighil. He pressed his eyes closed. What was he doing here? No. No. He could not allow doubt in. He shook himself. He was where he needed to be. Shaa. At last, Shaa.

Let the beast come.

This time no quarter would be asked or given. The air wavered and the woman's face tipped, shifted, and for an instant, the echo of Leiel rang even deeper. Decades crumbled beneath his feet, the rich soil of the Melbin prairie darkened, solidified, until the mineral smell of granite flooded his sinuses. Pressed through his entire body, the memory of the Spur threatened again for a heartbeat moment—

"Cleod!" The voice yanked his mind through the tumbled recollection and into the now-copper-light of the grasslands' dying day. Cleod drew himself straight as he turned. The action hid the shudder his body gave as he settled back into the moment, but his stomach churned and the skin on his shoulders crawled.

Trayor's smile creased his face, stiff, as though it had been forced into place. "She's of no importance." He glared upward. "Where is the beast?"

Cleod frowned. Yes, she is... The thought drifted into the smoke as he followed Trayor's glance toward the sky. "Shaa knows we're here."

"There's been a Draighil at every Sacrifice for the last twenty years. Of course he knows."

"About us both," Cleod said.

Trayor's smile broke at the edges. "How?"

Cleod looked over Trayor's shoulder at the woman crouched in chains by the post. She stared at her hands, a small frown bunched over her brow. Her face seemed to shift and reform in the dying light. He blinked the aberration away.

Behind her, the sky was purple-blue, bright, and empty, and the hills rolled away toward the distant horizon. The rooftops of Melbis were just visible in the deepening shadows and early stars salted the horizon as pinpricks of light. Cleod shook his head, instinct at war with truth. Leiel. "Open prairie," he said. "We didn't get here without being seen." Why did he not just speak what he knew?

Trayor looked up, back to Cleod. "There's been no sign of the beast. How could it see us?"

A glance at Teska, backed by a chill. "Witches," Cleod said. He smiled. "The Council said a witch came. You think she was not still in the city?" That was a better truth. A fierce truth, but made of sense and reality, and not at all of the worst of all possibilities. A truth he could face and conquer. A truth of corruption he might someday be able to correct. Old gods! If he could kill Shaa!

In the very depths of his belly, a half-contained hunger uncoiled. He shoved it down. It pressed back. Cleod dropped his head back and fought spiraling recollection. *The sky was wrong, clear and star brilliant. It should have been grey and heavy with clouds. Smoke filled the air, but no Draigon blazed heat across the earth. A woman awaited her fate, but the sense of her was wrong, not made of sarcasm and laughter and hope. And yet—*

The sky reeled and Cleod sucked in air. The spin slowed.

"The Draigon have always had allies," Trayor said.

"Something never mentioned in our training."

Trayor grinned. "Something mentioned to no one but Elders."

Cleod looked at him a moment, then turned away, scanned the deepening indigo of the sky. Trayor had just declared himself an Elder. Of course. Soibel. Rohl. Most of them had to be dead by now. Who else would be chosen to lead but Trayor? Who else had the knowledge, and the arrogant confidence, to head the Ehlewer? "Congratulations."

Trayor laughed. "Damn fool that you are, Cleod, you could have been one of us." He shrugged, bent to toss another bundle of cuila into the nearest fire, stepped to the side as the fire crackled and plumed smoke. It washed over Cleod, flooded his lungs, and Trayor *was right*. Cleod frowned. He *was* a damn fool. He could have been so much more...

The smoke coursed into his lungs and he swayed, fought vertigo. He closed his eyes and steadied, focused. Once, he could have done so as easily as did the man beside him, taken in the cuila and all it offered, and ridden the thrill of it to place where clarity of thought and action were undisputed. So long since he had known that comfort in Gweld, of self and purpose, carried from deep in his gut without fear of the pain that must follow. He breathed deep. He could get back to that place. From *this* place, he could find a way.

Beside him, Trayor laughed again. "That's it, Cleod. Here and now."

Cleod opened his eyes. "She'll come."

Trayor went still a moment, then leaned close, his features tightening and yet blurring across Cleod's vision. "*She*?"

"Shaa," Cleod blinked and shook his head. "Shaa will come." The cuila swirled, fading all hunger, fading all but the need to finish what he had started so long ago. The sun had vanished over the edge of the earth, and the dust filtered light and air and his ability to form thoughts. "She will come."

Trayor stared, but Cleod only half registered the intensity of emotion building in the other man's eyes. Nothing mattered but the fulfilling stench of vision herb on the breeze, and the distant sound of wings riving air. Real or dreamed, it did not matter. Eventually, heat would split the sky, split the very earth and all senses, and the waiting would end. A reckoning, long overdue, rode the night wind. Death would land with the Draigon and claim its due.

Chapter 2

Leiel - 23 years - 1179

She filled the sky. She *was* the sky. And she claimed the light and the air and every sound in the world, beautiful and terrible and watery dark, with eyes as green-gold as new leaves flashing in spring sunlight. Hope and death fell on pounding wings toward the mountain top.

Leiel sobbed out a breath and rushed forward until the chains slammed her to a halt. So beautiful! So terrible! Her heart was thunder in her chest and blood rushed in her ears. Regardless of Gahree's promise, how could the creature just arrived render anything but complete destruction?

Between her and the Draigon—Cleod, straight-backed, chin down, tension in the strong lines of his legs. She called his name, but he did not turn, made no sign that he heard her as he stepped forward.

"For the love of all things, Cleod, run! I don't want to witness your death!" Her voice broke, and she sucked in air to shout again.

"You won't," he said, hard and clear over the rush of wind. The certainty in his voice set her shaking. He slid the sword from its harness and the crystal crowning its hilt flashed in the shifting light. Seconds later, the light was lost in shadow as the giant body above blocked the sun.

The black Draigon landed and the ground lurched under Leiel's feet. She went down on one knee, screaming Cleod's name, but he was gone, lost from her sight in the billowing wave of debris kicked up by the great wings. She raised a hand to protect her face, and the pulse of heat that followed the wind broke sweat across her palm.

The Draigon began to glow. The fine edges of the scales over her body brightened and went fiery red, like old coals stirred to smoldering glory. All over the ridge, the vegetation wilted and began to smoke.

Leiel stumbled back from the grassy verge into the safer shelter of the boulders to which she was chained. Smoke billowed as the trees crushed under the Draigon's feet caught fire. "Cleod please! Stand down!" Leiel shouted. It was useless. If he had not heard her words, spoken in quiet spaces, why would he be willing to hear them now that the fight lay before him? She tried to call out again, but her voice formed only an inarticulate scream as he charged and the battle engaged.

Impossible, what she was seeing. Cleod moved in a way she had never imagined a person could. Motions river-fluid and as powerful as a cracked whip, he seemed to almost be dancing with the Draigon. The creature was agile as light, but Cleod matched her, as though he knew what she would do the instant before she acted. Dazzling and refined, the speed and power of his movement shocked thought. Power surged in him, beyond the physical. It reached out and echoed over Leiel's flesh, and the rocks beneath her feet hummed. Focused and ferocious, somehow suddenly *other*, he was a whipcord note of danger plucked and left to sing in the mountain air. *This*, then, was what it meant to be Draighil—to be more than human—more than wise and strong. *This* was what it meant to be the match of any enemy.

And yet, it could not last. In his mind, he faced a monster, a deadly beast out of legend. But the ancient intelligence harbored in that ferocious body was more than he could dream to face down. He would die. And part of her would die with him.

No. That could not happen. No matter the cost, no matter how much he had changed, he was still the first person to have ever offered her peace. And hope, that vital thing she had come to value so. And she loved him. At least the boy he had been. And perhaps the man he might have become had he not remade himself in a twisted attempt to be what he thought she needed most. Her avenger. Her protector.

The Draigon took flight, and the wing wind knocked her to the ground. Leiel clung to the jagged rocks until they bit into her hands and drew blood. She glimpsed him though the dust and ash.

"Gods of old! Cleod, stop! She'll kill you. She'll *kill* you!"

The Draigon folded her wings and plummeted.

"Cleod!" Leiel shouted again, though she could not see him amidst the smoke and wind and tumbling rocks and broken trees. Then the Draigon's great wings snapped open and the whole world became shaking and fire. Sparks showered the air and Cleod screamed. It echoed off the ridge and into her skull. Leiel cried out again as her need to *do something* ripped through her.

"Gahree!" she pleaded, raising her voice with all the air in her lungs. "Gahree for the promise you made me that I have choice—please! Spare his life!"

CHAPTER 3

Leiel

She awoke expecting to find the very air on fire. But there were leaves over her head, bright with autumn tones and flickering in a crisp breeze. She remembered smoke and ash and shouting. Her own cries. The roar of wing wind over scorched flora and rocks as they exploded from heat. And a sound she had never imagined even in her most terrible dreams: Cleod screaming.

A sob half-choked her, and she sat up, coughing. No longer on top of the Spur, she was in a rich, green place, on the edge of a sloped mountain meadow with the wide limbs of trees curving over her. The change rocked her senses. Only an ocean of water could have seemed more different from the fiery chaos of the Spur. Fresh air. A gentle breeze. Bird song. But the sound that lingered in her mind was a voice filled with pain and horror. She swallowed back the bile and panic rising in her throat and cried out, "Gahree! Shaa! Is your promise kept? Where are you? Answer me!"

Her response was something beyond silence and less than words, a low harmonic tremble that thrummed through the earth and the air, and up her spine. Tears slid over her cheeks. "Have you no words for me?"

Again the rippling tremble pushed through the earth and into her body. This time she found meaning as it vibrated through her. It filled her mind the way sight and scent did, combining late into meaning and offering clarity. *Not in this form.* The knowledge coalesced inside Leiel.

No words, as you know them, can I offer you until your journey is complete.

"I must know!" The taste of ash lingered on Leiel's tongue and the smell of charred flesh in her nose. She took hold, inside her mind, of the places she felt the pulse of the Draigon's connection, drew forth the bright horror of the screams that still rocked her heart, and *pushed* the sound and the ache inside her back at the presence that informed her. No longer abstract, her emotion crashed through the aloofness of the contact.

From across the meadow came a roar. The earth shook with the beat of thunderous wings. From the far side of the meadow, where it sloped away toward the fading ridgelines of mountains rolling into the distance, a great, dark shape rose into the air. *Yes!* Came the answer as the Draigon lifted on gigantic wings. *Yes, he lives. And there is a price both he and you will pay for the keeping of that promise.*

Whatever that meant, or might mean in the future, the answer was the one Leiel sought. She folded in on herself for a moment as the breath came fully into her lungs for the first time since she had faced Cleod in the chamber in the Tower. "Old gods, thank you for that!" She looked up at the great creature as it drew near, and all the air went out of her again, this time propelled by awe.

The Draigon soared up the slope of the clearing, its wings casting pulses of shadow like the drift of passing clouds. Watery dark, the edges of the scales covering the body no longer smoldered like bright coals. The Draigon was a piece of night wending through sunbeams.

Leiel wiped at her eyes and pushed to her feet. Her legs trembled, but they held her upright. The Draigon touched down, hind legs first, leathery wings pulled back to frame the powerful arch of the spiked tail. The ground trembled with the impact, though the arrival was all care and grace.

As huge as she had looked on the Spur, here, unfringed by flame and heat, the Draigon appeared larger still—an ancient, stoic presence that created the very space it occupied. Leiel's heart twisted, thudded at the base of her throat. By all that she had imagined, was *this* what she had chosen to someday become? She tried to swallow, but her mouth was dry and she could not force the action. She stared as the wide, rectangular head snaked out on its long neck and tipped down so she could look into the green-gold eyes. Leiel stared back for a few heartbeats, at the creature, then raised her gaze and took in the full aspect of the Draigon. This was myth made flesh, but myth knew not half the truth. The span of the wings was more than double the length of the lean body. The body itself was all muscle and scale and deep-chested power. Talons as long as Leiel's leg and broad as her chest curved from the five- toed feet. A creature of earth and water and air. A creature that pulsed fire, made large by time and knowledge, containing within wisdom and hope and death. The trembling in Leiel's legs found its way into the rest of her body. Her heart jerked and she had to concentrate to stay upright. Old gods! The *presence* of the creature! It was like walking into the mold from which the notion of the soul had been created—thunderous and shuddering and engulfed in a warmth that might be the root of *anything*.

Leiel raised a hand to touch the broad face, but stopped, her fingers outstretched and shaking. Was this creature anything of Gahree? Or something else entirely?

"Are you my friend?" she said, her voice a smoke-filled whisper, the vestiges of the charred Spur air roughing her throat.

The Draigon lowered her head still more and blinked a shining eye. Again the trembling filled Leiel's spine. *I am that and more, child of dreams. As you are to me.* Only caring permeated the force that touched Leiel, a gentle embrace in her mind.

Leiel drew a breath, let it out, and tension eased from her shoulders.

"And Cleod? I heard him—I heard—" A sob choked off her words. "He was—"

He chose, Leiel. There was pain in his choice. But he lives. What he does with that life now, what he can do, is not yours to guide.

Leiel closed her eyes. He was there in her mind, the straight-backed distant warrior on the ridge, the mischief-eyed boy of the schoolyard, the caring young man hugging her by the pond. And yet he was gone. So long gone, and so far, that she could not organize her memories of him.

She shook her head and tears gathered once again. "Where are we?" She opened her eyes to meet the Draigon's. "There is no drought here. The air is cool."

We have flown into the Great North. When you are rested enough to attend the rest of the journey, we will continue. Far, far, to where the snows have already fallen, and the world is more white than green.

"You carried me here?"

You cannot yet fly on your own. The thought held laughter.

"Fly?" Leiel said. Air caught in her scoured throat and she coughed, pressed a forearm against her mouth and turned away.

I am sorry for the smoke that filled you. Your Draighil fought like few before him. I could not finish the fight as quickly as I wished and still leave him alive.

Leiel coughed again, lowered her arm and met the timeless gaze. "I'm not hurt," she said. "This discomfort is worth it—knowing that he lives."

Shaa shifted her feet, her head tipping to the side and back again.

Leiel's belly flipped. How badly was Cleod hurt? What price had he paid in his fight for her, and her demand for his survival? Her chest ached as though gripped in Draigon claws.

"Gahree—Shaa—what—?" What had she done? What had she chosen—to be among such creatures as this one before her—to someday be one herself? Was this possible? Any of it? Was she truly freed of Klem by this choice? What price had been paid for her freedom?

How much can such questions matter, when their answers are beyond changing? Leave the mountain on the mountain, child of dreams. You cannot follow this journey to its end if you hold always to where you began it.

Leiel swayed as her legs shook again. A Draigon in her mind. She sat. The Draigon pulled her head back a bit and looked at Leiel and blinked. Could such a creature look quizzical?

"Are you saying this has an end?" Leiel asked. "I was hoping this was a beginning..."

All things are always both.

Yes. Yes, she knew that. "How am I to think of you? You are not the woman I have known, and you are not the beast I was raised to dread and hate. Are you a person? Are you a creature? How am I to consider what you are?"

Again the notion of laughter, this time tinged with approval. *When you are ready, Leiel Draigfen, we will continue our journey, to the end, and to the new start you seek. There are answers to all these questions, and more, where we are going.*

"But what am I to call you?"

The Draigon blinked, once again managing to look amused. *What you have always called me.*

What was that? Leiel frowned. Gahree, she had called friend. Shaa, she had known only as monster. The creature before her was both, perhaps more...and yet... "I have called you many things, many names. You have been my hate and my fear, but also my hope." She took in the immenseness of the presence before her, tried to sort through the heaviness and shaking that had taken over her body and mind. Too much. Too much to feel, and see, and know. So small was she, in all ways, before this ancient thing.

All that you feel is real and right. All confusion and possibility grows from a thoughtful mind, seeking. All fear comes borne on the wings of doubt. Call me nothing, or anything you wish. As I am, in this form, in this time and this light, the world knows me as Shaa. Think what you will of that title and legend. To all such things there is more than what is told or even imagined.

The Draigon took a step, turned, and bent an enormous foreleg toward Leiel. *Climb aboard, Leiel of Adfen. We have far to travel, and I would have us home before the sun seeks sleep.*

Chapter 4

Leiel

Home, the Draigon said. They were going home. How could some place Leiel had never been be home? But what else did she have now, what place? Not once in all the years of their acquaintance had Leiel considered where Gahree came from, or asked anything about what lay ahead.

"What is it called, this place we are going?" Leiel could barely hear her own voice over the rush of air, and the creak and whoosh of sweeping wings.

Climbing onto the Draigon's back had been very like climbing a breathing tree. Beneath her hands, the scales, bark-rough, radiated a pulsing warmth and hinted at the incalculable heat contained within the great body. Strange, strange, to be not just close to such a creature, but riding one. And stranger still to acknowledge that the same creature had, in less overwhelming form, offered her tea on a rainy day more times than she could remember.

Flying with a Draigon was not like riding a horse; the Draigon was too immense to straddle. So Leiel knelt in the low depression at the creature's withers and wrapped her fingers over the edges of ancient scales. They were soft to the touch, not at all the sharp armor she had expected, and her grip felt solid.

So smoothly did Shaa launch herself into the air, that Leiel did not realize they had taken flight until the great wings made their first pass above and around her and blasted her with tumbling air. She bent under the pressure, shoulders hunched.

Ease your mind, daughter of wings. I will not drop you. We fly low. Look upon the world as you have never seen it and breathe deep.

She was flying. Leiel let that thought rest in her mind before she raised her head and looked out at the world. For a moment all she could see was motion—the rush and change of clouds and mountains and sky flashing through her senses with a rapidity she had never imagined possible. The wind swept over her eyes, blurring the edges of her sight. She blinked and her vision cleared, even as her mind accepted the newness of momentum and speed. Ahead of her, the long, muscular neck of the Draigon arched like an arrow through the air, tipped by a squared-nosed head sloped to cut the breeze. They were not high above the earth, but rather riding the ridgelines, the tips of the fanning wings skimming treetops and rock outcrops. Forest and broken meadow and jagged edges of stone slipped beneath them and behind, fast as water flowing in a rushing river.

Breath caught in the back of her throat, Leiel let the spectacle take her, a blur of strange landscape and color and changing light. Then they crested into a low hanging cloud, and the damp swirl of white-crystal water droplets speckled her sooty clothing. The air was chill, and all she could see was swirling grey mist. Were they climbing? Falling? Turning through the sky? No, of course not, or she would have tumbled from the Draigon's back.

She fought to right her senses, guided only by the warmth of the Draigon and the rush of wings she could no longer see through the cloud.

Golden light flared as they speared out of the clouds and broke around the edge of a rocky peak. The world fell away beneath them, and Leiel's mind tumbled with it. Where they had been skirting the tops of the trees and ridges, they now winged out over an empty space so vast she had no hope of taking it all in. Clouds flashed both above and beneath them, whirled by the powerful beat of the Draigon's wings. A cry rose up in Leiel's throat, pushed forth by her pounding heart, and when it was released into the rushing air, she was not certain whether it was joy or fear or something else entirely.

From the Draigon came a rumbling that vibrated caring over Leiel's mind, and she laughed before she knew she was doing it—large, loud laughs of pure release. So free! So wild, this ride through the sky on the back of impossibility! Old gods!

Did she ride an old god, in fact? If the stories were true, if they held a thread of the heart of old mysteries, then yes. Again she laughed, leaning into the wind. Her body trembled and tingled in the chill air.

The world rushed far, far below her, and out of the distance rose another series of peaks, snowcapped this time, wreathed in clouds and pin-pricked with the tips of sharp evergreens. The Great Northern Range.

She had never known anyone who had actually seen it. It was a series of lines on a map, jagged and uncertain, marked dark and made dangerous by the word *Draigon* etched above them. In front of her now, it held the horizon, as real and staggering as her biggest dreams. Like the creature who carried her forth.

What awaited there for her? What knowledge and change? And *who* awaited her? A knot in her belly added weight to the thrilled pounding of her heart. She formed words in her mind and with her breath, knowing there would be no confusion at the simple question.

"Will she be there?"

Yes. She would be no where else on this day. A pause, a light thrumming without formed thought. *Long has she been waiting to see you again, and her heart races even as your does.*

"You can hear Ilora's heart from here?"

Not a thrum this time, but a roll, low and pulsing, that might represent laughter. *I hear yours, wild child, and the joy of Ilora's has long been a mirror of yours.*

The thunder of Leiel's heart did not slow, but her smile faded as her thoughts bore a new gravity. She flew not only toward the strange and new, but also toward something once beloved and familiar. Ilora awaited her, the mother who had left her so long ago, abandoned her to a life of fear and loneliness, one in which her mother's memory was a constant, aching ghost.

Judge her no more than you judge me in this moment. Let her tell her story, wild child, Leiel of Adfen, woman of wind and wings. Let her hear yours. Only then can all that you are feeling, and might feel, be measured and carried forward.

Rocked by the fierce pumping of shining, leatheren wings and borne through the sky in the face of unsurpassed splendor, Leiel took in the message. Could she do that? Listen? Forgive? So much ahead was change and learning. Many stories and many tears. She could only, in this moment, accept what was offered and what lay ahead. She willed down the tightness in her chest and let herself simply feel the moment.

"Fly!" she called as the legendary landscape ahead drew closer. "Show me this place that is to be my home!"

The mountain did not loom ahead of them, but rather formed the natural high point of the snow-capped range. They swept up the length of rolling peaks, sometimes catching the drafts rising off ridges and sometimes winging through great open notches, and gliding over sprawling valleys where the earth was still multi-colored with the many tones of fall. Ahead rose the mother peak, its great sloping summit falling away at many angles, lanced by slides and crevasses and waterfalls.

Leiel could see a great bowl on the nearest slope, a cupping of the mountain, as though an enormous hand had pressed the heel of its palm into the stone, like a child sculpting a giant pile of mud. As they drew closer, it came clear that it was not a smooth bowl before them, but a scree-ragged ravine, the upper slopes covered in jagged boulders the size of wagons, piled impossibly one on the next at wild angles, snow packed between them, with half- frozen cataracts tumbling toward the gentler angle of the tree-covered base.

Home. The word trembled in Leiel's mind. She need not be told that this place was their destination. The rhythm of the flight changed, eased, and if such were possible, some subtle measure of rigidity left the Draigon. For all creatures, then, there was a coming home. Leiel stared out at the untamed, rugged landscape, the magnificent cupped hollow of the mountain. Would this someday be home to her as well—not just in physical fact, or out of necessity, but a home for her heart and her soul? Would it be, someday, what the farm had been in her youth, before the world turned inside out and draped itself in fear?

The Draigon caught a rising gust as they approached and rode it high into the sky, banked left and swept along the southern ridge of the giant, bowl-shaped ravine. The updraft ceased, and the beat of powerful wings took over, carrying them in a massive arc around the upper line of the mountain.

Below and to the right, the ravine slopped away. Leiel glimpsed the dark openings of caves and the bright glint of falling water.

The Draigon lifted a wing and steepened her turn as the radius of the ravine's upper arc tightened. This side of the bowl was more treed, and Leiel saw scattered buildings, houses with smoke rising from their chimneys, barns and coops and pens, tucked along the forest edge. One structure, a large cabin with a wide porch, sat sentinel at the very mouth of the ravine, where the pitch of the mountain encountered the flattening downward slope of the bowl. No city, just a small settlement, dwarfed by the magnificence of the mountains that sheltered it. What had she expected? Had she ever considered how the Draigon might live? Gahree's story came back to her. The Draigon had been nearly wiped out in the great war. How many had been left to carry on? Too few, if the town below was an indication.

"This is where the Draigon live?"

Some, daughter of wings. For many, this place is too distant, too wild. Some cannot find their home here and leave us for lives elsewhere.

Women chose Sacrifice and came here, only to find themselves unhappy? Leiel's throat went dry. What if she was one such? Why had she not asked more about this place? What if this wild, cold mountain could no more be her home than Klem's basement had been?"

Small figures moved among the trees below. People then, as well as the Draigon, lived here. And didn't that make sense? Wasn't Shaa, the creature carrying her, also Gahree, the mountain witch who offered stories and crisp peppers at Fourth Market in Adfen? As home to Draigon, this place must be home to them in either form.

Village. Mountain. This strange and magnificent landscape. Her question remained unanswered. "This place—does it have a name?"

The reply pressed into her mind. *Many. The oldest among us call it Cyunant.* The contact no longer seemed strange. Should it be this easy to accept all of this? Or was she just unable to feel shock anymore?

Leiel raised her chin a little, called to the Draigon, "You are not one of the oldest? Are you not Shaa?"

Again, the wavelike rumble of laughter washed over her mind. *I am Shaa, as others have been before me. Long since, has the name become a title, for she among us who has grown to fit the role.*

Never had it occurred to Leiel that Shaa might not be a creature as ancient and long-lived as her legend. But of course that could not be. The creature carrying her through the goldening light was as mortal as she, and while the Draigon's life probably spanned centuries, it was unlikely that she carried the knowledge of a millennium.

"What happened to the others?" she asked. "How many have there been?" They swooped high and dropped at a sharp angle toward the huge ravine. Leiel caught back her breath and tightened her hold on the warm scales. For a moment the Draigon made no reply as she banked hard and made a turn over the angled side of the ridge.

I am the third. Draighil claimed the former.

Leiel took that in, as the ground rushed toward them and the Draigon flattened her wings and beat back hard, slowing their descent. She touched down with a force that shook but did not shatter, stone and earth and bones. Leiel rocked with it, sat still for a moment recovering as the sound of rushing wind and wings, and the sense of speed, left her for the first time in hours. She smelled snow and fir trees in the thin air. Her senses began to settle, but her mind did not. Draighil had claimed the others. Draighil like Cleod.

"He could have killed you," Leiel said.

Of course he could have. But I did not let him.

"But—I put you at risk—in a way I never thought about. Somehow—"

The Draigon brought a green-gold eye to bear on Leiel. The bright orb compelled complete attention. *Such risk was well-measured. The choice was not yours alone. We know how dangerous they are. They learned to be so by studying us. Let go this troubling idea, Leiel. All is well. Lift your eyes and take in Cyunant.*

Chapter 5

Leiel

Leiel looked around, and the Draigon drew back her head and bent lower toward the ground. Seated where she was, Leiel was at the same height as the tops of the tallest firs. They were the prominent tree in this place. The bare-branched deciduous trees were smaller, tucked low among them, slender and wind-bent. The air hung rich with the tar-heavy scent of balsam and pine, crisp and tangy like crushed rosemary and dry bones. So different from home, where those scents where carried on high, and the common odors were of loamy earth and human living.

So very different, but just as real, this here and now, and whatever change it meant she must face. "I am ready," she said.

I have no doubt. The Draigon dipped and extended her leg. Leiel unbent and rose carefully. Not as numb as she expected after the pounding flight, she found her balance, and then climbed down.

They had landed at the lower edge of the giant scree-field. The ground was rocks and moss and low shrubs protruding from a light dusting of snow. Well-walked paths wove over the earth. Farther down the slope, a few people were gathered. Leiel's heart resumed a frantic pounding. People. She did not see a familiar face among the small group, but somewhere on this mountain, among these strangers, was her mother.

Leiel's stomach turned over, and she bent double and closed her eyes. The great creature beside her pressed a leg against her body, steadying her. For a moment, Leiel just held on, let herself sway with the breathing of the Draigon. By all that she had ever dreamed, was this real? Would she awaken in the dank basement of Klem's house, to the smell of Elda's cooking and the sadness of another day under her brother's hand? Another breath. Still another. She opened her eyes and forced herself upright. No. She stepped away from Shaa's support.

The true chill of the mountain air claimed her for the first time, raising goose-flesh over her arms and neck, and her breath turned to mist before her with each exhalation. Shivering, she folded her arms across her chest and rubbed her arms. How warm Shaa had kept her during the flight!

She looked toward the strangers at the edge of the trees. Most wore only light clothing, less layered than even her heavy skirts and woven shirt. They were not dressed for the weather. *Draigon heat.*

Leiel nodded to herself, then dropped her chin and studied the group a moment longer. She looked up at the Shaa. "So few of you?" she asked. Only half a dozen women waited to greet her.

Of us. The pressure behind the idea as it formed in Leiel's mind was a message. *Not so few as this. But only those you need to meet this moment are here to greet you. Child in a new wilderness, how much more do you want to take on, this moment?*

Again Leiel shivered, but a stiffness she had hardly realized she had been holding across her shoulders eased. Of course. In their meetings at the market, Gahree had been wise and kind. Had she expected less in this place? After all, she was not the first woman to come here like this. Not the first shaken spirit to arrive on the wings of legend, with her whole life strewn upside down behind her.

Leiel smiled up at the Draigon, then turned and moved down the rocky slope toward the waiting women. The way was uneven, but not steep.

A lean, long haired woman in grey pants and a light tunic stepped forward and offered both her hands. A second of hesitation, and Leiel took them. Hot fingers squeezed her wrists, strong and trembling slightly. Leiel gazed into the stranger's lightly lined face and saw only kindness.

"Welcome, Leiel. We have waited so long to meet you. I am Gydron. We are so pleased you have chosen to join us."

Choice. Yes—that was it. That was the reason she was here. Because she had made a choice. Been offered a true choice for the first time in her life. Leiel nodded. “Yes,” she said. “Yes. Thank you.”

Gydron nodded, squeezed her again and let go. She half-turned and gestured to the others. “This is Wynt.” She indicated a vibrant, copper-haired woman in scarred leathers and worn boots. “And Lista and Kinra. Teachers all. You will come to know us over time.” The two she named were both thin, and the taller of the two had a small scar under one eye that shone white against her skin. Leiel swept her gaze over the group again. Their faces did not hold the marks of age to match the life and certainty that was conveyed in their expressions. A firmness at the edges of their eyes, the steadiness of each gaze, spoke experience and confidence in ways Leiel had not experienced with anyone but Gahree.

Gydron beckoned forward another woman. “And this is Gemda. She is the finest cook in Cyunant and lives to feed others. I think you will like her cooking. She is cousin to your friend, Elda.”

Leiel whipped her attention to the small-boned woman. She was Elda’s height exactly, and when she pushed back her hood and met Leiel’s gaze, the family resemblance was clear.

“Oh!” Leiel raised a hand to her mouth. Moisture welled in her eyes and suddenly, for the first time since she had said goodbye to Elda in the kitchen of Klem’s house, she cried.

“Yes, my dear,” Gemda said, and enfolded Leiel in her arms as Elda had done so many times through the years. Truly warm, the embrace radiated through her.

Leiel grasped the woman who was both stranger and strangely familiar, and let herself sob for a few moments, her thoughts tumbling, caught between sorrow and joy. At last she pulled back and looked at Gemda. “I never thought—I did not consider that you would be here. I don’t know why.”

“You were considering your meeting with someone else,” Gemda said, and reached to brush the salty traces of tears from Leiel’s cheeks.

“Your mother is down the valley,” Gydron said.

Leiel tore her gaze from Gemda to meet the other woman’s.

Gydron answered the unasked question. “She wanted to stand with us here, to greet you. But then we thought—she and all of us here—that it would be best that you chose the time to meet her again. It has been so long, and we are aware, Leiel Draigfen, of the pain we caused you when we took her.”

Leiel blinked. What had she been expecting? Not this. Not this casual admission of damage inflicted. And her mother...as much as she longed to see Ilora, was she ready to meet her again? When would she really be ready?

Suddenly, Leiel was more than tired. All the strength flooded out of her, and tears came again. "I'm sorry," she said. "I think I have no words left in me. I don't know what to do but stand here and cry."

Gemda laughed, slid an arm around Leiel's waist. "Come with me. You need food and rest. Time enough for talking and greeting when you know more of what you are about. Let me show you your house."

The others murmured assent and gave her room as Gemda led her over a smooth, stone path along the edge of the trees. "My house?" Leiel asked.

"We have a cabin waiting for you," Gydron said. "One all your own."

Her own? An entire house all her own? Draigon lived in houses and were giving her one? The idea tilted through her mind, and for a moment her vision swam. Or perhaps it was just the altitude and finding her feet after the wildness of her flight. Flight. She had *flown* here... Leiel closed her eyes a moment, paused her steps. "I can't—" she started, but a warm hand touched her face. She opened her eyes to see Gydron looking back at her, and Gemda's worried expression.

"You can," Wynt said and her eyes sparked and shimmered, metallic copper like her hair. "You've made it this far, even though your own family wanted you dead. There's nothing you can't do. But you might need a hot meal first." She winked.

Leiel stared at her a moment, then looked at the other faces around her, all warm and certain. Each kind, and perhaps wise, in its own way. She looked over her shoulder, back to where Shaa waited, huge and patient. Behind her, the white-capped peak loomed over the sweep of the bowl. The mountain surrounded and crowned, a fitting setting and throne for the creature that pulsed, each breath, with knowledge both formidable and ancient.

The familiar green-gold eyes made a sense in the giant form of a Draigon that they never had in a human visage viewed through the steam rising from a cup of tea. The slow blink of those eyes, comfortable and relaxed, offered Leiel enough reassurance that she turned and let herself be led down the uneven path toward the small cluster of tiny houses.

Sturdy structures constructed of weathered logs, most of the cabins would have fit into the kitchen of the farm house Leiel had grown up in. The roofs were split-shingles, worn by wind and rain and snow, and those houses more in shadow wore a glamour of snow that glinted crystalline in the afternoon light. Homes, small and normal. Somehow, it made more sense to her than a great city of gold ever could have. This was, after all, Gahree's home. Gahree with her worn boots and dusty skirts and tales of freedom and loss. Where else would such a being come from?

Ahead, Gemda moved with relaxed purpose over the chill ground. The cold from the stones pushed through the soles of Leiel's shoes as she followed. They had dressed her to die, back in Adfen, in light shoes and long skirts. If they had let her pack, the first thing she would have stowed were good winter boots... She smiled at the absurdity of the thought.

With a quick glance back, Gemda waved Leiel forward, ushered her past homes with small garden spaces lying fallow against side walls or door paths. Some homes had large windows hung with bright curtains. A few stood blank-faced, with just single, solid doors to break the faces of the front walls. Others were hung with racks holding skis, or snowshoes, or tools. Each house, rough used or wildly decorated, projected a character, or a humor that, Leiel could only hope, carried over to the personality of whomever resided within.

Around a bend, a new path forked to the right. They followed it, and a short climb through some trees, they approached a cabin set a little off from the others. The area around it had been cleared, and bronze sunlight filled the space, warming the air despite the mountain breeze.

The yard was mossy near the tree line, but filled with browned, patchy grass closer to the house. Chunks of wood marked areas that could, in proper season, form garden spaces. A small shed was visible beyond the corner of the house.

The main structure was simple, with a red-painted door and a single window to the right of it, and a chimney rising from the back corner.

"This is mine?" Leiel asked, a low tremor in her voice that she did not try to conceal. Some of the worry that had filled her upon seeing Cyunant from the air faded. So simple, the little house and its grounds. So simple and so perfect.

Enough space for a pig. The shed could host chickens. And the yard she could fill with flowers and herbs and—

"Yes," Gemda said as she stepped past Leiel and opened the door. "Your mother chose this place for you. She said you would know what to do to make it home."

Her mother. Who else would know what would signal comfort in the deepest part of Leiel's being? Of all the houses she had passed on the trail, this was the one that spoke to her, offered hints of something that might take hold of her spirit and allow her to label it truly *home*. A hint of the old farm lurked in the color of this building's faded wood. The angle of the light this time of day was reflected memory of chill spring mornings. But the clearing, the thin mountain air, the smell of the wind, were all different enough from the farm for the echo of home to hold mostly comfort, with little of the pain of lonely, later years.

"My mother chose well." The words were strange in her throat. Her mother choosing for her, like mothers were supposed to do, to help guide their children through the years, and yet Ilora had been absent so long. Elda and Gahree claimed more of the shaping of the person Leiel had become than Ilora. So many years...

Gemda beckoned. "Come inside."

Leiel stepped over the threshold and paused a moment to let her eyes adjust to the diminished light. Two more windows on the southern wall spilled sunlight into the room, but it took several seconds before she could clearly discern the interior space.

An iron cookstove dominated the back right corner of the room. Shelves and counters, complete with a sink boasting its own pump, lined the back wall to the left of the fireplace.

In the center of the room, a plank table and six oak chairs stood, the table set with stoneware in preparation for a meal. A pair of chairs and a smaller table filled the room's front right corner, and against the left wall, two narrow beds, set end to end with a trunk between, were visible beyond partly drawn privacy curtains.

The air, sweet with burning birch, was warm, and pressed comfort though the space and into her bones. Leiel sighed.

"I hope you'll find nothing lacking, at least this first evening. Delhar made you some clothes, just simple items based on what Gahree told her of your size and preferred way of dressing. Of course, you'll be able to choose or make new items if these are not to your taste. But they should work for a start. Have a look in the chest between the beds."

"Who is Delhar?"

"She's our lead clothier. She dyes fabrics and patterns clothing for most of us. She has a knack for making clothes we feel comfortable in. Take a look."

Leiel stepped to the chest, knelt to open it and pulled out soft pants and a warm sweater of boiled wool. Dyed a deep red, the piece was light, and cut large enough for her to comfortably fit a second shirt beneath. She found just such an item, made of soft flannel, folded beside thick socks at the bottom of the trunk. Next to them was a pair of heavy, leather boots with thick soles and felted liners. She smiled. Just what she would have packed. Everything was finely made and practical, in the style of Spur clothing, and looked to be just her size.

"Did Delhar make the boots as well?"

"No. Those are Lista's work."

"Does everyone in this place have a craft?"

"Most of us have more than one. We've a lot of time here."

Leiel looked over her shoulder at Gemda as the woman stepped to the stove and began pulling bowls off the shelf. So like Elda in build and movement, with the same ease in the kitchen. But different as well, with a quicker smile, and a firmer glance.

Gemda looked back at Leiel, flicked both her eyebrows up a few times, and turned back to the pot simmering on the stove.

"I'm sorry for staring," Leiel said with a laugh. "You remind me so much of your cousin." Where was Elda now? Still in Adfen with Klem, most likely. Had she heard what happened on the mountain? Did she believe what Leiel had promised her, that everything would be all right? That Ilora was alive, and so Leiel would be as well? Leiel frowned. She could hope so. She had, after all, decided everything based on hope.

"I want many stories of her." Gemda stirred the soup. "I've long since gotten everything out of Ilora."

A little skip pinched Leiel's heart. All these years, others had heard Ilora tell stories. The woman at the stove knew Ilora the way Leiel knew Elda, knew her laugh, and foibles and annoyances and charms. How strange to think that Elda had been something of what Ilora might have been. "You talk often?"

Gemda laughed. "We're a small community. Most days don't pass without all of us tripping over each other at least once." She smiled, looked over with a nod. "It's well to feel uncertain in the face of all this." With the lift of her chin, she indicated a wash stand near the foot of the second bed. "There, dear, clean up. Change clothes. Then we'll see you fed. There'll be time later for a real bath."

Leiel took a breath, held it, then let it out. Later. After she met with Ilora. How much of what Leiel recalled about her mother was even close to the reality that awaited her? Her belly tightened as she rose, fresh clothes in hand, and went to the stand in the corner. The pitcher beside the basin was full, but Leiel waited a few seconds to calm her nerves before she lifted it and poured.

"Do all the women in your family love to cook?"

Gemda laughed. "I hear her breads are legendary."

"Yes. The best baker in The Spur." Leiel pulled off her shirt, stepped free of her skirts and let them pool around her feet. She found a bar of soap, a folded cotton rag, and a wooden comb on a small tray beside the basin. The small act of wiping dirt and soot from her body cleared tension, even as her thoughts turned to the reason why she was so filthy. If she was this dirty, what must Cleod look like? His screams. He had to be hurt. Blood and dirt and smoke. She shook her head. Gahree had promised he would live. She had to trust that.

The water wasn't warm, and by the time she had done all she could with the cloth, the liquid was dark with soot. Leiel dressed, and picked up the comb, worked at the knotted mess of her hair. It smelled of ash and fear, and she tugged at it to little avail. She would need an hour to bring the unruly locks under control, and a real bath to remove the smell. Her shoulders rippled with chill, and she pressed her lips together and blinked hard to back down the sudden turn of her stomach as the memory of screams and smoke again filled her mind. No time to think on that now.

Turning the comb on end, she worked at a tangle. It snagged like stray threads on a worn coat, and hung up on the wooden teeth. She worked for several minutes, then paused. Threads. Threads in need of trimming. Or ripping. Cleod.

She bent and used the comb to tear at a seam of her old skirt. A moment later, she retrieved the smoky crystal he had given her on her last day of school. She turned it in her hand, studying it. For so long had she kept it hidden that she had forgotten the look and feel of it. It wasn't large, and the natural facets were angled and uneven, but its subtle translucence held an unexpected beauty. She rolled it with her fingers. What to do with it? For now, it was safe. She straightened and placed it on the tray.

She turned back toward Gemda, and smiled at the other woman. With a sigh, Leiel scanned the room again, and her gaze landed on a shelf on the back wall. Two small books leaned against a tiny statue of a bird. Leiel's lips parted and she crossed the room, reached out to touch the volumes. Truly, this place was meant to seem like a home. She set the comb down on the shelf and picked up the books. The worn, familiar bindings settled into her hand as tears filled her eyes.

"Hungry yet, dear?"

Leiel blinked and looked up. She smiled. "Yes." Wiping her eyes with the back of her wrist, she returned the books to their place and retrieved the comb. "It smells wonderful."

"Come sit."

Stomach rumbling, Leiel came to the table and slid into a chair. The mess that was her hair would take some time to deal with, and the demands of her belly warranted immediate attention.

Gemda set a steaming bowl in front of Leiel and took a seat across from her. "Eat. Then I'll help comb out your hair. When we're done, I'll tell you where to find your mother."

A fresh shiver touched Leiel's shoulders as she picked up the spoon and dipped it into the soup. Her mother. So many years… The utensil seemed frozen in her hand. She stared at it, then shook herself, lifted the spoon and sipped the hot broth. It warmed her straight to her bones, and her next spoonful included a heap of vegetables. A hint of tang flavored the meal, like nothing her mother or Elda had ever cooked. "What is this, the bite, like…sweat on my lip?"

The voice that answered her was not Gemda's. "It's called salt, wild daughter. It comes from the northeast coast."

Leiel looked toward the door. Gahree closed it behind her, and smiled. Instead of the heavy skirts Leiel was used to seeing her in, she wore tan pants, but she was Gahree as Leiel had known her through the years. Not strange or mythical. Not dark and fiery. Just the woman who had offered comfort and knowledge for more than half of Leiel's life. And she was just the person Leiel needed, as she had always been.

Without a word, Leiel rose from the table and crossed the small space. Gahree pulled her close, and Leiel sighed as she took in the familiar scents of herby tea and fir. Something rolled back into place and settled inside her. A few heartbeats, and Leiel pulled away and met the green-gold gaze. "Salt?"

Gahree laughed a little. "Back to your meal. Such a savory soup must not be left unattended for long." She put a hand on Leiel's shoulder, and warmth chased down her arm.

"Sit and eat," Gemda said. She pulled Leiel's chair out a little and gestured her into it. "There's plenty on the stove, Gahree. I know the change has left you hungry."

"Many thanks." Gahree moved around the table to the stove to fill herself a bowl.

The change. Shaa. Gahree. What must that transition be like? How was it possible? Was she to learn that? Become something like the creature that had carried her here? She had to. That was why she had come here, why she had given up every hope of a normal life, given up on Cleod. Her heart picked up pace.

"Eat," Gemda said. She took up the comb and stepped behind Leiel, began to work at her snarled hair, pulling Leiel from too-heavy thoughts and back into the moment. Her stomach rumbled, and she looked over at Gahree, now settled across from her and starting into her own soup.

Pushing down the wild doubts that has suddenly risen inside her, Leiel lifted her spoon again and ate. The gentle pull of the comb through her hair and the hearty warmth of the food settled her racing thoughts. She shoved everything but those simple comforts away and finished the meal.

"What happens now?" She did not know how to make those simple words encompass everything she meant, but no others came.

Gahree set her spoon down beside her own empty bowl. "Now, your mother awaits, if you feel ready to see her."

Leiel's belly flipped. "How can I be ready for that, Gahree?"

"Willing, then." Gahree smiled. "The choice is yours, when you wish to see her. But you cannot put it off long. Cyunant is a small village, and the need for this meeting is large."

"Whose need?"

"All of ours," Gemda said. She ran her fingers through Leiel's hair, and the path of them along Leiel's scalp was both comfort and pleasure. She tugged and turned the locks, and Leiel felt a braid take shape over her head.

"All?"

"Your mother has longed for you as you have for her," Gahree said. "The path of healing between you will be long, and the more of it you choose to walk together, the more you will find of each other along that way."

So familiar was the half-riddle message of Gahree's words, that Leiel smiled despite her worry. "Where is she?"

Chapter 6

Cleod - 16 years

Cleod sat on his heels in the slanting rain and stared across the plains toward the Spur, though he could not see the mountain range through the heavy clouds. Grass waved, bent by the onslaught, occasionally lifted with the breeze, and its colored tips shifted from green to lush purples with the motion. A chill in the air increased as evening crept close. Icy water slid under his collar and dripped off his nose, soaked his exposed shirt cuffs where they protruded from the sleeves of his coat. The muscles of his thighs burned, but he did not move until they trembled. He rose slowly, controlling the motion, until he stood straight and stiff, with the wind pushing at the raindrops and tears on his cheeks.

The grave at his back was piled with fresh earth, and its existence echoed through an empty place inside him. *So fast.* Only a few weeks ago he had driven Leiel's family wagon into the yard of his father's house. Just days after that, his father had stood at the edge of the woodlot and waved farewell. Cleod had promised to return in the spring...but Ellan had not even survived the autumn.

The small crowd of family friends now milled in the yard as they said their goodbyes. A dozen people to mark a life. So few, despite all the years Ellan had worked around the city. How many hundreds had been able to cook, or spent the hard Spur country winters warm and safe, because of Ellan's labor? Were they absent now because they did not care, or because they feared the woodcutter's son, made strange, and a stranger, by his time with the Ehlewer? Those who had come had offered what comfort they could, while eying him with a wary unease that translated in restless motions of their hands and quavering words. Fear of the Ehlewer or contempt for a son who had left his father to die alone? Did it matter? He blinked hard, swallowed down new tears.

"Cleod, we must return." Trayor's voice seemed out of place in the thick air of the lowlands.

Cleod nodded, but did not turn. This was not a Farlan place, this low hill where the rolling plains met the forest. It was just a short walk from the little homestead where he had been raised. The person who should be with him in this place, this time, was not Trayor. Did Leiel even know of his loss? To have her beside him, hug him tight, and press her head into his chest and tell him she was sorry—he wanted that with a need that choked him. But it was an impossibility. She was Draigfen and had no place here, at a ceremony as sacred as this.

"We can't stay." A note of insistence this time, tugged through Trayor's words.

With a sigh, Cleod pivoted to face him.

Trayor wiped rain from his face as he walked around the fresh grave to join Cleod. "We've been here all day. There's snow coming. It'll be dark soon." He glanced at the northern horizon where thickening clouds built above the tree line.

Cleod did the same, then looked back at the grave, past it. Across the packed-dirt yard, the house he had grown up in sat flanked by tall oaks. The possibility flickered, that they could stay the night, but no. Ellan had died there, alone, in the cold. "It's a short ride to Adfen." Tears tightened his throat and put a guttural edge to the words.

"One I prefer to make in what daylight we have left." Trayor nodded toward the horses tied at the tree line. The yard was nearly clear of funeral goers. The last of them climbed into a buckboard and turned his team toward the road.

A frown pulled at Cleod's lips. Was this how little friendship was worth? Ellan had called many that through the years. On random summer evenings, those who claimed to be just passing by had managed to stay for hours, singing and talking until the sun was nearly down. Where were those people on this day? Where had they been during Ellan's long illness? Were they truly friends, or had they, for long years, simply found advantage in his hospitality?

"There's nothing more we can do here," Trayor said.

The back of Cleod's throat went dry, and he had to force a breath. "He was my father, Tray."

"And he's gone. It's time to leave this place."

Cleod turned away again, counted his heartbeat, and watched his breath mist in the air.

Trayor stepped closer. "There's nothing left here."

Almost, Cleod protested. But this place was no longer home, and the only person in all of Adfen who might understand the ripping knot in his stomach, was Draigfen, and unwelcome in his life. Only Trayor stood with him. Did that make them friends, any more than songs and laughter had made those who used to visit this house? No. But perhaps that was for the best. Standing without undue emotion might, over time, be worth more.

The wind kicked up, and he glanced at the sky. A strange storm, to slide in from the north against normal weather patterns. He let out the air in his lungs. What more was there to be done? "All right."

A hand landed on his shoulder, and then slipped away. Trayor's footsteps crunched on the brittle ground as he walked away. A few more seconds, a few more rough breaths, then Cleod turned to follow. Instinct pulled, but he did not look at the grave as he passed.

Chapter 7

Leiel - 23 years

She left the cabin behind, but paused a few steps down the path and glanced back. A house. *Her* house. A tiny flip repeated itself in her belly. Despite all the doubts filling her, the little building was already a small source of joy. Morning and night, a place she could shape and attend and take comfort, as well as shelter, within. A place she was glad to know awaited her, no matter what came of the meeting that lay ahead.

Small rocks skittered under her boots as she started down the trail again. Trees creaked around her, their tops swaying in the wind funneled down the ravine. Snow and dry leaves flitted off branches and swirled sparsely, speckling the thin air.

The main trail crossed her narrow track. She stopped again for a moment, then sighed through a heavy breath and turned downslope, following Gahree's directions.

The way snaked through the forest, so steep in places that she had to slow her pace and catch at small trees for balance. A few hundred steps down the trail, the left side dropped away in a steep embankment, and a glint of water bounced up at her though the branches. The small pond she had seen from on high became visible through the gap in the trees. She paused and stared at it. Then a small smile found her lips. A pond, something to make this place feel like home.

Ahead down the path, open space beckoned. A rock-strewn clearing sloped in rough tiers down the mouth of the ravine. A weathered grey building with a long porch sat at the top edge, just beyond the tree line. In front of it, two trails merged with the one she was on.

At that junction, a woman waited.

Leiel stopped on the path and stared at the person she had spent most of her life missing. Heat surged through her again, a heavy anger that shocked straight through the core of her. Shaking, she dragged in a breath and stared. Ilora was dressed in layered shades of greens and auburns, loose cut, and strange to Leiel's eyes. She remembered Ilora in pale greys and browns, farm clothes, worn boots, but this different look seemed somehow more her mother, more all the things she had sensed in Ilora's laughter, and in the stories she had told.

A breeze picked up and tossed Ilora's hair over her face. Only a hint of grey brightened the dark locks. Leiel caught her breath. Ilora's face seemed barely touched by age, despite the years that had passed. Only a few lines that marked time or laughter or pain had left their paths on her face. How was that possible? Was this person before her at all the mother she remembered? Leiel trembled, took a half step back, then stopped herself as Gahree's green-gold gaze filled her mind. Uncanny eyes in a human face, in the countenance of a creature out of legend.

Did the word impossible have any meaning at all?

Wind gusted again, and sent a scattering rain of yellowed leaves and snow dust tumbling loose from grey branches and into the rocky yard. The limbs might have been her bones, brittle and rattling, and the leaves, with their random whirling, a mirror of her skittering thoughts. They swirled into the space between her and her mother, like all the things left so long unspoken between them.

Leiel blinked, swallowed hard, and asked the thing that mattered most of all. "Why?" Of all the things to be shared and all the questions to be asked, this was the only one that had bloomed in Leiel's mind since the moment Ilora's name had been called in Adfen Square. Gahree's explanations had eased some of the pain—but to hear the answers from Ilora, to see her face as she spoke and hear her tone—that was vital. *Why* was the need that kept expanding. Why could you not explain more? Was it simply that I was too young? Or did you not trust me?

Or not trust yourself to go if you tried to explain? Why did you never tell me you were alive? *Why*? Why was everything.

Ilora offered a faint smile that held no humor. "You never did care to wait for the niceties. That is part of what has always made you a danger to the Farlan and their ways." Her voice was the same, husky and filled with warmth. It echoed into Leiel's skull, a memory made real.

Leiel stared at the ghost made flesh. Though her heart pounded her ribs, she folded her arms and met her mother's gaze. "I don't remember you making light of my questions. Much less one as important as this." More than the altitude made it hard to catch her breath, but she managed to keep her voice steady. She was not going to rage or rant or cry—or throw herself into Ilora's arms and beg to be held. Not yet. Not before some part of her question was answered.

"No," Ilora shook her head. "But the answer is both simple and bitter, Leiel."

"I am bitter already." The words formed before thought, true in a way she did not wish to admit. What to do when faced with the thing she wanted most of all in the world, and yet which turned the hardest emotions inside her? Her throat was dry, and a headache pressed at the back of her eyes. "Tell me. I have waited so long. I need to know. You left us. Left me. What choice was that? Tell me! Gahree said it was to keep me safe."

Ilora took a few steps forward and opened her hands, shook her head. "I made my choice because you were already a Councilman's choice."

Leiel's heart skipped. "What do you mean?"

Ilora's lips parted, but she did not speak. Then she took a breath and said, "There are some men who are so caught up in the power they have obtained, and so afraid of losing even one bit of it, that the smallest slight can send them into a rage. Do you remember Councilman Swillon?"

"Swillon?" What did the old man have to do with anything? He had been dead for years.

"At the Market—do you recall arguing with him? Do you remember refusing to sell him the last pumpkin that you had promised to Ils?"

Leiel stared. Vaguely, a memory stirred. A rainy day. An angry man. Her father gone from the stall at the end of the day to get the mules, Gial off flirting with Corra. And that last pumpkin, already promised, and the strange rage of the man when she refused to sell it to him. "Yes..." She frowned. "Why would such a thing matter?"

"Because it marked you. It brought you to the notice of a man who needed little excuse to hate women, and none at all to exercise his power to destroy them."

Such words, a few years ago, would have sent a chill down Leiel's spine. Not now. She had seen too much of the Councilmen on their visits to Klem's house, seen desire for power and control turn her brother's heart. And the anger and lust in the eyes of the other members. Heard their twisted jokes and dodged their clammy hands as she served food and refilled drinks. Neither age nor decency played a role in some of their stated desires. As cruel as Klem had been, at least he had not allowed the twisted fantasies of some of his friends to engulf her. But what Ilora spoke of was even more petty and horrific than any of that—an insult to pride, of all things, might have led to her destruction.

"Swillon? Over a *pumpkin*?"

"Over your refusal to obey him."

Leiel took that in, shook her head. "Couldn't you have stopped him? Couldn't father have?"

Ilora shook her head. "Once you are noticed by such a man as that, there is no hiding. He would have, at best, offered you as Sacrifice purely for spite."

"But—" Leiel stopped. She had heard of such thing, rumors from others cities and distant regions—of girls and women offered up before any sign of Draigon Weather appeared. It had been said such action kept the Draigon at bay, satisfied them in advance and warded off drought.

How old had she been? Seven or eight? What would she have been, had that happened? Gahree has spent years preparing her for the truth of the Draigon and still the knowledge had overwhelmed her. If she had simply been chained on the Spur, given as Sacrifice...who would she have become? Would even being brought here and told the truth, have been enough to preserve her spirit? She shuddered, but managed to speak.

"How did you know? That he wanted to hurt me."

"You were bright and curious and fearless. Things which likely brought you to the notice of that terrible man. But you were also noticed by the Draigon for those same reasons. And a woman came to me, one day in the Market. She warned me of Swillon's plans for you and told me the most fantastic stories. She was strange and brilliant. She told me truths. She said she could bring a Draigon. And she did. The weather changed, outside all precedent, very soon after the last Sacrifice. The Draigon sent word to the Council, and they had no choice but to honor the Draigon's demand. And they sent word that *I was to be named, not you.*"

The words rolled over Leiel, only a portion of them making contact with her mind in any way that formed understanding. A Councilman had wanted to have her killed? A woman had come to her mother, just as Gahree had come to Leiel? The Draigon could give the Council orders? The ideas ricocheted against each other, competing for attention. Her breath left her in a rush and she sat. No thought or control marked her descent, only the sudden inability of her legs to hold her upright. Her hands came up to cradle her head. Too much, she thought. Too much to make sense of. Too many emotions.

The scent of ice-touched earth, weighted and sharp, filled her nose. The ground was cold under her. She concentrated on that, on the solidity of soil and stone. "You should have let the Draigon come for me back then."

"You were too young. You would never have understood what was happening." Hands wrapped light over Leiel's shoulders, a touch once familiar but for so long known only in dreams.

Leiel shifted a hand from her face to grasp her mother's fingers. The *reality* of them, their warmth and remembered, slender strength, drew forth a sob. "Old gods! You're *here*. I'm *here*. I can't think!" Caught between need and anger, she shook.

Ilora's voice came close in her ear, gentle and strong, haunting in its familiarity and its strangeness. "Let go, Leiel. Let go your doubts and fears and let me hold you. There is time enough—ages of time to come—for all your questions and all your anger."

Leiel twisted her body into the waiting comfort of Ilora's grasp and, for the moment, gave up on the rage and the doubt blazing inside, let herself fall back into the best moments of her childhood, held safe and warm and loved in her mother's arms.

Chapter 8

Leiel

Comfort seeped from the walls of the little cabin, if anything, richer and warmer than when she had first stepped inside with Gemda. Leiel folded her hands around the stone mug and sipped her tea. It was the same earthy blend Gahree had offered her in the Market that chill, rainy day she had learned the truth about the Draigon and her mother. The scent of it mixed with memory, and eased a hint of familiarity through the ongoing strangeness of the day. At length she sighed and raised her gaze, looked between her mother, who sat beside her at the table, and Gahree, standing by the stove pouring water from a steaming kettle.

She wanted to find pure joy in being here, in Ilora's presence, but long years of loss tugged. "You didn't just leave me," Leiel said. "I might understand if you had just taken my place. But what about Klem and Gial? What about father? I need to understand. Did you think we would all just be *all right*?"

A few heartbeats passed, the silence deepening, then Ilora said, "Your father and I were never in love. Our marriage was arranged for money and convenience. We liked each other well enough, but never had real understanding, or passion. I hoped he was stronger than he turned out to be. Strong enough to keep the farm a home for you. I was wrong in that."

The jolt was less than it would once have been, to learn her mother had never loved her father. To hear it said aloud was more cutting than the actual news; the knowledge of years, torn through her youth, had been enough to prove the lack of caring. Leiel pressed her lips together, breathed deep through her nose, and continued. "And Gial? *Klem*? Do you know how they changed? Do you know what they did? How much do you know, mother?" The edge on the words left a bitter taste on Leiel's tongue. She swallowed, blinked back a glaze of moisture.

"I know." Ilora drew a breath and let it out. Her face looked drawn in the lamp light, but her eyes were bright. "I know enough. Gial was always the one with his head in the clouds. He was always looking to the next thing, not concerned with where he was at the moment. He was the dreamer, though he never had great dreams. I knew he would find a way to be satisfied with whatever came his way. He would take on whatever role was laid out for him, without questions or introspection. He would always choose the easiest path. He would miss me, and he would be hurt, but he would move on. And he has."

"But not Klem," Leiel said.

"No." Again silence fell, uneased by the words that had recently filled it. "No," Ilora repeated. "Klem was the most fragile of you. He probably needed me the most." She smiled the faintest bit. "Don't look so startled. You know it is true. My judgment was clouded by that knowledge."

Judgment? What did that mean? "I don't understand."

Ilora took a deep breath. "Klem always needed more than you or Gial."

Leiel went still, a nearly intolerable idea uncurling through her mind.

"You—you *told him*?" Leiel stared at her mother. She bit back the desire to repeat the phrase, then surrendered to it. "You told him you were going to—to be—?"

"I told him I would be going away." Ilora shook her head, met Leiel's gaze. "To protect you."

Leiel's jaw fell open.

"The worst mistake of the many I made. I had hoped to give him purpose, something to focus on—"

Leiel scoffed. That had indeed been accomplished.

"Not in the way he *blamed* you." Ilora gripped her mug harder, shook her head. "But to take on a role as a true brother. To protect you. I did not know then, that the Sanctuary Priests would have the impact they did. That they would turn my words in his mind."

"He believed them, mother," Leiel said. "When they told him *I* was the reason for what had happened to you. With your own words to back them, why would he ever have doubted them?"

"I have lived long with my regrets. Klem—Klem is the deepest of them. I expect you to be angry with me, for as long as you feel you must be. About leaving, about lying, about your brothers. But I do not regret my choice. It set you on the path that brought you here—brought us together again—and I cannot feel bad about that."

"*Brought us together*? There would have been no need to bring us together if you had never left in the first place." Leiel set her mug down hard and got to her feet, paced away, criss-crossing the small space with tight steps. Every part of her was shaking, and she could not find a place for her gaze to rest.

A few seconds passed before she turned to face her mother. "I know," she said through a tight breath. "I know you had to leave—I just—It was so *hard* without you." Heat trembled in her chest as she met Ilora's gaze. "I am going be angry for a long time. And I don't know how to reconcile that with how glad I am to see you."

Ilora nodded without smiling. "I don't expect you to be anything but angry," she said. "And I am having trouble seeing you before me as a grown woman. In my heart, you are the little girl I left on the steps of the Tower."

Leiel looked at her mother, still trying to fully accept that Ilora looked so little different from that day. If only she could go back and reclaim the heart of the little girl she had been... "You still look like the mother I lost that day."

"A simple suggestion can be of use in times like these," Gahree said, as she came to join them at the table. "Start by coming to know each other as you are now."

Ilora laughed. "Simple logic from you, Gahree?"

"And you have a way to best do that?" Leiel asked. How many answers, through the years, that should have come from Ilora, had come from Gahree instead?

"Questions." Gahree tipped her head. "A thousand, thousand questions asked and answered, and raising more of each with every reply."

"Not simple after all." Leiel smiled, wry and tight. Many answers, though never direct. "You have never been good at giving me an easy reply."

Gahree laughed her bone-echoing laugh. "That never stopped your questions. Why should it now?"

Leiel shook her head. With a sigh, she came back to the table and reclaimed her seat. "Tell me what you meant," she said, looking at Ilora, seeking something to focus on besides the pressure building in her skull. "About the Draigon sending someone to tell the Council what to do."

Ilora folded her hands on the table. "It is not a role I have chosen. I am more comfortable here in Cyunant, where I teach lore to the new arrivals. I always feared that if I left this place, I would seek you out before it was time. That would have put us all in danger."

Leiel started. "You would have done that?"

"Each day after she first earned her Great Shape, I spent hours talking her out of it," Gahree said.

Leiel eyed Gahree. So, she had truly kept Ilora away. Leiel frowned. She had trusted Gahree. Did she still? The answer came from her gut—yes. Beyond the fact that she had little choice, here in this new place, Leiel realized she believed in the woman now even more than she had. More than she, anymore, believed in Ilora. No comfort lingered within that realization.

"How much is betrayal, and how much is caution and need?" Gahree said. "Turn that question in your mind, wild daughter, before you let your heart conclude anything."

Leiel pressed her lips together, frowning. "You know my thoughts almost before I do."

"I have sat through many a conversation like this," Gahree said, "with anger and joy and fear and hope all becoming one thing. You are not the first to struggle with hard truths. But you heard the story of the Draigon and recognized the truth of it. Time will be needed before we all come to what understanding can be reached."

Leiel nodded, dropping her gaze to the table. She was weary in a way she had never thought possible, a way that ached to her bones.

Ilora reached out a hand, folded her fingers over Leiel's, and the touch was a hard combination of both comfort and unfamiliarity, welcome despite the strangeness and her unease. A slow, deep breath. Leiel let it out and met Ilora's gaze. Not all answers would come this moment. Not all scars would be healed or soothed. But there was time now. And time with Ilora was something Leiel had never thought to have again. She shook herself internally, focused again on the question she had asked. "But the Council."

Gahree brought her mug and joined them at the table. The chair scraped a little over the floor as she pulled it out and sat. Steam from her cup tumbled toward Leiel. "Some of us seek among all the girls of the world, and find those who have the born strength, minds, and learned will, to make this journey. Do you think the Councils always wish to be rid of those we want? I, and others, play many roles. One has long been to assure the Councils select those we have chosen and prepared to come to us."

"Those prepared as I was," Leiel said. Shaa, the mighty form that had carried her here. Could she really ever be prepared to become something like that?

"Sometimes," Ilora said. "You were different than most."

"Because of what happened to you." Leiel looked at Ilora. "I suppose you don't often have two generations of women from the same family arrive here."

Gahree nodded. "Not often in succession."

"What do you do? March into Council chambers and demand they chose who you want them to chose?"

"Yes," Ghahree said. "That is exactly what I do."

"You—what?"

Gahree grinned at Leiel, and her ringing laugh filled the small cabin as it had so often filled her market stall in Adfen. "I would have thought, after all you have seen, nothing I could say could return that look to your face, daughter of wings."

Leiel closed her mouth, spoke when she could. "You...you walk into Council rooms all across Arnan, and *tell* those men what to do?"

"Stride," Gahree said. "I prefer to stride into such rooms. Setting the tone when speaking of Draigfen is of vital importance."

Leiel blinked, smiled. "And you do this often?"

"Only in the rare circumstance that they have not already decided to name the woman we have prepared."

"They usually have already picked the person you want?"

Gahree sipped her tea. "Women with minds of their own have always marked themselves. Most of the time, we need not say a word, or show ourselves at all. There are few things more dangerous than a woman who speaks freely. And few things more predicable than the man who fears her."

Leiel put a hand over her mouth to hold back another bark of laughter, then she took in where she was, the cozy warmth of the space, and the smiling faces gazing back at her. This was not Adfen where laughter was dangerous and such words were sacrilege. Ilora and Gahree. Could she be in safer company for stinging words or joy? She let the laugh come, rolling through the small room with the scented steam of the tea. "Old gods!" she gasped. "It's truth you speak as usual, Gahree." For a moment she forgot that she was tired and angry. A lightness filtered beneath her ribs, a sense of air and mist and things washed clean and put into motion.

So, the Draigon had more power than she had ever imagined. And the Councils—the Councils, on some level, feared women. If the people of Adfen ever knew that! Klem would die of frank humiliation if such a thing were ever to become common knowledge. Klem...did he *know*? No. How could he? She had, all along, been the Draigon's choice. No need had existed for Gahree to *stride*—Leiel turned the word in her mind, the image it called up, fierce and perfect—into Adfen's Council Chamber and demand her way. But someday there might be...gods and dreams! The shock he was in for if the Draigon needed to direct him on the choice of the next Sacrifice in Adfen! Oh, how she would love to be the one to present him and the rest of the Council with that order! But logic forced knowledge. She could not, in the lifetime of any of those men, return to Adfen. To do so would invite disaster for herself, the imperiled women of Adfen, and for the Draigon and all that they guarded.

The women...

"What of the others? What of the women the Councils target, but who are not among your chosen? What happens to them?"

Gahree gave a nod. "They are guided to better places, where appreciation for their spirit can be found."

"But where?" Leiel said.

"Places like our farm." Ilora spoke through a smile.

Leiel stared, shook herself as realization dawned. "Elda," she said.

Gahree nodded. "She did not have the depth of strength for such a choice as we offered your mother, or you. But within her there is a certain pride of will. It was always enough to nurture and sustain her. We see that such women as Elda find their way to women like your mother."

That good news settled her some, but Gahree's words, as usual, woke more questions. Elda, and others did not have the depth of strength...and yet Gahree thought that she, Leiel, did? Had strength the way Ilora had? Or Gemda? To live in this high, cold place, and find a life beyond what she had been raised to know? And perhaps a purpose in that? What would that be for her? Old gods, what if they were wrong about her and this was all a terrible mistake? If someone like

Elda, who owned the caring of a man as strong as Torrin, lacked the fortitude to come here...

Trying to sort her thoughts, Leiel looked between Ilora and Gahree. Leiel's head ached and her limbs felt weighted, as though the things she was learning were somehow heavy, pulling at her, mind and body. "Torrin, too," she said after a moment. "They both found their way to the farm, because you were there."

"No," Ilora said. "Because *we* were there, you and I. There are some havens, for the misfits, in our little piece of the Spur country."

Leiel sat a moment in silence. Havens and warm hearts. The pond by the old mill. The old oak tree. Cleod. Safe spaces. Caring. "So, I have always been part of this." Was she really meant to be here? She shifted her grip on the mug she held. "But what of them, now?" She would not make Cleod part of this question. Not in this moment. She had given up everything to come here. Given up on *him*. "Elda is in Klem's home. I've had no word from Torrin for months. What will they do now, separated from each other and with no one who understands?"

A chuckle from Gahree. Leiel cocked her head and met the woman's green-gold eyes. "Do you think, child of wild spaces," Gahree said. "That I am the only stranger to be met in the market?"

Leiel smiled. "I suppose I should trust that you wouldn't leave good people to fend for themselves." Did that include Cleod?

"The Draigon guided Elda and Torrin to a home once," Ilora said. "Calm your worries. Be assured we will do it again."

We. That word again, this time expanded in meaning. It hung in the air, not cutting the tension, but filling the space with it. Silence added its tingling pressure. In the hearth, the fire crackled low. The mountain wind gave the window casings a rattle. Time stretched, then collapsed, gentle as a whisper.

"Am I...to become part of *we*?" Leiel asked at last. Could she really? What if she, like Elda, like others, lacked something vital that would make such a thing possible? Cleod's screams filled her mind again. She had mistaken the cost to him, of her choice. What else had she been wrong about? What if Gahree was wrong to bring her here?

"Should you choose to," Gahree said. "We offer knowledge and possibility. There are lessons to be explored. Decisions to be made. Few deny the change, when they have learned enough to have the choice. But there are years and years to come in gathering knowledge and seeking truths. Many long seasons, before your preference must be made known."

That shook away some of her swirling thoughts. Gahree was so certain of Leiel's worthiness. She pushed doubts aside as the prospect offered by Gahree's last statement unfolded in her mind. Long seasons. Learning. *Learning.* As much as she wanted. Anything she wanted. No rules. No limits. Time to discover if this was really where she belonged. She drew in air, and closed her eyes. "I am still trying to believe I am here," she said. "To take this all in. I don't know how."

Ilora's hand wrapped her wrist. "Time to rest. We'll be here in the morning. All of us. All this. And all your questions as well."

Leiel raised her head, met the eyes she had never dreamed to see again. "You'll stay with me, tonight?" she asked. "You'll be here in the morning when I wake, baking bread and singing at the stove?"

Ilora smiled. "You would have to drive me from this house to get me to do otherwise."

CHAPTER 9

Leiel

"What is this place?" Leiel followed Gydron up the rock-strewn path toward the dark, oval opening in the cliff wall. The cave loomed large, its depths shadowed and uninviting.

Gydron smiled over her shoulder. "From what I was told about you, a place you will appreciate. It's our library."

Leiel stumbled up a step before catching her balance again. The Draigon had a library? Somehow she had thought they would be above such mundane things as books. But why would they be? As much as Gahree valued stories, what else would be as important as the places where stories were kept? Yes, a library. But here? In this place? Weren't caves dark and damp? "A library?"

Gydron gave a crisp nod. "A fine one." She stopped and turned, reached down a hand to help Leiel up the last jumble of rocks.

"Your paths could be smoother." Leiel let Gydron steady her up the last few steps.

"They could. And they were once, when Desga was here and loved to polish and build them. But Draigon feet are heavy on the ground, even in our human form. We wear on things a bit."

"Desga?" Leiel started. "Desga Hiage? The woman who built the Tower in Adfen?"

Gydron smiled broader. "Built *all* of Old Adfen. Yes. She learned, in building Arnan, to love stone. Many of her works across Adfen still stand. Here, however, we are a bit harder on things, over time. And we do a lot of coming and going from this place."

"No one else can repair these?" Leiel looked down at the partly upended flagstones. "Oh we do, from time to time. But nothing we do lasts like her creations."

Leiel hesitated, then asked. "And Desga? Is she...where is she?"

"Long since passed along the chain of light."

"You mean she's dead."

Gydron nodded. "Just so. But there are finer ways to say it, and I prefer them. At the very least, it is prettier to think of the passage to the next realm as a well-lit path, rather than a hole through which we plunge." She turned and gestured for Leiel to follow her. "Come. The way is easier from here." Her steps were sure as she moved away.

Leiel stared after her, blinking. From books to stonework to death in the space of a few heartbeats, the Draigon were able shift their attention from subject to subject so quickly she could hardly keep up. If Gahree's strangeness had become familiar over the years, it had done little to prepare Leiel for the rambling wisdom of the rest of the Draigon. Even Ilora seemed touched by it. Could she possibly measure up to minds like those?

Shaking her head, Leiel followed Gydron toward the mouth of the cave. Perhaps something in whatever led a woman to become a Draigon—whatever that entailed—also shifted her mind. Perhaps hers would shift as well.

The path was smoother, the rocks still in place tightly enough that she could see the quality of the construction. Worn and cracked though the stones were, there was an artistry to the way they had been placed and joined that made her want to stop and get down on her knees and look closer. She shook herself and turned her attention back to Gydron.

The woman stepped over the lower lip of the cave entrance. The fall of her boots on the rock rang in the enclosed space. Then the ringing turned to echoing as she descended, moving down and away at an angle. Leiel watched, cocked her head, and listened. The echoing expanded, faded, then washed into slow silence.

Leiel stepped to the edge of the opening. Stairs cut into the stone sloped downward, but not into darkness as she expected. A warm glow rose from where the steps slanted away beyond sight. Leiel's heart skipped like a hopping sparrow. A library! How long had it been since she had been in one, been *allowed* in one?

Her steps clicked and echoed like Gydron's. Darkness surrounded her for a few seconds, then the light from below fanned over her feet and the reverberation of her steps faded. A turn of the stairs brought her into a great, open cavern, stretching distant until it met the curve of the mountain wall and arched away into new patterns of flickering shadows.

Cabinets built to match the shape of the uneven stone walls and floor were placed wherever they could be made to fit. They were stacked with books, and not neatly. An awkward, teetering madness seemed to guide each placement. Books, upon books, upon books, upon shelves, as far as she could see. Rugs scattered over the floor deadened echos and added warmth to the space. And the air—it was dry and comfortable without a hint of the mustiness she had expected. Leiel stared, her eyes wide, then laughed.

"You expected more or less?" Gydron asked from where she sat on a plush rug to the right of the nearest shelf.

Leiel smiled. "I am not sure, but not this. It's so..."

"Delightfully chaotic. Just like most minds. There are parts that are more organized, rooms deeper in, for those who think differently. There are always those who think differently."

Again Leiel laughed. "Yes," she agreed. "How it is so dry in here?"

"We excel at keeping things warm and dry."

Of course. A touch of Draigon Weather in a place like this... "You mean there's a Draigon somewhere in this cave?"

"There is a Draigon sitting in front of you," Gydron said.

"Yes, but another—in—I am not sure what to call any of you—one form to the other."

"The Great Shape. That is what we call the winged form we take."

"And...like this? When you are...human?"

"We are always human, Leiel. Sometimes we are simply no longer contained by our original form. When we stand on two feet and move as only what we once were, we are sometimes called Draigfen."

"Draigfen? That's what they call us back home—those of us who had family taken by the Draigon. I would not—" Leiel stopped. What was she saying? Her face burned.

Gydron laughed and got to her feet. "It takes time to understand it all. We are still 'them' to you. 'There' is still home. We understand. Change and comfort take time." She beckoned Leiel to accompany her as she moved deeper into the cave. "And either term, or neither, will suffice."

The casual tone of Gydron's words eased the tension from Leiel's mind. Taking a breath, she followed the Draigfen, weaving between the uneven aisles that mazed among the cabinets. Books everywhere, thick and thin, standing, stacked, and leaning, filled every bit of shelf space. Leiel ran her fingers over the spines, brushed at the pages as she passed. Oh, to spend days and days in the place! What she could learn!

"May I...?"

"Yes, of course."

Leiel stopped, examined the nearest shelf. Few of the spines of the books faced out, and of those that did, only some were marked in any language that she knew. But one, small and edge-worn, caught her eye. The cover was dark and cracked with age. She drew it from the middle of a teetering pile, held her breath that the other volumes would not topple to the floor. The stains of many hands discolored the leather, and she smiled. Much loved, this book. Much read, like the one her mother had given her so long ago. She opened the one in her hand, turned a few pages. The print was faded, and she did not know the language.

"Is this of Arnan?" she asked.

Gydron peered over Leiel's shoulder, shook her head. "No. This story is from Dyil Across Water. Do you know of it?"

"Only by mention in a story Gahree told me in the market. Is it not where the Farlan came from?"

"Not quite. The Far Landers came from a land near there. But they tried once, as well, to change Dyil as they changed Arnan. But the Goddess there would not have such, and she gave her people the power to resist and drive the Far Landers out."

"And if we had such a Goddess here, would things have been different for Arnan and for the Draigon?"

Gydron smiled and dipped her head. "Perhaps. But things are as they are, and the story of Arnan is not the story of Dyil. It never could have been."

Leiel considered. Stories again. Each different from the last and from the next. "And what story is this? Is this Goddess named in this book?"

"She is. That is the story of Yishi, Goddess of the North Wind, and how she was born in the heart of fire to see kindness prevail in the world."

Leiel turned another page, as though the words would come clear simply through her desire to gain their knowledge. "Will you tell me the story?" she asked, looking at Gydron.

"No," the woman said, her smile broadening. "You will read it yourself, as you learn the language in which it is written."

"I am to learn this?" Awe opened inside her.

Gydron swept her arm wide. "You are to learn all of this, in time. As you choose."

Leiel gazed around her. They were deep enough in the stacks that she could see just how far they extended. And farther on, more light spilled from openings in the darkness, indicating still more levels of knowledge contained beneath and all around her. "All of this?" she said aloud. "You know all of this?"

"I know some of it," Gydron said.

"And how long have you been studying?"

"Only a few centuries. I have much to learn."

A few centuries. Old gods! For the first time, Leiel considered that phrase as it crossed her mind. Who were the old gods? Had she ever heard any of their names? Did she know any gods except those named by the Farlan? Who were Arnan's true gods? "We have no gods here, do we?" Leiel asked. "Though some might call you such, you Draigon. Or perhaps Arnan once called you gods?"

"Perhaps they name us so only now," Gydron said. "We never were. But people seeking hope will build faith or curses on many old things."

Leiel looked back to the book, closed it, and returned it to the shelf. "Did Arnan ever have gods besides what we have made of you?" What was she doing among gods, if the Draigon were such?

"Perhaps." Gydron shrugged. "I am not old enough to remember. Gahree might know. Or there might be stories of them named within a book somewhere deep within this place. Come. I have much to show you."

Leiel followed through the stacks, past pillowed nooks, and up and down winding staircases, until the space became a maze from which she had no desire to ever escape. So much knowledge! So much history and humor and wonder! Was there anything she could ever want to know that as not contained somewhere within this space? I like being smart. She remembered saying those words to Cleod the day they met. Was she smart enough for this place? To take in all it offered? Her hands itched. She could pick any book, start reading, lose herself here for days and months and years... Heat bloomed in her stomach like hunger, expanded through her chest, and pushed into her throat with a pounding need that startled her.

Always, she had loved to learn, but this space awakened something new in her mind—the possibility of endless new understandings. She trembled. Had she ever dreamed to have such wealth around her?

"Gydron, where do I begin?" Her voice sounded strange, tight, yet somehow big enough to fill the echoing chamber through which they moved.

"With histories of Arnan, since you seem curious of our past."

"True histories?"

Gydron laughed. "There are no such things. There are only the words of those who lived in the past and their stories of the things they saw or studied. Histories are written by those who bother, or are allowed, to write them."

Leiel frowned. Had she not learned the history of Arnan as the Farlan had written it? The stories Gahree had told her were of those times, and yet the differences between the same events had been what had turned her heart and set her on the path that brought her here. "So, there are always more histories," she said. "Always different stories of the same past."

"Pasts," Gydron said. "Because whose past is the same as yours? And who can tell yours, but you?"

"Why would anyone tell my past?"

"That depends," Gydron laughed, "on what you do with your future."

CHAPTER 10

Cleod - 24 years

By all gods old and new, I didn't believe them."

Cleod rolled his head on arms folded on the table, and cracked an eye upward. The shape that loomed over him was a back-lit blur. Blinking, he lifted his chin, pressing his hands into the scratched tabletop to steady himself. A shape swirled into focus, but it was not the man standing beside him. It was the mug just inches from his nose. Good. He was too damn sober. He lifted a hand toward it, but another descended and snatched it away.

"Blood of the Elders! Cleod!" The voice was louder now, and he recognized it. Trayor. Trayor was here. How fitting.

The mug was slammed back down on the other side of the table, and someone yanked around the bench on which he sat. He swayed on the seat, still half asleep. The hands that caught his arms were not gentle, and he snarled as the still healing burns on his body sent a wave of complaint to his brain.

"Hold him up, Hoyd," Trayor said. He put a leg on either side of the bench and sat, caught Cleod's face in his hands and stared at him.

"Let go," Cleod jerked his head back, and the motion set his skull pounding. He slanted an eye up at the man who gripped his shoulders and recognized the young Draigre he had mentored. "Hoyd! Tray! Have some drink. Is the best thing for healing wounds. I'm better every day."

Hoyd uttered a fluid curse.

"Oh, come." Cleod raised a hand toward the mug. "The stuff is cheap and plentiful."

"I never thought to see such a thing." Hoyd's voice was rough in Cleod's ears. "When they said he refused to return to the Enclave—"

"Be silent," Trayor said. "He's in need."

"No need," Cleod said. He shrugged off Hoyd's hands, jerked free of Trayor. "Leave me be. I am no Draighil. Go back to your mountain."

"Rotting cefreid, we're here to help you."

"Haa!" Cleod leaned across the table and dragged the mug back to him. "This is the help I need. I am done with Draigon. And you're fools if you don't quit, too."

"You can't quit," Hoyd said. "You've done so much, Cleod. There is too much you have to teach the rest of us."

"He's right. You've faced Shaa and lived. Your knowledge..." Trayor reached out to take the mug away again.

"I didn't *live!*" Cleod shouted. He grabbed back the mug and hurled it away. The impact with the stone floor sent shards of pottery skittering under the neighboring tables. He shook his head and dropped it back onto folded arms. "Leave me be. Leave me."

"Cleod, let us help you. We came—"

"*Burn*!" he said. There was something he needed to say. Something important. Words he could not find. He could help these two if he could find the words. But whatever truth he sought slipped away each time he reached for it. If he could not save them, he could drive them away. "Burn with the Enclaves. They did this to me. Fool's bounty. Cursed life. Wander and rot, Draighil fools. Be gone. I want no more of you."

He shoved back from the table and staggered upright, his legs tingling from sitting for so long. "No more from you," he repeated, and lurched away through the crowd, struggling for balance as feeling returned to his limbs.

Cursing sounded all around him as he shoved people out of his way. More rough language came from behind as Trayor and Hoyd followed him. Didn't they understand? He was done. Something—something he knew now— made him done. He should tell them...what? His thoughts skittered away, and his stomach heaved as he shoved at the tavern door. It slammed open and he stepped into the street.

It was snowing. His feet crunched on ice, and he slid the next step, caught himself against the wall. Blinking as a cold wind whipped snow into his eyes, he shivered. Coat. Didn't he own a coat? No matter. Somewhere would be warmer. The tavern across the street.

The door behind him banged, and someone said his name. He snarled a curse. Not the other establishment then. Somewhere that he could make certain the lesson he needed to teach his stubborn followers could be laid out in a way they would never forget. He took a sliding step and slammed again into the wall of the building. He put hand against the building's wall for balance, planting each step carefully so as not to slip again. An alley opened beside him, and he turned into it as footsteps sounded behind him.

Snow swirled his vision—not just snow, but that didn't matter. He let himself lose focus and shoved away from the wall. More footsteps, this time on the snow. Hands grabbed him and tried to spin him around. He went with the turn and raised a stiff elbow, cracked the point of it into someone's lower jaw.

He knew before the howl of surprise issued forth which of his two followers he had connected with. Trayor would not have been so foolish as to try to grab him on open ground. The blur that was Hoyd faced him with a bloodied lip.

Cleod took a step backward, trying to remember why Trayor would know better. So much came and went now, between drink and pain and exhaustion. So much, everything like the snow falling, all the time, cloudy things, always in motion. Ercew's view of the world. So much better than what had come before.

"Hands off, Hoyd," Trayor said. "He's drunk, but he's still Draighil. And almost as good as me. If we have to drag him back, I'll be the one doing it." His black-clad shape half-blurred into place beside Hoyd. The younger man held his hand to his face, blood bright between his fingers.

Something shimmered in Cleod's mind. "Almost as good as me..." The statement was meant to provoke. But what? Violence? Anger? It was laughter that rose in him and barked out. The frown on Trayor's face sent a clear message that amusement had not been the response he had expected. You always expected me to be predictable, Cleod thought. You should know better by now.

Where had that come from? Cleod shook his head. What did he know? So many lies. Again it came, the thought that there was something important he needed to tell these men. But it slipped away as Trayor stepped forward.

Cleod brought his arm up and moved into the blow. He twisted at the last instant, let Trayor's arm slide down and slam into his shoulder. The strike rocked through his knees, and for an instant, he fought the power of it, pressing back upward against Tray's weight. Then Cleod let himself give way and collapsed into the building snow. Part of him expected the other man to follow him down. Something about balance? But it did not happen. That was wrong. Or not. He wasn't clear.

Cleod crunched his body inward and rolled, not toward or away from his attacker, but toward the wall of the alley. A foot came down where his head had been a second before. It was wrapped in a boot of black leather that had no laces. Too bad. He might have considered tying them together to see if he could get the owner of the boot to join him in the snow.

Being in the snow was not right. He grabbed the foot and yanked, trying to pull himself upright. Above him, a fluid and creative series of curses burst forth, then the slickness of the ground took charge and brought the owner of the boot down beside him after all.

"You said something about dragging?" he said, bracing his hands in the snow on either side of his feet and shoving himself upright. Across from him, Trayor did the same.

"You always were a damned cheat, Cleod."

Cleod laughed. "Not just me," he said. "I—I—am the least of the cheats. Ask Soibel. Burning gods—ask them all."

"What in all the blooded lands have you been drinking?" Trayor glared at him, but it was hard to find the look intimidating when it kept disappearing from focus behind a veil of blowing snow.

"Don't," Cleod said to the shape drifting toward him from his right.

Hoyd stopped.

The sound of snowflakes hitting wood and fabric was, for a moment, the only noise in the alley. Then Trayor hissed out a breath, and Cleod tipped his head at the sound. "Don't," he repeated. "I'm not going back. Not ever going back. I'm not sober, but I can do enough damage to both of you that you'll be as useless as I am for the rest of your lives." He had trouble making all the sounds come out right. They drifted as though blown by the storm. But the meaning got through. Hoyd took a step back, and Trayor raised his chin a little.

Cleod frowned. Damn the rush of fighting. He was too sober. Small things were starting to become clear again. His throat felt dry and swollen. There was more ercew to be had if he could just get rid of these two. "I'll break you as I was broken," he said. "They don't even know you are here. You came for me. All the way to Sibora. And no one knows."

"Tray. There are two of us." Hoyd's voice was hoarse and a bit muffled by his swollen lips. "We can take—"

"We can end up bloodying the snow," Trayor cut him off, his gaze never leaving Cleod. "We came to help you, Cleod. The Ehlewer will understand that."

Cleod glared back. Too much clarity brought on by adrenaline. He was aware of things again. "You're not here to help me," he said. The slur was fading from his words. Damn them. Gods of all, he needed a drink! His stomach flipped, but he swallowed back the sudden rise of bile. "You're here to help yourselves. Poor Tray. Poor Hoyd. Friends with a traitor. Better bring him back and show you're not the same." He wished they were the same. That would be best. Why? It would be better for so many if they did quit. Why was that? Damn them for keeping him from the ercew. "Won't work. Can't save yourselves by trying to save me."

"I'm not—"

"Course you are. Always have been. Share the glory. Share the fall. Come on down to the hard earth, Tray. I'll buy you a drink."

Trayor took a half-step forward, reached to grasp Cleod's shirt. A fight it would be, then. Cleod's stomach heaved and the potential for battle vanished as he rendered up the rewards of the last three days in the tavern across Trayor's uniform.

"Gods and fire on high!" Trayor backed away, his arms raised, looking down at his ruined clothes, his face twisted.

Cleod stepped away. "Best to let me be," he said, spat into the snow and wiped his lips with the back of one hand.

Hoyd stood beside Trayor, his mouth hanging open. The two Draighil looked as stunned as a pair of squirrels that had fallen out of a tree. Cleod laughed. "I'll fight you both," he said. "Filth and all."

Trayor ran his hands down his chest, flicking away the foulness covering his shirt, then bent to rub his hands clean in the fresh snow. "What in the name of all that breathes have you done to yourself?"

"Not so much that I can't bloody the likes of you. Imagine what your shiny clothes will look like then."

Trayor stared, then looked at Hoyd. "He's ruined. There's no Draighil pride left in him."

"No," Hoyd said. "He can't stay like this. We have to take him back."

"How?" Trayor shook his head, looked at Cleod. "You'd rather try to kill us than return? Or stay here in your own stink?"

Cleod laughed, bitterness lingering on his tongue. "You're wearing the worst of my stink. Go back to your mountain top. What's left of your pride matters not at all to me." Was that true? He shook his head. The next drink was what mattered. Rot these two for keeping him from it. The cold was seeping in and even his anger was not enough to keep it at bay. He was done talking. "Go away," he said. "Or I'll break both your necks."

Snow whirled around them, tapped at Cleod's exposed skin. Laughter rang from the tavern and on the street behind him, feet and the wheels of passing carriages crunched in the snow. The moment folded in on itself, then stretched and flattened. Fight or leave. No more patience for these games. Could they force him? It was likely. But would it be worth the cost in the moment? And worth the consequences of his fully sober anger in the near future?

Trayor took a step away.

Cleod smiled. "Don't come back." He turned and walked carefully back toward the street and the drowning warmth of the tavern and its many charms. Training acknowledged the flex of tension through the air, but no action followed. Cleod did not look back as he made his way back onto the street. Pride or fear—it did not matter which —had won his desired outcome.

CHAPTER 11

Leiel

Is this a school?" The quaver in Leiel's voice spoke of wonder. She looked at Ilora, then back around the room. The cabin where she had met Ilora on her first day in Cyunant was thick-walled, and the storm outside was barely noticeable once the door closed behind them. The inside of the building was a single room with a huge wood stove at one end and shelves stacked with books along both long walls. Tables and desks and chairs huddled in tight spaces. Seated on cushions near the stove, a handful of young children looked up attentively at Gemda, who was holding forth with broad gestures, telling a story. Leiel blinked. She had not expected to see children in this place. And not since she was a child herself, had she been in a place where learning was encouraged, expected, considered important.

"It's many things," Ilora said. "Gydron usually teaches in the Library, but this is easier for the children in harsh weather. And for the newest arrivals, this space is sometimes more comfortable than the cave."

That made sense. The library was so huge it overwhelmed. And it was just one of many new things, and people, to keep straight in her head. This place, smaller and more intimate, was easier to take in.

She glanced again at the young students listening to Gemda. "Where do the children come from?"

Ilora followed her gaze. "They are born here."

"Born? I haven't seen any men."

"Some of the women we bring here arrive pregnant. Some take lovers before they become Draigon."

Heat rushed to Leiel's face as she stared at Ilora. "Lovers?"

"Sometimes."

"And you?" Did she know this woman at all?

Ilora shook her head. "No. I did not make that choice."

A lover. She never thought of her mother in terms of such an option...never even really considered for herself whether or not such a thing might be possible. Had there ever been anyone but Cleod with whom she might have...? She let the thought drift away. "I never thought to ask what life might be like here. I was too caught up with my life at home and Klem and—"

"You had enough to make sense of in Adfen without wondering about a place you hardly knew existed. You're here now."

Leiel nodded, looked around again. She smiled at two women, a few years older than she, seated on a couch next to the door. One waved. The other looked over her shoulder and smiled back.

"That's Simmini and Shorr. Sim came from Melbis five years ago. Shorr was the last Sacrifice from Giddor—on the southeast coast. They will be able to answer many questions for you, about settling in here. The rest of us have been in Cyunant so long that we have forgotten, a bit, what it is like to be strangers here."

Leiel smiled back at the two young women, they both nodded, turned back to the papers spread between them. For a few more seconds, Leiel watched. The two laughed, relaxed, at ease and confident. Would she feel that someday, here in this strange place? With the woman beside her? She looked at Ilora again. "What are they doing?"

"Translating fairy tales."

Leiel looked at her. "Like Gahree had me do, with the story of the Witch in the Wood."

Ilora nodded. "Familiar tales are easy to follow."

"Is that what is taught here? Stories, and more ways to learn them?"

The laugh Leiel was still learning to believe was real, not just a memory, escaped Ilora. "Among so many other things. Stories have always been the best and easiest ways to share knowledge. You already know that."

Leiel considered, nodded a little. "But what else is taught here? Who teaches?"

"Come." Ilora led the way across the room. A small slate hung on the end of a shelf. "This is a list of everyone who will be teaching here this week. They mark when they will be here, and what they will be teaching in that time."

The list was long. Some of the names Leiel recognized, like Ilora and Gemda, and even Gahree.

"I need to learn all these things?" Leiel ran a finger down the edge of the slate. *Origins of the Draigon. Defenses of Cyunant. Diplomacy Across Arnan. History of Gweld and Expansion of Awareness for Transformation.*

What most of it meant, she did not know, but something caught at memory. Gweld. Why did she know the word? It was something important. Something Cleod learned in the Enclave.

She touched a finger under the word, and looked at Ilora. "What is this? Cleod spoke of this." Memory came clear.

"He *learned* this! He said it was what made him powerful enough to face and kill the Draigon!" Her voice rose and cut the air.

Ilora met Leiel's gaze. "I am not the best person to answer that question. But Gweld was not created by the Enclaves. It was a skill the Draigon learned, long ago, to reach the level of conscious perception needed to take on the Great Shape. Gahree will tell you more, when you have learned enough history to ."

"Gweld is *Draigon knowledge*?" Leiel half-choked on the words. Her stomach was again in hot knots.

"No," Ilora said. She reached out as though to take Leiel's hands, but stopped the action short and just spoke instead. "Gweld is simply *knowledge*. How it is used, and by whom, determines whose power it is considered to be."

Leiel frowned. "Mother, I think you have been in Gahree's company far too long."

"You may be right." Ilora shrugged. "Gweld is complicated. It is not anything you will learn soon, but that's just what it is—something to learn. What is done with that knowledge, and how complete that knowledge is before it is used, will vary based on the teacher. And the student."

"Cleod said it would make him sick to learn it." What had he gone through that she simply did not understand?

"The Enclaves are not known for their subtlety."

Leiel shook her head. "So, learning this...skill...doesn't have to be painful?"

"Not painful in the way the Draighil experience it. It is not something easy to understand or master. But the Enclaves choose a different path for their students. They choose one of pain."

"But why?"

"So they have a way to control their students, body and mind."

"Then Cleod—"

"Some part of him will always belong to the Enclaves. You can only hope that the rest of him is strong enough to survive beyond their influence. The life ahead of him is not the one he planned. It won't be easy for him."

"Something not being easy is different from his survival being threatened." Leiel frowned. Her chest ached. "Is this Gweld dangerous?"

Ilora shook her. "Not in itself. But there are dangers in its misuse."

"And Cleod has somehow misused what he was taught."

"Not exactly." Ilora sighed. "I'm not the best person to explain."

Heat rushed through Leiel's chest, pushed into her voice. "Then who is?" But she already knew. Where had all her answers come from in the years since Ilora left?

The cabin door slammed behind Leiel as she crossed the porch and went down the steps into the packed snow. Where was the greenhouse? Gahree had shown her the way a few days ago. Icy rain sleeted into Leiel's eyes as she turned, spotted a hard-beaten path running around the north side of the cabin. She wrapped her scarf over her head and started up the trail. Behind her, the cabin door creaked open, and she glanced back. Ilora stepped onto the porch. She raised a hand, offered an understanding tip of her head. Leiel turned her gaze up the ravine and worked her way along the snowy path.

Made slick by the sleet, the trail grew treacherous as she climbed. Her breath heaved and hissed in the thin air, and she had to slow her pace. What had she left Cleod to? What fate had she asked Gahree to save him for? Was he so damaged, so far beyond help, that there was no real life left for him? Her chest burned from more than lack of breath.

She turned the layout of the village in her mind, trying to recall from her few days in Cyunant, the location of the building she sought. Sheltered along the north wall of the ravine, were glass walls exposed to the eastern light and the southwest track of the sun, it should be below the trail to the library cave. A gust blew the sleet away, and she caught a glimpse of shining glass in the grey and white landscape. She pushed through the weather. The patter of icy pellets on glass greeted her as she reached the building and with a shiver, pulled open the door and stepped into the bright space enclosed by shining walls.

Heat rocked her, as it had when Gahree had brought her here to explain the mystery of the year-round fresh peppers. But Leiel pushed the wonder of the building to the back of her mind.

Gahree stood halfway across the room, watery-dark hair braided down her back, and arms bare and flecked with dirt. The scene was so unlike what Leiel had expected, that she just stared for several heartbeats. At last she said, "My mother spoke as though Cleod might not survive." Her voice was not shaking, but her hands were, as she unwrapped the scarf that covered her hair. The cloth was soaked through, and she wrung the fabric a bit, both to dry it and to occupy her fingers. Drips hit the stone floor, left dark circles on the rock. Overhead, the ping of rain and sleet was an echo of her nerves.

Gahree turned, watering can in hand. "I should have had you wring that over the plants." Gahree motioned her forward. "Take off your coat, wild daughter, or you will soon be too warm in here." She set aside her watering can, and lifted a pot, half-filled with soil. "Cleod Draighil is a plant, grown strong in one soil, but now being transplanted to a new one."

Leiel peeled out of her coat and folded it over her arm. "No metaphors, Gahree. Please. I need to know. You told me he would be well."

"I told you he would live." Gahree shook her head. "Your friend is strong, but he has been twisted by his time among the Ehlewer. He will need time to heal. And his future will not be easy, but we will not leave him to suffer alone. We will find a way to help him, if we can." Gahree tapped at the bottom of a small pot, lifted out a young pepper plant. She brushed gently at the dirt packed around its roots to loosen it and set the small plant into the larger pot.

"Like you helped Elda and Torrin find mother?" Leiel asked.

Gahree nodded. "In a way."

Leiel was silent for a few seconds as she watched Gahree place fresh soil into the pot. "You won't tell me more?"

"Have I ever?"

A short laugh escaped Leiel.

Gahree nodded, flicked a smile over her shoulder. "What would you ask me now?"

Leiel trembled, then paced away toward the glass wall, stopped and came back, the need to do something burning her belly. "I would ask you why. Why do you let the Enclaves exist at all? Why do you let them train boys to be killers? Why do you let them create danger for you? Why do you let them twist good people into—into—" She stopped, unable to find the word she wanted. "*Why?*"

"Because we believe in choice." Gahree lifted a hand spade from the table and turned to the bin beside her, stirred the rich compost stored there. "We cannot promote such for women like you—for all of Arnan—and yet take away the choice of those who decide to hate us. Thus, we mark the difference between how the world is now, and what we would have it be, with what we hope to return to the land. Those who rule Arnan would have the world be only one way. They would have every living being believe only one thing, and behave by only a handful of rules. They would dictate every breath of every creature under their power. Were we to destroy the Enclaves, we would be acting as they do—deciding for every person what they need or are allowed to want."

"But you tell me they lie to those who join them. That they make them sick on purpose. How can that be freedom?" Why had she not asked these things sooner?

Gahree lifted soil into the new pot, patted it loosely around the roots. She paused and looked over at Leiel. "Do you think freedom is such a simple thing, daughter of wings, that it should always lead to good? Choices are painful. Every person lives with every decision made through life—good or bad. It is the freedom to make them, even decisions that lead to pain, that matters most. Without even the opportunity to decide, no wisdom is gained, no strength acquired."

Leiel stood in the hot space, listened to the sleet against the glass walls, and tried to accept Gahree's words. Nothing in their logic eased the twisting in her gut. "You cannot help them."

"I choose to let them choose," Gahree said. "How many men, of those you have known, Leiel Sower of Adfen, would listen to anything I had to say?"

"You said the Councils listen to you."

"The Councils listen to the representative of the Draigon when Draigon Weather reigns. On a street—a chance meeting at an old mill—how many men would hear me then?"

"Cleod would have," Leiel said.

Gahree held her gaze a moment, gave a nod, then turned back to the plant before her. "Perhaps he would have," Gahree said. "And perhaps my choice not to go to him, as I went to you, was wrong."

Leiel pulled her head back, breath caught sharp in her throat. Never, in all the years of their acquaintance, had she heard Gahree admit any doubt, or weakness, or possibility of wrongdoing. For a moment, she found no words. She watched Gahree work, her hands darkened by the rich soil, then she asked quietly, "Why didn't you?"

Gahree brushed her hands against each other over the pot. "I was more concerned with your mother. And with you. I had much to teach you both. And so, that was my choice. If you wish to hold me to some blame for it now, that choice is yours."

Blame? Leiel frowned. Was that what she was doing? Looking for someone to blame? Someone to push her doubts and guilt and fears off on...as Klem had done for so many years to her? Her next indrawn breath had a weight behind it that she forced herself to swallow. "No," she said. "No, that is not what I want to do."

Gahree smiled. "And I am glad of that choice."

Leiel stared, then gave a laugh. "Lesson brought to my heart," she said. She paused, then asked, "My mother said you were the one to ask about Gweld."

"Aaaahhh. To speak of something as powerful as the Gweld, we will need much work. There are some things that are better learned by the mind when the hands are also busy." She gestured to a coat stand beside the door. "Put your things there and join me." She turned back to the potting table.

Knowing she would get no answers until Gahree was ready to give them, Leiel hung up her coat and scarf and moved to join the woman.

Gahree set a large pot before Leiel, and handed her a trowel. A tray of seedlings sat in the center of the table, and Leiel smiled a little as she pulled it toward her. She had come to the top of a mountain in the Great Northern Range in the company of the greatest of the Draigon, only to find herself doing the same work she had done all her life back on the farm, and somehow that was not strange at all.

"Why is work necessary to learn about this Gweld? Cleod said it made him sick. Is even talking about this thing dangerous?"

Gahree's haunting laugh burst into the air with an enthusiasm Leiel had not heard since their first meeting at the mill pond. "Oh, daughter of dreams, all knowledge is dangerous, if learned by half, or taught by half. All knowledge has the power to change the learner, and should be treated with respect."

"You are saying that the Enclaves do not respect this Gweld."

Gahree shook her head as she lifted compost into her pot. "No, they respect it greatly. But they only understand enough of it to bend it to their purpose—which is to give advantage to the Draighil."

Cleod's blinding speed and economy of power. The complete confidence with which he had faced Shaa on the Spur. "And it works."

A nod from Gahree. "In a way. The best of their warriors move within it well enough to outmatch some of us, but they never fully understand it."

"What is it?"

"Awareness."

"Of what?"

Gahree lifted the trowel and gestured in a small circle in the air before her. "That is the power of Gweld, Leiel Sower. Gweld is earned knowledge—but so much more. It is understanding how knowledge changes the learner. And it is accepting those changes—accepting that there will always be more to learn.

"The beauty and difficulty of Gweld is that no one learns the same things, or absorbs even the same knowledge in the same way—therefore, Gweld manifests itself differently for everyone. The one constancy of it is expanded awareness, and the ability to react to events at a speed beyond normal human action. Acceptance and knowledge allow access to Gweld states—and those things combined allow some of us—those able to take enough into ourselves and offer it out again—to take on the Great Shape. It is what makes us Draigon."

Leiel paused in her work, hands deep in the dirt, looked at Gahree. "Gweld makes you Draigon?" Was that all it took? Unease tugged at her mind, but no clear idea formed to tell her why.

"Gweld allows me to pour my knowledge into a shape that can contain it all, and allows me to access all of it with the shift of a thought."

"But it also allows the Draighil to kill you—"

"Gweld allows many things. But it is, itself, neither good nor bad. It is just a space inside each of us, that allows us to be more than we think we are."

Leiel was silent. She twisted her fingers through the soil, brushed the roots of the tiny plant. Gweld was within? Yet it changed how the world was seen and experienced? She thought again of the unearthly speed and grace with which Cleod had moved on the mountain, how he had seemed beyond the moment, yet able to act with a quickness that defied thought. "Will I learn to use Gweld? Has my mother?"

"All in Cyunant learn it. Some sooner than others. Some deeper. Some only enough to be able to communicate with those in the Great Shape."

Leiel looked at Gahree, met the green-gold eyes. "Communicate?" Leiel pulled herself up a little straighter. "Like we did, when you brought me here?"

"Just so," Gahree said with a tip of her head.

"Then...I already have some knowledge of Gweld?" Leiel asked. How was that possible, when she hardly knew what it was?

"You saw the leaves on my tree dance in the firelight, Leiel. You knew the power of the stories told to you when you were but a small girl. You sensed the truth in my tales, even when they were difficult for your heart to hear. You have an imagination and a spirit suited to exploration and challenge. You have always been able to touch Gweld. It is part of why I wanted you among us."

Leiel pulled her hands from the soil and brushed them off against each other. Was it possible? Did she somehow already know something about the very thing the Enclaves existed to teach the Draighil? The thing that made the Draigon creatures of legend? A tingle swept from her toes to the top of her skull. "But I was never sick," she said. "Cleod said learning Gweld made him sick. He said it made them all sick."

"Gweld makes no one sick who comes to it naturally," Gahree said. She traced a dirty finger over the edge of a leaf on the plant she had just transferred. Its delicate green shivered under her touch, gold light slipping along the edges. "What makes the Draighil sick is not Gweld, but being forced to learn it—each Draigre being forced to all learn the exact same aspects of it, and the same manner of accessing it. The forced conformity of Gweld expression is what brings illness. No two beings should feel or understand Gweld in the same way. To force such uniform condition of the experience is traumatic to body and mind."

Leiel faced Gahree fully. "You are telling me that there is not one way to learn this?"

"There are as many ways as there are people," Gahree said. "Over the centuries, we have learned patterns of knowledge that seem to speed understanding for many, but the student must commit to her own learning, and follow her heart and her interests, to reach Gweld. It should never be rushed. It should never be forced. When you have learned what you must know, you will find your expression of Gweld."

"My expression?"

"How it changes your interaction with the world around you. And how that allows you to seek the Great Shape." "So...you can't teach me how to become Draigon."

Gahree laughed. "Of course not," she said. "I can only teach you how to teach yourself."

"More riddles." Leiel shook her head. "I don't think I can bear such now."

"Daughter of dreams, you have never truly learned anything from me or anyone else. You have always only learned either what you must to survive, or what you cared to learn. *You* learned it. I only offered you knowledge. You had to choose to take it in. This is always the way of knowledge. There is no riddle in truth."

CHAPTER 12

Leiel - 24 years

Leiel's voice rose and fell with the reading, her words both softened and lent a subtle echo by the tapestried walls of the library chamber. The passing months had not lessened her thrill at the warmth the space added to the sound of her voice. It let her forget how small she felt before the knowledge surrounding her.

The worn book spread open on the table before her claimed her focus, as she studied the faded ink on the yellowing parchment, and gingerly turned pages made soft at the edges by time and use. Around her, the golden glow of lanterns brightened all but the darkest corners and alcoves. Some of those held more books, some were tucked full of small carvings or other treasures of history that Leiel had yet to explore. Would she ever be able to explore and understand it all?

Across the vaulted chamber, Simmini perched half-way up a ladder. Shorr waited at the base, one hand steadying, the other handing up books to be shelved.

"Wait, read that again?" Sim said.

Leiel paused, then repeated the last phrase, and looked up. The two women were watching her, their faces animated by suppressed laughter. Then all effort at containment failed, and Sim nearly doubled over on the ladder, giggling.

"Glorious, not farcical!" Shorr wheezed, her south-coast accent heavier for the laughter caught behind it. "Glorious sunset over Pentryp!"

"Here though—farcical sunset—that's original!" Sim said, behind fingers pressed to her mouth. Her eyes crinkled. "Glorious?" Leiel said. She looked down at the book in her lap. Yes, there it was, the accent mark over the second high-twist. Glorious. And farcical sunset. How had she even managed to say it without bursting out laughing herself? She half-choked on a snort.

"I have to wonder just what that would look like," Ilora said from over Leiel's shoulder.

Leiel looked up with a start, then shook her head. "I'm sure we'll arrive at a terrible description if we dwell on it for long."

"I'm certain," Ilora said. "I'm here to interrupt."

"Oh, that's just as well," Shorr said. "I'm done in now. We'll not get more work done now for laughing. Is this a call to lunch? I think it should be. We'll finish after. Join us, Ilora?"

"We'll catch up," Ilora said.

Leiel looked at her. An interruption with purpose it seemed. The passage of months had managed to ease some aches in their relationship, but added new ones. Conversations sometimes delighted and sometimes frustrated beyond reason. Good, all of it, but trying. Last night, they had argued through most of the late meal. Leiel looked at her friends, then shook her head. "Talking to be done."

"Here then, all right," Simmini said. She climbed down, hopping off the last rung. "See you in a bit. Speak of nothing farcical."

Ilora smiled. "You two enjoy the afternoon. We'll finish the shelving."

"Thank you," Shorr said. "Come on, Sim." She grabbed the Melbian woman and led her out of the chamber, their footsteps quickly muffled by the thick carpets in the passageway.

"Join me?" Ilora asked. She crossed the room to continue the abandoned project.

Leiel put the book aside, marked her place with a thin-shaved bit of wood as she studied her mother. Stranger than Leiel had expected, had been the shift to having Ilora back in her life. From a bubbling joy that vibrated her body from top to bottom like a plucked string, to a tight-throated anger that choked speech,

Leiel found her emotions sliding and teetering, until the only release she had was to either run screaming down the mountain, or burst into tears. Of late, more laughter than tears had been the norm, but the logical understanding of Ilora's choices was so different from facing the still-present anger of childhood loss and loneliness. Last night's rough conversation was likely the reason Ilora had sought her out.

Leiel rose and joined her mother. "Shelve?"

Ilora nodded, and Leiel braced the ladder. It creaked as Ilora climbed up.

"Ready to finish our talk?"

They had both gone to bed, not angry, but with little resolved between them.

"You always did know when I was feeling low."

"And I know I'm the cause," Ilora said, reaching down.

A smile lifted Leiel's lips. "Not the only cause." Leiel placed a volume in her mother's hand. "You can't expect me to not be angry, no matter how glad I am to be here with you."

The ladder swayed a fraction as Ilora leaned to tuck the book into place. "Leiel, your ability to be angry at the right things is one of your best traits. If you simply accepted what I did, and all of this, I would be truly concerned for your sanity. But we're here, both of us. We have time in plenty. We can make all the use of it we need to, to set things right between us."

"You say that as though that's what must happen."

"You think it won't? That you'll be angry with me forever?"

Leiel smiled. "Do we have forever?"

Ilora shook her head as she accepted another book. "No. But we'll have longer than most creatures."

Was that what she would become? Was that what Ilora was now? A creature? *Could* she? The passing weeks, if anything, had redoubled the doubt crouched in the darkest corners of her heart. All this knowledge—were even her best efforts half enough? To become Draigon—a creature of fear and legend. "You think of yourself so?"

A chuckle. "We're all creatures, always. Draigon are just stranger than most."

"Just stranger?" Leiel blinked up at her mother. "That's all?" Strange and learned and powerful and fearsome. So much to be measured against.

"Well, we're not the most interesting, or well understood. We might be wiser than most, but that's the nature of both time and our purpose."

Ilora glanced down, smiled. "Are you thinking it's odd that I consider myself part of something else—something more than I was, and not quite human?"

"Are Draigon at all human?" Leiel asked. The question rolled in her mind more each day. Strange, to ask it of the woman who had birthed her, but Leiel was not certain of the answer. Draigfen, Gydron had said. The women moved and spoke like people. They trained and cooked and studied and worked and ate and laughed—yet—their thoughts moved more quickly and more deeply than any people she had ever known. And their hearts welcomed so much. It seemed too impossible, that human frailty and failing could assume such power, express so much kindness and strength.

Ilora slid another volume into place. "Of course we are human. Otherwise, we would not care about Arnan. So few creatures can care for anything other than themselves. Humans are more capable of it than most. The natural-born Draigon learn compassion from those of us who can *choose* the Great Shape. They are born loving knowledge and adventure, but it takes more for them to understand how to love others as much as those things. It takes contact with us."

Leiel passed up another book, then blinked a few times as Ilora's words sank in. "Natural-born Draigon?"

"Like Wynt. Both her parents were Draigon, when she was conceived."

"Both...? *Men can be Draigon?*" And she remembered Gahree's brother, Glau, called *Drip* in the old language. Had he been Draigon as well? Could Cleod become Draigon? Could he join her here? Leiel's throat went dry, and her heart thudded until she felt it behind her eyes. When she asked Gahree about Gweld...a thought that had only half-formed then, now leaped clear into her mind. If Gweld was what it took to become Draigon...

Ilora nodded. "It's rare. But some men love knowledge, and giving, enough to open themselves to a Great Shape. Some men feel a truth greater than their own power."

That was Cleod, ready to dedicate himself to more than he was. And yet it was not. The pride in him. The calm arrogance. Was that born? Learned? Could such things be unlearned? And, if so, would that be enough?

"My friend—"

"The Draighil." Ilora slid a book home, then looked down at Leiel. "The boy you were so close with."

"He hasn't been that boy in a long time."

"But you're wondering—"

"How can I not wonder, mother?" Her head was hot. "He is what he is because of me."

Ilora shook her head. "It would be easier if it were that simple. He chose what he is, just as you have chosen what you are. He was trained to kill us. I don't see how he could overcome that to become one of us. Not even all born among us can do that."

Leiel's heart skipped. More than Gweld, then, was needed. What else? Will? Knowledge? If not even those born in Cyunant could access the change, was any amount of study guaranteed to bring her to it? She pushed the thought down. "What do you mean? How can a child born here not be Draigon?"

Ilora reached down and, instead of taking the book Leiel held up, curled her fingers around Leiel's. "You know Torrin's story—what happened to his mother."

Leiel nodded. The tale of that abuse was not something she would forget.

"Torrin's mother is far from the only woman of spirit to have faced such horror. Some end up here. Sometimes, a child is born here after a woman arrives."

The heat at the back of Leiel's skull was swept away by the chill that ricocheted between her shoulder blades. "Where are they? These women? These children? Are they still here? Are they Draigon?"

"Some." Ilora nodded. "Most women who choose to come here are strong beyond their own knowledge."

Leiel considered. Yes, the women of Cyunant were, to a person, steadfast and smart, willing to both learn and share. Women who, day by day, promoted their own strength and that of those around them. And here she was among them. Gahree believed in her. "Who?"

"Those stories aren't mine to tell," Ilora said.

Leiel looked at her mother for a few seconds. Stories. Everyone in Cyunant had one. Stories had led her to the Sacrifice, to this village high in the mountains. Had she thought they would not continue to be the most important thing of all? "It's been so long since you told me a story. As Loremaster, I think you should remedy that."

Ilora laughed. She squeezed Leiel's fingers, took the book, and put it away, then climbed down to join her daughter. "Sit. I think I will tell you how wisdom came to the Draigon."

"Wisdom?"

"So we like to think."

Leiel didn't try to hold back a grin. "I would like to learn how wisdom comes to anyone."

Ilora moved to the table and settled herself in a chair. Leiel joined her, an old tingle flickering over her shoulders. Worries, she shoved aside. A story from her mother's lips! Too long a time had passed since she had heard one. For all her anticipation of Gahree's tales through the years, it had always been her mother's voice, her mother's words she longed for. Leiel pulled her knees up in the seat and hugged them, settling back as Ilora spoke.

"From the north came a wind, laced with notes of cedar and ice. It bent branches, and rustled frosted grasses, and carried upon its current a falcon. The bird's name was Wisdom, and it had never before been seen in the land.

"In a wide vale marked by a winding river, a woman named Draigon looked up from her work and saw the creature on wing. Its head crowned with silvered feathers and eyes so bright they pierced across the length of the valley, it flew closer. Draigon raised a hand to see it better, outlined against the clouds. Then the falcon's gaze hooked hers and drew her spirit from her body.

"Up, up she rose, while her body waited in the sun. No fear touched her spirit as the falcon carried her high, into darkness, where the arc of the sky bent to reveal the curves of the world and the day-lit spark of stars. Its wings beat hard to reach that height, but it did not slack its effort once it reached elevation, but powered forward, holding its gain and sweeping through the sky until so much of the world was visible below. At the sight, shame filled Draigon — for she had believed her small land was all that mattered.

"'See here,' said the bird. 'This is what tenacity can achieve. This gift of vision so clear it encompasses the whole world. We rise, through patience and work. And once we rise, we see all that matters, and all that we do not yet know.'

"On beating wings, they soared, balanced between heavens and earth, until the woman knew she was connected to all that she could see, and all, also, that she could imagine. Daylight and nightshadow, the land and sky spun, and she with it, seeing and feeling all, knowing every part had a place within herself.

"At last, the bird tipped its wings and began the long slide back to the valley from which it had claimed her.

"The spirit of the woman cried out with loss. 'Falcon, great bird, how can I know this again without you?'

"'Seek knowledge. Seek that which opens you to others. Learn their stories. Believe their truths. This is the way of Wisdom. And as you grow, you will learn to soar, for this you will have to do in order to share what you learn.'

"How little she knew! How much there was to learn! 'So much,' said the woman. 'And I am so small.'

"'But you will not be,' said the falcon as they banked over the river. In the distance, the woman's body waited, hand still raised to her eyes. 'Once you grant yourself permission to be free, to reach the joy that your heart desires.'

"And Draigon's spirit poured back into her body, full of what she felt more than knew, and with the desire to replace emotion with learning and truth. As the falcon stroked its wings and climbed away, Draigon knew that long work and study would also give her wings. If she committed her strength and accepted the bird's great gift, one day, she would join it at the arc of the sky, and offer to others what it had offered her."

With a sweep of her arm, Ilora indicated that the tale had ended.

Leiel steepled her hands and clapped them lightly together a few times. "A woman named Draigon." Like the moment Leiel had learned Gahree was the witch in the old story, the idea warmed her very core, that Draigon was more than a title or a descriptor. She had been a person. "Was she real?"

With a smile, Ilora shrugged. "Perhaps. We are called Draigon for some reason."

"And the falcon? Draigon are not birds."

"But we fly."

Leiel grinned. "On wings of wisdom?"

"What else is the Great Shape but a way to expand and contain all we know?"

"Is that why Shaa is so large? She knows so much?"

Ilora nodded. "Did Gyddron show you Gahree's books? The ones she's written through all the years?"

Gahree had written down her knowledge? Leiel shook her head, trying to imagine how many wondrous stories must be contained in those pages. "How many books?"

"Every book on the fourth level, and most of the fifth."

Leiel's jaw fell open and she stared. "Every...?"

Ilora laughed. "And probably more that I don't even know about. If you want to understand what you might become, there is no better way to continue your learning than to continue delving into what Gahree has spent her life understanding. She writes every day, and she learns every day. I try to do the same. Knowledge will lead you to the Great Shape. If that is the path you wish to follow."

"You chose it."

"I did."

"Why? You don't leave here. Why learn to change and fly, only to stay in one place?"

"Just because I don't travel Arnan does not mean having wings is pointless. There are lands beyond ours, daughter. And, now that you are safe, I intend to visit many. Imagine the stories to be found in far places. Imagine what creatures take care of others' sacred knowledge."

Like a thrown spear, Ilora's words pierced Leiel's gut. Every part of her tensed. "You're leaving?"

"No, no!" Ilora shook her head. "Not now. Not for years. Not until you, if you so desire, have wings of your own to fly with me."

The ache in Leiel's belly faded, replaced by a warmth that pulled laughter up into her lungs. To spend time with Ilora, wander out into the world and leave everything behind and start anew... But she had already done the leaving, and still the past lingered. A twist pulled through Leiel's chest. Some things needed, quite firmly, to be remembered. She bent her head. "A tempting dream."

"But not the future you will choose," Ilora said. "I am a keeper of stories, like Gydron. I could have been content on the farm, gathering wisdom and keeping my family safe. But you—you are more like Gahree. You want to understand more. You want choice and change. You'll be a seeker, a teacher. You'll stand before Councils and shift the future of the land."

Could she really? Was she worthy of the trust Gahree and every woman in Cyunant had placed in her? Only a few months ago, Leiel would have laughed at the idea of facing the Councils. But now—things she thought she had known had gained new meaning inside her. She looked around the room, at the tall shelves stacked with wisdom and humor and flights of fancy. Stories and truth. She looked at her mother. Family and friendship, and a wider idea that might be akin to justice. She looked inside at the anger that she was beginning to think might never quite fade, and realized much of it was no longer directed at Ilora, but rather at the loss she had chosen, at the idea that so many others still had no choices at all. At herself, for those she had left behind.

Leiel sat up straighter. She could ease some of that anger, some of the guilt. She could be part of offering more women choices and chances that they had never dreamed might exist, bring real knowledge back to the land. A spark caught inside her, where the base of her throat met her chest. "I like that dream, mother. As much as you like yours." If she was worthy. If her will and hard work were enough. If not...

She refused to imagine what she might become if she failed.

Chapter 13

Leiel

A whistle split the air and cracked an echo, sharp and brittle, through the ravine. The hair on Leiel's arms tingled and rose, and she lifted her head quickly, her gaze flicking up the mountain.

"Take care!"

Leiel stepped back, feet moving awkwardly back into pattern as she half-brought her attention back to dance practice. It wasn't enough. She stumbled, bumped into Simmini and grabbed at the other woman to keep from falling. The other woman made a sound that was part laugh and part yelp of irritation, as she clutched Leiel back, each trying to steady the other.

Shorr gave two hard, final beats on her hand drum and brought the rhythm to a halt, shaking her head at their wobbly conundrum.

Leiel looked between the two women, her teeth clenched for a rebuke. Instead, they both burst into light laughter. A few seconds later and Leiel joined them. "What was that noise about?"

"Oh, hah! Here, stand up." Simmini, chuckling, extricated herself from Leiel's grasp and the tangle of their feet.

"What's she into now do you imagine?" Shorr asked, setting the drum aside.

"Who?" Leiel pushed back her hair and looked upslope again.

"Wynt of course. Oh that's right, you've not heard her let go that warning of hers before. Now that spring's nearly here, you'll hear it bouncing off all the peaks. She's—" A whoop from above, followed by a repeat of the long, piercing whistle, cut short Simmini's words.

Leiel looked up to see the copper-haired Draigon appear on a large boulder above them. Wynt's grin cracked like late-summer lightening and her iridescent locks whipped around her shoulders. The air filled with the chill scent of melting snow and new-sprouted grasses, as though Wynt ushered in the first breath of spring. "Come see!" Wynt's voice was mischief the way Gahree's was music. "The ice is cracking on the upper falls. Winter's turning loose at last!"

"By the wind!" Shorr said. "That's worth a whistle!"

She got to her feet and started up the trail between the rocks, Simmini fast on her heels. Leiel followed with more caution. The way was patchy with ice and hard-packed snow. She stepped as quickly as she could, climbing between the thin trees bent by the mountain winds, up into a boulder field, and then onto the rocks themselves. Laughter bounced and bounded ahead of her, for the freedom of the climb and the wonder that lay ahead.

"Leiel, feel the heat! Life is rising! Can't you feel it?" Wynt's voice was bright, and Leiel met her eyes with another upward glance. Shorr and Simmini stood beside her, and the frozen ribbon of water that marked the main stream feeding through the ravine, snaked through the rocks beyond them, then Leiel heard the hard pop and crack of ice breaking free.

Wynt reached down a hand. Leiel grasped it, and Wynt half-lifted her up the last few steps to join them. More laughter echoed from below, and Leiel glanced back to see Gahree and Gemda and a line of other women working their way up to witness the arrival of spring. Ilora waved from the back of the line.

"Is this a tradition?" Leiel asked as she raised a hand and returned the gesture.

"We don't watch for it," Wynt said. "But if one of us notices it happening... Even our own heat can't match spring warmth hitting the mountains."

Draigon heat. Leiel was still grasping the concept. She'd spent the long winter bundled in layers of wool, hats and coats and scarves and socks upon socks, to hold a temperature that was endurable. The Draigon moved over the mountain as though winter had hardly arrived. She'd have felt the fool, but for the fact that all the newer arrivals shared her love of layers. Would she ever master the skills that led to the Great Shape, and the ability to generate her own warmth at will?

And even growing up in the Spur country had not prepared her to travel month after month over this rugged terrain, with its wildly varying rockiness, and unruly growths of lichen and slick mossy wood. But Wynt had taught her, all the long winter, all the little things that made life in this harsh season easier. How to move in the snow: the slow steady actions of climbing and traversing, careful not to break into a running sweat, careful of the feel of ice and snow under her feet, the possibilities of slip and avalanche. The thoughtful nature of walking in snowshoes: how the pivot point of the platforms changed, and yet didn't alter, the action of each step. The importance of drinking more water than she thought she needed, and of regular breaks to eat, even before she realized she was hungry. How to sleep comfortably and well, using the very snow as an insulator, and the angles of the land and trees, to block the worst of the weather. Difficult lessons, some such a struggle that she had at times doubted her ability to met them. So far she had, but every day brought new lessons, new challenges.

Hard days on the farm flitted through her mind. Sometimes she fell back on those memories, when the studies she undertook among the Draigon seemed too great, and her mind and body too outmatched. She had survived Klem and Gial and Addor. She had survived the loneliness and loss. Such memories buoyed her when her doubts in her ability to achieve her goals weighted her most.

If Elda and Torrin could see her now...

A hard *pang* rang above and Leiel swept her attention back to the frozen waterfall, just in time to see the first large chunk of ice break free and slide into the crevasse below. It slipped, trembling down the face of the falls, then caught an edge and tumbled, shards shattering and ricocheting into the crack in the mountain. It landed without impact, only a muffled splash, a sign the waters were flowing beneath the ice and snow, trapped under the concealing cover of winter, but rising now, to meet awakening life.

Leiel gasped as another piece broke loose. Beside her, Wynt laughed, and Gahree spoke over the sound of shattering winter as she stepped up beside them. "Frozen things awaken, a sight so welcome and joyous we laugh as things break open."

"Wisdom in wobbly words," Wynt said. "It's what Gahree is known for!"

Gahree smiled. "And this daughter of the mountain rises with the sun, and runs for days with the creatures of the forest. She weighs the impact of each stride, but rarely that of each word."

"Rambling words aren't as easy to track as animals," Wynt said. "Look!"

The very air fractured as the main ice sheet spidered, streaks breaking blue through the hard-packed glistening white surface. It rocked, shook, and let go, splintering and snapping through the air and over rocks as it roared past them into the crevasse. Leiel stepped back with a gasp as the impact broke through the ice below, and raised a mist of icy water blasting upward, coating them in chill vapor.

A shout of appreciation broke around her as everyone cheered, and a second later she joined in. Old gods! To witness such a sight! Above, the long-trapped creek spit and sputtered, releasing a few sparse jets of water. Then it burst through the remaining thin barrier of ice, and sluiced wildly over the rocks, down the ancient channel in the mountain, freed at last from the constraints demanded by the seasons.

Cheers and laughter bloomed around Leiel, and she smiled and smiled until the muscles in her cheeks ached. Natural beauty. Freedom. How had she ever survived living where those things were considered the purview of the few? She glanced over at Ilora, just climbing the last few paces to join the group, and at Gahree, standing relaxed beside her, as though this was the way all things should always happen, surrounded by joy and wonder. Her throat ached with contained tears, and she blinked hard.

Leiel turned and threw her arms around Gahree, and smiled through the Draigon's dark locks at Ilora. "Thank you," she said, her words for both of them—shared and beyond measure—these two women whose choices had led to her having her own, and to this place, and this stunning joy.

Ilora nodded, smiling back. Gahree returned the hug, her preternatural warmth sinking into Leiel's very bones. "You're welcome, wild daughter, always. Imagine all the wonder still to come."

Leiel pulled back and met those green-gold eyes. Still to come—so much to learn, to explore. Water rushed free behind her, going new places, turned loose to carve stone, bring life, expand over the entire land.

"You've made me want more," Leiel said. So much too learn. So terrifying, the thought of failure. "And not just for me."

Gahree threw back her head and laughed, the ringing sound a true companion to this spring-born moment. "Then more it shall be, Leiel of Arnan. On a day like this, all possibilities flow free."

To be believed in so completely, when her own heart held so many questions. Leiel forced a smile. "Yes," she said, but the thought rose unspoken in her mind—I hope so.

CHAPTER 14

Leiel

Slash and bash and stumble had been the pattern of the morning, imprinted on Leiel's arms and knees in bruises and scrapes. In a few days, the mosaic they formed would be worthy of the term 'art.'

Heaving air into her lungs, Leiel advanced again, seeking an opening. She stepped right and struck out, catching nothing but empty air as Kinra sidestepped easily, not even winded. Leiel turned to follow, over reached, and skittered to one knee yet again. Tension ripped through her, dark frustration a shaking tightness across her chest. A hard phrase cursing her own ancestry rose and burst from her lips, and brought a grunt of amusement from her instructor.

"The sword is not for you, my dear," Kinra said, lowering her wooden weapon. She shook her head and reached down a hand to help Leiel up. "You have the speed, but not the extended focus."

Leiel brushed at the dirt on her pants. Training with Kinra was worse than baking with Elda had ever been. The difference was, this was something Leiel wanted to learn. But her body and her will could not seem to agree on an outcome.

Please let that not be a sign of things to come. "I can learn." She said it as much to convince herself as Kinra.

"You can and will," the other women agreed. "But your natural inclination isn't toward a blade. You'll make better use of your intelligence than you will of any weapon."

"My—?"

"Your mind, Leiel. The same thing you have always used. Be smart and quick and you'll have little use for fighting."

"I need to learn to defend myself." She tightened her grip on the hilt of her practice sword. Never again would she passively accept a blow from anyone.

"You've always done that. Every woman has." Kinra shook her head, as she reached out and collected Leiel's weapon. "Some with more skill than others. We need to make use of your quickness. There are techniques that will let you use attackers' actions against them. You can turn their size and momentum back upon them. Put down the sword. I'll show you." An easy hop carried her off the training platform, and she made her way toward the little stone building that housed her training weapons. "Show me Gweld?"

Kinra smiled. "Not yet. You've far too much else to learn first."

"But the Draighil—"

"Study for three years before they even attempt it. And the price they pay is ridiculous. For them, Gweld is a crooked stick used to prop up their will. For those willing to study longer, Gweld is a connection that is only ever a thought away. You can find it, moment to moment, like the air in your lungs. It's not something you call upon; it's always there."

"Do *you* feel it all the time?"

"Yes. It hovers on the periphery." Kinra looked over her shoulder as she pulled open the door of the storage shed. "It's a powerful tool for us. It can keep us in balance, aware of when things are not right. It gives us the ability to anticipate, and lets us fight off outside influences, even poisons, like snakebite."

"You mean it makes us immune?"

"In a way. The Great Shape, once you learn enough Gweld to reach it, will confer many unexpected gains to your natural inclinations."

"When I learn how to change."

"Yes. When you're ready. Which you're not. Now come on, grab your pack. We've a new route to run today."

Gods of old. Leiel imagined the stiff complaints of her body in the coming days and groaned. She shook her head, pushed back her hair, and climbed down to follow.

"Here!" Kinra called, and beckoned Leiel onward before turning and leaping to the next protrusion of granite.

Panting in the thin mountain air, Leiel raised her eyes to the wedge of sky visible at the top of the rock-strewn ravine. Not even a third of the way up yet. Three days of chasing Kinra all over the slopes of the Great Northern Range had worn Leiel's feet to blisters and her hands to rawness, from grasping at rocks and trees. She caught a flash of movement as Kinra made another leap among the rocks above her. Sucking in a breath, Leiel took two running steps and crossed the gap to top the next boulder. She teetered a moment, then shifted the wobble into forward motion and leaped again.

"Better!" Kinra said. "I told you, the sword is not for you. This is what you are good at."

"How—" Leiel called as she spread her arms and jumped to the next rock. She braced herself against a tree thrusting up between the stones and used it to lever herself up another level. "How will—scratching my way—up—these—rocks—help me fight—anything?" She gasped out the words as she pulled herself over the edge of the boulder and stared up at Kinra.

The older woman smiled and moved on, leaping up through the steep sprawl of giant rocks like a locust hopping from blade to blade among prairie grasses. "When you can move on this terrain, you won't need to fight. And if you do, once we find you the right weapon, you will never be unsteady on the ground beneath you. Besides, thinking ahead can be as important as any battle. Come along. We have to get to the top by high sun if you want enough time to eat lunch. We have another ridge to top before dark."

Leiel sighed and followed. When she had been a little girl, she had jumped from porch to rail to wagon bed with fearless ease. But it had been years since she had played such games, and now, she felt so much farther from the ground, as though her center of balance had moved all the way to her head, and with every move she made, she was threatened with tipping over. Had she the breath to waste, she would have cursed her frustration. Muscles burning, she worked her way up the ravine, wary of both crevasses between the boulders, and the slickness of moss and lichen. A misstep would be painful at the least. A broken limb or a broken skull were not remote possibilities.

"Look ahead," Kinra called. Her voice was not breathless. Leiel grunted and paused again, looked up at the woman. Kinra had expanded her lead by double. How did she move so easily over this terrain?

Leiel took the moment to sample more gasps of the thin air. "I *am* looking." In the distance, through the tree limbs rocking in the wind, she could see other peaks of the Great Northern Range. Accomplishment. Now that her training had begun, what did she want of it? And what did the Draigon want of her? She had never asked. But did they have something in mind, to have brought her here? A library full of knowledge. A world of people without access to it. Her desire to know. Her fight to know. A mountain to climb, unending, always more to endure and to seek...

"You are looking only at where your feet will land." Kinra said. "You are not planning your route. Look *up*. You'll be surprised at how much easier it is, when you see the whole of what lies ahead."

"I wish I knew when I was a girl that I needed to keep practicing childish acrobatics," Leiel called.

Kinra laughed. "You can relearn what you have forgotten. And you can learn a thousand, thousand new things. You've nothing but time, unless a Draighil kills you. And you won't see one of those for years yet. Now, come on. We've a mountain to run."

Chapter 15

Cleod - 25 years

Two days ride from Giddor, all that the merchants talked about was the seafood. How fresh. How well-cooked.

How well it filled platters and bowls and bellies. The trade city on the southeast coast of Arnan was known as the finest deep-water port in the east. It was also famous for its fare the way Sibora was famous for its gardens. Cleod had heard so much about it, he dreamed he could smell salt air and taste scallops. Seeing Giddor had been a goal since he heard the first tales of it—even the most stoic traders became long-winded when they spoke of the place. Would the reality, now that it was within a few day's ride, be anything close to his imaginings?

At the caravan's back, building storm clouds on the edge of the sky signaled yet another reason to be grateful this leg of the journey was drawing to a close. Cleod pulled his bay mare to a halt beside Nae's gelding and looked back at the darkening horizon. At least the wagons, circling to set camp among a copse of wind-sculpted trees, would be somewhat sheltered from any rising wind.

He resisted the urge to hunch his shoulders. "Clouds like that remind me of home."

"Spur country has nothing on the winds kicked up here," Nae said. "Only a Wing Wind hits harder."

A grin flashed over Cleod's lips. Everything, for Nae, was worse, in the moment, than anything that had come before. Before Cleod could reply, the pounding sound of a horse at a full run interrupted conversation. Cleod looked back. A chill crossed his shoulders at the sight of Kilras riding toward them.

"Turn them." Kilras pulled his dancing mare up beside Cleod, flicked his gaze between Cleod and Nae. "We ride back the way we came. *Now.*" Kilras reined the mare away and rode for the far end of the line of wagons.

Cleod stared after the Dorn, then turned to Nae, but the question he started to voice was left hanging as Nae responded with an immediacy that brooked no argument. The older man kicked his horse into a canter toward the stopped wagons. Cleod's mare skittered at the sudden action, and his attention went to calming her. By the time she settled, Nae was halfway to the trees, already shouting orders.

A glance over his shoulder confirmed that the wagons at the back of the caravan were already turning. What in the name of every long dead god—? He clucked to the horse and reined her around to follow Nae. Convincing the merchants to reverse course this close to Giddor would not be easy. How was he supposed to answer the questions they were sure to ask when no explanation had been given?

He swung toward the lead wagons, leaving the near ones to Nae.

Despite the weather, no merchants argued with the new order. Kilras's orders, passed on, brought instant response. Cleod watched, brow furrowed, as they dismantled the fresh camp. Even in the Enclaves, where discipline was demanded in all things, there was always grumbling under the breath when orders were given without explanation. Not here.

In the slanting rain, Cleod spotted Kilras working on the far side of the camp. Cleod started across the distance. Then he watched Kilras speak a few words to an old man and his son, traders from Giddor itself, just days ride from the comforts of home. Without hesitation or argument, the two turned to harnessing their weary team of oxen.

Frowning, Cleod halted. Whatever had motivated Kilras's strange directive, no one else seemed inclined to question it. Cleod thought of the trail behind, of the decisive logic of the Dorn's past orders. Whatever had motivated this odd turn of mind, perhaps he should just trust it as the merchants seemed to. One by one, they refocused their energy and packed their goods into the wagons. In only moments, they were rolling back the way had come, the shelter of the trees abandoned for the driving force of the chill rain.

Gweld trembled the edges of Cleod's senses. He fought it back. What good would the fighting trance do him on a night like this? There was nothing to battle but the weather and the strange order of the man he rode for. The pure instinct that roused the skill in times of stress served him not at all this night. He swallowed and set his jaw, turned with the reloaded wagons and took his position on the forward perimeter of the train.

They plugged north, away from their planned destination, through rain so slanted that it pushed through every loose seam and fold of oiled canvas. Clothing soaked through. Even goods in the wagons wetted out as snapping winds pulled free lacings and whipped open the snuggest panels. Through the long night, they struggled against mud and chill and exhaustion, until, just before dawn, the rain and wind abated, and the caravan stopped nearly within sight of the spot where they had broken camp the previous morning, having gained nothing for their travel but a shivering weariness and half-ruined animals and goods.

Cleod stripped his saddle from his mare's back and rubbed her down with care. What in the name of all dead gods had prompted the night's ride? Such exhaustion as they had willingly sought would slow their arrival in Giddor by far longer than just a day, could bring illness, and worse, to the animals, as well as the travelers in their care. What was Kilras thinking?

"Wondering what he's about?"

Cleod looked over at Nae, caring for his own mount in the misting, grey light. The trees around them dripped the remains of last night's deluge onto the mucky ground. Drops pattered, some absorbed by fallen leaves, some plopping into puddles. "Aren't you? Our first run since Kilras bought out Haggris and he does this?"

Nae shook his grey head. "Nope. Kilras says ride, we ride. Would have thought you knew that by now."

"I thought I did." Cleod shook his head. "But I missed the point in exhausting us all on a night like this."

Nae grunted. "Kilras does things. Always has a reason. I don't have to know it."

Lips pressed together, Cleod passed a hand over his tired eyes. Every part of him ached. The scars on his hips pulled at his legs and spine, twisting a sharp pain that would keep sleep at bay despite his weariness. What could make any of this worth the suffering? "Well *I* need to know."

He gave the mare a final pat and left her to her portion of grain and such wet grazing as she desired. Hefting his gear across his back, he made for the cook wagon to find the Dorn.

Kilras looked up with no surprise in his expression when Cleod dumped his saddle by the fire.

"Coffee?"

Need jolted through Cleod's gut, but the craving that backed it was not for the bitter drink Kilras so favored. Cleod swallowed, shook his head. "How you drink that foul, burned bean, I will never understand."

A grin cracked one corner of Kilras's face. "It's a habit I acquired in my youth, for good or ill."

Cleod pulled a mug from the shelf embedded in the side of the wagon and pried open a tea tin. A few leaves went into the bottom of the cup, and he made his way to the fire to add water from the kettle tucked among the coals. "How did Sehina get a fire started in this wet?"

"Never question that woman's skills," Kilras said with a chuckle.

Cleod shook his head.

Kilras blew across the hot surface of his drink. "What's your question?"

With a glance at the older man, Cleod said, "I don't understand why we're here." In the Enclaves, Cleod had followed orders, assumed an ethic and a knowledge that, in the end, turned out not to exist. Until now, Kilras's decisions had seemed based in logic and clear-eyed simplicity. But that had been while he was Dorn to Haggris Ritt. Now, on Kilras's first journey as not just Dorn, but as a Ritt himself, he had issued orders that made little sense. This night's inexplicable change in destination and dangerous slog through the storm, twisted a knot in Cleod's gut he did not know how to untangle.

"Sometimes leading's not about doing the easy thing."

"You speak as though I don't know that."

"You don't," Kilras said. He sipped his coffee, met Cleod's gaze. "There's no obvious reason for my orders last night. Don't bother looking for one. There're times when I don't want you to question, just act."

The muscles between Cleod's shoulder blades bunched, and tension crowded up his neck. He ground his teeth together, wrapped his fingers tight around the steaming mug, crouched across the fire, and stared at the Dorn.

Kilras met Cleod's gaze. "What answer would satisfy?"

"The truth."

Kilras threw back his head and laughed. "I've been riding these hills since I was barely a man. What explanation do you expect, besides time and knowledge? Unless you think those couldn't suffice for me."

Cleod straightened. He was on the verge of insult, of accusation. And neither of those was an acceptable offering to the man before him, not after all Kilras had done for him this last year. What was he thinking? Why did he feel the need for a greater explanation for the Dorn's demands?

An image of Soibel, the tight-lipped Ehlewer Elder, formed in Cleod's mind. The vision was hazy, as though the last pain-and-drink-filled encounter between them had blurred the edges of memory. But the old man's face—livid and stiff with anger—was clear, eyes bright and narrowed, focused as though to pierce through Cleod's very flesh. He flinched.

"Cleod?"

A hard breath and Cleod gave his attention to the Dorn. With a shake of his head, Cleod dropped his gaze.

"Whomever I remind you of, I'm not him."

Cleod laughed, glanced back at Kilras. "Remind me of?"

"You've not questioned much about me or my decisions since you joined us. But we get some rain and you look at me like you've never seen me before. Either it's me you're unsure of, or you really hate riding in the rain."

With a grunt, Cleod got to his feet. He took a few steps, then stopped, came back to the fire. "You never asked me why I quit."

Kilras shook his head. "We all relinquish things, over time."

"You really don't care?"

"I respect that you felt a strong enough need to leave the Enclaves that you'd rather drink yourself to death than return. That's all I need to know, unless you feel something more's important."

A tremor laced Cleod's spine. "No." Kilras knew the story of the failure on the Spur—the Dorn had known that before he walked into the Rock Digger. All of Arnan knew what happened. But Kilras never asked for details. Never asked what about that horrible day had broken Cleod. And what was he doing now to return that kindness? Pressing. Well there would be time enough for that later, if it came to that. Did he need anything more today?

"His name is Soibel," Cleod said at last. "He is head of the Ehlewer. The master of the Ehlewer. And he lied to me from the day I met him."

"About?"

"About everything."

"Everything?"

"Everything that matters."

"And what matters? Rain?"

Cleod blinked, and then laughed. "Rain can matter," he said. "When it's the first to fall after Draigon Weather. Or the last before." He held down a roll of nausea as he spoke of the beasts.

"What else matters?"

Again, Cleod glanced at Kilras. "Honor." He shrugged. "At least it used to. When I thought there was such a thing. When I thought the Elders taught truth and wanted their students to succeed."

"The Enclaves didn't want you to kill Draigon?"

This time he could not contain the ripple that coursed through him at the mention of the creatures. He held still a moment to contain the sharp reaction of his senses, because that question mattered. When control was certain, he said, "If we kill all the Draigon, then what is the point of the Enclaves?"

Kilras grunted. "A question worth asking. I'll be glad to have you around if you keep thinking."

Cleod smiled. "No. You don't remind me of Soibel. He was always worried that I would think too much. He called me too bold." Too bold by far and by half again.

"You don't need to worry about that with me." Kilras reached to pour himself more coffee. "I'd appreciate it if you dared a little more. We're still learning to trust each other. You've proved your worth to me as I hoped you would. I'm doing the same, if you'll give me the chance."

Dropping his gaze for a moment, Cleod watched the steam curl out of his mug. Need pressed out through his gut. In the third wagon behind him, a corked bottle of ercew was poorly hidden under the driver's bedroll in the front left corner... Three months. Three long months since he had last taken a drink, despite the cramping need that woke him in the night.

Why had Kilras driven them through the night? The answer should be readily offered, and yet... Cleod looked at the Dorn. The calm, expectant expression on the older man's face was a clear message.

Cleod glanced around the camp, the activity of arrival had settled into the silence of bone-weary slumber in the thin morning light. Not a soul had questioned Kilras's orders. Not one. But Cleod had been lured to such seemingly mindless loyalty once; he did not intend to follow that route again. Still, the other scouts were not drones trained to a single cause and purpose. They were smart, strong-willed, with minds of their own. And they followed Kilras through the storm without hesitation or complaint.

Trust. Since Cleod had joined the caravan, never once, until last night, had Kilras's orders seemed based on whim. The response of the other riders made it unlikely that these were either, despite appearances and the potentially dangerous consequences.

Cleod turned his gaze back to Kilras, nodded once. "All right. I will try." Though unease still lurked in the pit of his belly, he was too tired, and, if he was honest, too in need of something to keep believing in, to let his doubt bend the hope that he had found someone worth trusting.

"Sehina put dry clothes for you in the community wagon. We're not going anywhere for a couple days." Kilras paused. "I'll take watch tonight. Get some sleep."

"You won't tell me why?"

"Better to show you. If you've the patience to wait."

Kilras's tone held the promise of comfort, and he had not dismissed the possibility of future clarity. Patience, Cleod could manage. The Dorn had not failed him yet. For now, it would have to be enough.

A muddy swath more than a bow-shot wide and jammed with logs and boulders obliterated the trail. Cleod stood with Sehina atop a low rise at the edge of the mudslide. Looking east toward the foothills, as far as they could see, the land had been sluiced apart in lines of devastating slides. Masses of mud and rocks and broken trees had wiped the hills bare, pushed down the valleys and creeks, and left waves of wreckage over the trade route into Giddor. If their intended campsite from two nights ago looked anything like what lay before them...

"How did he know?"

Sehina shrugged. "Kilras has been riding this land a long time."

Cleod glanced at her. Though true, her explanation left more questions than answers. Nothing in the weather should have led anyone to think *this* was to be the result of the rain they had ridden through. Cleod shook his head.

She grinned, grabbed her thick braid and tossed it over her shoulder. "Snap your mouth closed, Cleod. Kilras just knows things. You'll come to be glad of it." She clapped a hand on his shoulder and turned to make her way, ginger-footed, back downslope to the waiting caravan.

Cleod watched her go. She reminded him of Leiel, the way she said what needed saying. But Sehina followed her words with actions in a way Leiel never had. How did Kilras allow Sehina such freedom? Cleod checked the thought, his throat suddenly dry, his eyes anything but. Leiel had died because of that kind of thinking. Sehina was unwelcome proof of what he was coming to understand—that Leiel had died for what was little more than an archaic set of rules.

His gut churned. Don't think on it. Don't. Don't regret. Don't rage. Don't *need*. He closed his eyes and breathed deep. A long series of heartbeats passed, and then he opened his eyes and forced his attention back to the ravaged land before him. For a moment more he studied it, only half seeing, then looked back at the caravan.

Kilras, his hand wrapped around a steaming mug, stood with Nae and a small group of traders. Sehina joined the group and bent her head to Kilras's. The Dorn's frown at whatever she said, held no surprise. The problem Sehina presented to Cleod's sense of propriety faded as the true trouble of the day reasserted itself. The distance they had retreated in a day, would take them several times that to regain. The question reasserted itself. How had Kilras known?

The Dorn looked up at Cleod, flashed a smile and went back to his conversation. No one else seemed bothered by Kilras's canny knowledge. What had the man shown Cleod in the last months but a stalwart kindness and a purely capable mind? Were the events of the past couple days so much different than any others he had witnessed since he took up with the Dorn and his people? Not in substance, but definitely in scale.

Cleod sighed, took another look at the ruined land they must cross to reach Giddor. Did he really want to question the actions that had kept him alive to see the city? What was the point? Kilras was not Soibel. The caravan team was not a band of focus-driven Dragihil in the making. And the storm-made disaster before him was not a mystery to be solved—but simply a problem hard work and determination could see them through. The doubt that turned his gut gave a last shudder. Cleod looked down at the people gathered around Kilras. They were relaxed, confident, even in the face of the work ahead. No unease or confusion marred their posture or their faces. They trusted Kilras without reservation. Cleod took a breath, let it out. Perhaps he could find a way to do the same.

Chapter 16

Leiel - 25 years

Pure Draigon, tireless and fearless, Wynt lived with a confidence matched not even by Gahree. Just the week before, she had climbed to the top of the ravine, made a run at the edge of the ridgeline, and transformed in mid-leap off the cliff. She caught an updraft Ilora said most would not have even believed would support the Great Shape. Old gods, would Leiel ever possess that kind of confidence? She had once, in her work, with Cleod. And though she gained ground daily in her studies, the possibility of the Great Shape still seemed so far away. The only consolation was seeing new arrivals struggle with the same doubts and fears—even Simmini and Shorr, who had been here longer than she.

But Wynt saw things differently. And she acted on what she saw. The dive off the cliff was just one piece of the reckless certainty she radiated. Whether she thought through her actions or just committed to them blindly, Leiel had yet to decide. But interrupting her was always risky, so Leiel kicked a few rocks across the trail as she made the turn toward the workshop. Whether Wynt was half-napping or sharpening weapons, her reflexes often outmatched thought. An extra rattle of the gate handle as Leiel swung it open brought a grunt from the copper-haired Draigon across the yard.

"Excessive?" Leiel asked as she crossed the packed-dirt space to join Wynt under the pavilion that served as her work area.

"I heard you with the first four pebbles." Wynt looked up from the sword hilt she was wrapping. Seated on a low stool with the shining blade angled across the table in front of her, she pulled the leather into place, weaving a durable, intricate, pattern down the hilt. Fine twists of hide covered the maker's mark on the tang, but something about the weapon's craftsmanship tugged at Leiel's mind. "That's a beautiful blade."

"You've need of a sword after all?" Wynt asked.

Leiel laughed. "No. Not one of that caliber anyway. Kinra's judgment of my potential in that area is accurate. I'm barely fair. Kinra has declared I'll not be a warrior outside the Great Shape."

Wynt cracked a half-smile. "What brings you here? If you're looking for a lighter blade, I'm out. You'll have to ask Gahree to bring you back one when she next goes out to the world."

"The world?"

Wynt waved a hand. "Any place that's not here. Not that we're not part of it. We're just a smallish part."

Leiel nodded. Cyunant was the center of Draigon culture, but there were other villages out there, other small pockets that contained their own portion of Draigon wisdom. "No. I came to ask if I could borrow a honing steel. I thought the finest hunter in Cyunant would be the first person to ask."

Wynt chuckled, accepting the compliment as fact, and took a moment to pinch the leather twisted through her fingers. "On the bench. Far right. Are you sharpening swords, if not training with them?"

Leiel laughed. "No. Just Delhar's scissors. She promised to teach me how to mix dyes, and she said I need to put a better edge on the shears to cut the bloodroot cleanly." She moved to the bench and found the steel.

"You'll never find a more skilled clothier than Delhar, but she does like to make her students do the dull work."

"Ever the learner's lot," Leiel said and laughed.

"It's worth the trouble with Del. Gahree sells the cloth in Sibora for more money than the King's tailors dare to admit they spend. If they had the slightest idea where it came from…" Wynt laughed. "They'd die from shock before the King got a chance to chop their heads off."

Leiel almost looked around to see if anyone had overheard that outrageous statement, but she caught herself before the old habit took hold. She smiled. "I am still learning to live with so many people who say exactly what they mean." She took the honing steel, balanced it in her hand. "Only in stories do women speak as you do."

"Ha!" Wynt said. "If that were true, you wouldn't be here."

Leiel laughed. "I always loved the stories a bit too much."

"My friend," Wynt said with a shake of her head and a gleam in her eyes. "That's not possible."

"You've never heard a story so turned into a lie that there's no point left to it except to make you angry."

"You're talking about Farlan tales."

"Some of them."

"Tracking down true stories is like hunting." Wynt turned her gaze back to the work in her hands. The sword shifted, flashed in the sunlight as she returned to her task. "It takes a while to get on the trail of something worth following. Until you learn what makes sense, you waste a lot of time chasing useless sign."

Trust Wynt to find a way to weave her personal passion into any conversation.

"I'll try not to chase too many false tracks." Leiel flipped the steel in her hand. "Thank you for the loan. I'll have it back by evening."

Wynt shook her head, attention fixed on her hands as they twisted and pressed fine leather into shape and place. "Greetings to Del. See you for twilight meal in the Common? You can bring back the hone then."

Leiel accepted the friendly dismissal. "See you then," she agreed, and left the Draigon to her work. Leiel smiled. By the time she spent the afternoon stirring Delhar's dye vats, she might be too tired to bother with eating. But she turned Wynt's smile in her mind. A lifetime could be spent stalking stories, and she had gotten to a point where the hunt was half the pleasure. What stories could she ply from Delhar over an afternoon's work?

Glad for sharpened scissors and thick gloves, Leiel put the last of the cut roots into her bowl and faced Delhar across the cobbled yard. Three iron kettles, each at various levels of boil or soak, were set over stone-rimmed fire pits that formed a half circle in the yard. Delhar stood at the righthand vat, carefully stirring a length of linen into the simmering water. Leiel walked to the center kettle and dumped the cut roots into the water. They swirled slowly downward, their juices darkening the water as they fell. She glanced at Delhar. Compact, with bright eyes, and a brow with a constant hint of furrow, Delhar was the Draigon Leiel knew least well. Unlike so many of the others who loved to share endless tidbits of information, Delhar reserved most of her words for answering questions—the more direct the better.

"We could use some more heat, here," Delhar said without looking up from her work.

Leiel nodded and crossed the yard to fetch more wood. She studied the Draigon as she came back. Delhar's hair was streaked with grey. So few among the Draigon had that look. Most, like her mother and Gahree, had maintained their relative youth, studying hard and claiming their Great Shape as soon as possible. The change preserved their human age, casting the progression of time and growing wisdom into the body better designed to contain both.

Curiosity won out. "Have you been here long? You seem—older than most."

Delhar's arm never slowed its steady arching as she stirred the dye vat. "Not as long as most. But longer than your mother."

Leiel wrinkled her nose, shifted as a breeze wafted pungent steam into her face. She bent, fed more wood into the firehole, then brushed bark flakes from her hands and looked at the other woman. "You were not young, then, when you came here?"

Delhar laughed a little, flicked the barest glance at Leiel. "Oh, I was. Younger than you. One of the youngest ever chosen."

"So you—what—never Changed?"

"I did," Delhar said. She brushed sweat from her forehead with a forearm, kept stirring. "But I spent time here, first. Many years."

"Why?" Leiel asked. She would, before long, have enough knowledge to make the Change, to let her knowledge bloom into a new shape that overwhelmed her born body and raised her into something entirely new—something that could bear the weight of ages to come. But the Gweld still had to be mastered, and then the choice was hers, when to take that step. And some, as Delhar, had clearly chosen to delay that moment. Why? What did Delhar know that perhaps she should? "Why did you wait?"

Delhar continued her stirring, silent for several passes. Leiel waited. Then a sigh lifted Delhar's chest. "Shaa fetched me too late."

"What do you mean?"

The Draigon did not answer right away, a frown clouding her face. Then she shook herself. "I was raised in Sibora. That was my home, when I was young. But my father sold me when I was chosen. Because I brought him shame by being the one the Draigon wanted, he let men bid for my body. One of the merchants handed over money. He forced himself on me, the last night in Sibora. So, when Shaa came for me, I was broken, and I was pregnant."

Leiel held her breath. Her last night in her old life had been full of wonderful dreams. There had been uncertainty, yes, but mostly excitement, a thrill that, the next morning, the change in her world would be for the better. The threats she had faced in the Tower had never included this. What would that night have become had it been shattered by violence like what Delhar had lived through? "I am so sorry," she said, her throat dry. What else should she say? She shuddered to imagine such a thing. She did not *want* to imagine it. "I didn't know—something like that was allowed. How was that allowed?"

A low grunt of almost-amusement came from the older woman and she paused her work, looked at Leiel. "Money. Gahree had already taken her Great Shape. There was no one to stop it."

"And you...here? Did you..." Leiel stopped. The question she wanted to ask was not one she could find words for. It was too callous. Her curiosity was not worth cruelty. She picked up more sticks, gathering her thoughts along with the wood. A few moments passed before she glanced again at the dyer.

For the first time, Delhar smiled. "It's all right, Leiel. I had the child. And I healed. It took time but, as I raised him, I forgave him for being his father's child. And he forgave me for needing to." She switched the heavy spirtle to her other hand and resumed pushing fabric through the bubbling dye. The earthy scent of the mixture erupted anew. "It wasn't until he left here, that I took the Great Shape."

Leiel stood, the wood in her arms, staring at Delhar. People left here? Not just Draigon moving to other villages? But as people? How many? Where did they go? "Where is he?" she asked, the only question she could form of all those turning her mind.

"Roaming Arnan," Delhar said, a low, warm note in her voice. "He lives as a man—a good man—as the Hantyn tend to be."

"Hantyn?" Leiel asked.

"The half-children. The ones born here, Draigon-touched—but who cannot find the full purpose of their life among us. They need the wider world. And they often make it a better place by being out in it. Kilras is one such."

"Kilras. Is that your son's name?"

Delhar nodded, the warmth in her words reaching the smile in her eyes and the wrinkles that crowned them. "Yes," she said. "Kilras is my son. A good man among so many who aren't."

"And he is not Draigon?"

"No."

"No?"

"He could not reach the Great Shape."

Leiel pulled in a sharp breath. The old fear gripped her. If the son of a Draigon could not be a Draigon, was she really capable of such change? "Did he want to be?" she asked.

"Very much," Delhar said. "But his path through this life lay elsewhere."

"Out in Arnan." Leiel frowned. Skill. Knowledge. Desire. Which of those things mattered most? "You watch him? From here?"

Delhar laughed, a springing joyous sound. "Oh, no. But I hear of him. I'm brought stories, by the others who choose to travel Arnan. They tell me of his life, and his joys and sorrows. And when they can, they bring me his letters."

"Letters." Was it possible? Communication with those she loved, left behind in Adfen? Could she write to Torrin or to Elda? For a moment her heart raced with the possibility. But no. No. Any letter to Elda might find its way into Klem's hands, and only something horrible would be born of such an accident. And Torrin...she did not even know where he was. Had he stayed at the farm as he had said he would, or had he sought a new life? He could be anywhere. Leiel shook away the thought, turned her attention back to Delhar.

"He writes when he can. I've had four letters since he left." There was something in her voice, something warm and lifted, a quiet pride.

"Four letters? How long ago did he leave?"

"More than sixteen years ago," the other woman said.

Leiel stared at her. "Sixteen years?"

"If I count correctly," Delhar said. "It's difficult to know. Time seems different here."

"Four letters," Leiel said. "In all that time...four?"

"Leiel," Delhar said, "those letters fill books. They're his life. He writes them through the years and sends them when he can. How often do you think a man can willingly meet with a Draigon?"

"But Gahree—she came to me so often, in the market. She talked to people. I saw her. Why is it so hard?"

"My son is a nomad. He travels far each year. It's not often that he and a Draigon are in the same city. We're few, and Arnan is large. Our energy is best spent finding women to join us."

Of course. The Draigon's first need was to search out girls like her, women to be offered a chance to come to Cyunant, and learn, and grow, and guard knowledge for the future. "Books," she said. "Your Kilras writes books for you?"

"Poorly," Delhar laughed. "His handwriting is terrible."

"His..." Leiel blinked. "His...handwriting." A smile switched at her lips, and before she could stop it, she was shaking with laughter. The son of a Draigon could not become Draigon, and had terrible handwriting. A hand to her mouth could not dilute her chuckles. If Delhar had not joined in, Leiel would have turned away to hide her unrestrained amusement, but the older woman was laughing even harder than Leiel.

"Atrocious!" Delhar said.

"His skills must lie elsewhere."

"Oh, yes!" Delhar took the spirtle in both hands, leaned back from the dye vat, and laughed. "His books—his books are in the library Leiel, should you wish to endure their scrawl."

The library, once again. The heart of Cyunant. The place she spent so many days and nights, working toward what so often seemed an unreachable goal.

"And do you have books in the library? Ones about your life?"

Delhar shook her head. "No. My handwriting is worse than my son's."

Leiel smiled at that. "No one else will write your stories down?"

The dyer paused in her stirring. "Perhaps someone has. Gydron likes to listen to everyone's tales. And she's always scribbling."

"She wouldn't tell you if she was doing that?"

If I asked." Her words went quiet again.

Leiel studied the dyer, working steadily. If she were Delhar, she wouldn't want to write her own life. And she might not want to know someone else was recording it. But Delhar had offered the story willingly enough. Leiel nodded to herself. Gydron, it seemed, had her own wisdom when it came to dealing with people. That was something Leiel put attention toward—understanding how stories were best gathered and shared. Attention and, just maybe, purpose.

Delhar's son had left Cyunant to find his. Delhar found hers in the arts of weaving and dying. Ilora kept stories. Gydron guarded the library. And Gahree—Gahree traveled Arnan seeking women to help.

Leiel frowned. She cared about all of that, wanted to learn everything, from Wynt's lessons in tracking and survival to Shorr's ability to play a hand drum for hours. She wanted to learn. And she wanted everyone else to be able to learn as well. Elda and Brea and all the others in Arnan who were kept to half their potential, half their laughter, half their skill, simply because they were not born male. Or, like Torrin, not born Farlan.

She wanted to learn, and share knowledge, to free it for all. The Tower at Adfen. The great crossbeam that topped it. The Square below, now filled with merchants and shoppers and, occasionally, sweating hordes awaiting brutal announcements. Her lips parted with a sharp breath. But what that place had been when it was built… Other places like it must exist in Arnan.

Her heart jumped, quickened. To see those places restored—that was a purpose worth turning toward. Could she really do it? Was her strength of will enough? It always had been. But failure now…what would she be if she could not be Draigon? Where would that leave all her dreams?

Chapter 17

Leiel

Leiel fitted her hands under the notched log, nodded to Wynt and Gahree where they waited along the beam. The cabin was more than half built, so it had to be close to noon. The summer sun beat down, and the gnats buzzed around her head, attracted to the sweat pouring down her face and back. She blew in vain at a strand of hair as it flopped into her eyes. Her muscles burned and her joints ached, and her chest was tight with a happiness she had not known she could find in physical work. But, sure as the day was long, she needed a cool drink of water after this log was in place.

"One, two—lift!" Leiel counted them down, then pushed up from her knees, using the muscles of her back and legs to take most of the weight of the beam. Wynt gave a half-laugh, half-grunt of satisfaction as they dropped the log into place on the wall.

With a sigh of relieved effort, Leiel reached up and shoved back the offending loose hairs. She tucked the loose strands back into her braid, but they instantly sprang free. With a shake of her head, she walked toward the water bucket on the table set up beside the work site.

"Leiel, you've a talent for cutting those notches," Wynt said as she passed. The copper-haired Draigon dusted her hands against each other. "These logs fit like they grew together." She patted a hand on the log they had just set. "Whoever gets this house is going to be pleased."

"When is the next Sacrifice?" Leiel dipped a ladle of water from the bucket. The water, cool and sweet, passed her lips.

"Next summer, in Bajor." Gahree came to join her.

Leiel handed her the ladle. "And we build her house this early?"

"The house needs time to settle. And we've limited time to build," Wynt said.

"What if she doesn't like it?"

"She might not. Some don't," Wynt said. "Some don't wish to be here at all. Or turn out not to be as capable as we hoped. We find other places for them to be and grow." She took her turn with the water dipper, but instead of drinking, she poured the water down the back of her neck. "Ahh—I'm looking forward to a swim in the lake. I'd be happy to make the change and fly all the way to the northern ocean."

"For women who've learned to control the weather..."

Gahree laughed, and the sound, as always, went straight through Leiel's bones. "We warm, and are warm." She took the ladle back from Wynt, dipped more water.

"There's a reason we live on this mountain." Wynt tugged at her shirt, fanning herself. "When you reach the change, you'll see."

"What do you know of it?" Kinra asked, as she came around from the side of the half-built building. Sweat stained her shirt and her hair was matted flat with it. "Are the three of you planning on getting back to work?"

Leiel shook her head. "Some of us still need to eat regularly for more than just pleasure."

"Wynt wouldn't know about that either," Kinra said.

Leiel shook her head. "I brought some bread and cheese," Leiel said. "Feel free to continue without me."

"Your change can't come soon enough." Wynt turned back to the building. "The faster we finish, the faster we get to the lake."

"A small feast sounds as good for the spirit as for the belly," Gahree said, and Leiel smiled. At least Gahree remembered some of what it meant to be human. At least enough to agree that a break was needed.

Wynt held up a dismissive hand and went back to the stack of logs still to be notched for placement on the cabin walls. She measured a log, turned and looked at the wall, then laid her hands flat near the end of the wood. A moment later, a charred pattern darkened the log, marking the exact place where the log needed to be notched. She moved on to the next, and Kinra went to help her.

Leiel watched, shook her head. Someday she should be able to do that, mark wood, or even stone as needed, with just the power of her will, and the heat of her body. Old gods...more heat than this? For all her fears the day of transition might never come, today it was the last thing she wanted! She found her packed lunch in her bag tucked under the table, and pulled out the hunk of wrapped cheese and half a loaf of the bread she had baked the night before, perfectly browned. Elda would be pleased. "It took me leaving a life in the kitchen to learn to bake properly," she said.

Gahree settled on the ground, cross-legged, and pulled a small sack of fresh pea-pods from her pocket. She bit into one, crunching happily.

"Is that what you've been snacking on?" Leiel asked as she sat beside the Draigon.

"The sweetest greens of the season have always been my favorites." She passed the little bag. Leiel pulled out a few pods, handed it back, and offered a hunk of bread.

Gahree took it and sampled a bite. "And it took you baking for pleasure to learn to bake."

Leiel crunched a pea-pod, sighed at the sweetness. "I've always learned best, the things that interest me." She frowned. "Imagine if everyone could learn whatever they wanted to—like here."

"Arnan was like that, once. At least a large part of it. When Draigon were teachers, and the land was younger."

"Is that true? Or is it just the story that's been passed for a thousand years?"

A smile crinkled Gahree's eyes. "More truth than not. I'm not what I was that long ago, but I remember, flying free across this land, to a warm welcome wherever I landed, with gatherings of all those curious and interested in learning. Not everyone was, of course. But so many were—and so many are to this day."

Leiel remembered a longing, tight in her belly, the ache in the back of her throat that came from knowing how much of the world she wanted more of and how little of it was to be hers simply because she was a girl. How many others lived with that feeling, because of who they were? Not how smart or curious they were, but because they had been born a girl or poor or in the wrong place. "Why isn't that what we work to change?" Leiel asked.

"It is, wild daughter. We gather the brightest, the most able to add to our knowledge. We keep light in the world. The library here—the other small storehouses of stories and wisdom and curious things. We find help and homes for as many people as we can, among those we cannot bring here."

Leiel nodded, frowned as she chewed.

"You're thinking that it's not enough."

"It isn't."

Gahree smiled. "Why do you think I brought you here?"

Leiel started, turned to look at the watery-haired woman. So much conviction, that Leiel would achieve all Gahree hoped for... What if she turned out, after all this time, to be one of the ones Wynt mentioned? What if she was not capable of becoming what she hoped?

A whoop of joy from across the small lot interrupted her thoughts, and Leiel whipped her attention toward the sound. Kinra had her arms wrapped around Shorr and they rocked together, laughing. Sim stood beside them, laughing, until Kinra reached out and dragged her into the embrace. Wynt just grinned from a few paces away.

"Well, at last," Gahree got to her feet and reached down to help Leiel up.

"What's going on?"

Gahree just laughed and walked toward the happy gathering. Leiel followed, trying to make sense of the happy chatter as she approached.

"Gahree! Leiel!" Simmini broke loose from the triple hug and bounded toward them. She grabbed Gahree, then pulled back and hugged Leiel. "Oh, it's happening at last!"

Leiel found herself laughing, even though she had no idea at what. Happiness poured out of Simmini, out of them all, and wrapped around Leiel as though it had been directly born inside her. It flowed between them, warm and rising, bubbling. What was this? The grass beneath her feet shivered and started to wilt. With a gasp, Leiel pulled back, stared at it. "What—?"

"Oh yes, you're one of us!" Shorr said. "Just a little Draigon training cracking through."

Leiel stared at the grass. Was it true? Finally possible? That some change was at last at work deep within her?

"Gweld, Leiel," Gahree said. "A bit of Draigon joy and a bit of Draigon heat, channeled to you, by laughter and love. And through you, because you are becoming more, every day, what you are deciding you will be."

Gweld, manifesting in Draigon fashion—through her! A rush a wild joy went through Leiel, then she looked into Shorr's grinning face and pushed down her own elation. "This moment is not about me," she said. Though what had just happened tingled every part of her and quickened her heart, it was not the most important thing happening this moment. "What's the news?"

"Annaluft Rayyat!" Sim shouted.

"The desert?" Leiel frowned.

"Yes! Pentryp! They want us to come!"

"Pentryp?" Leiel fumbled a moment, trying to place the word. Then it came—a note written on the edge of a map—her farcical mistranslation of an old story. "The artists' village! Haha!" She shouted the last word and pulled Sim back into her arms. "They've invited you! Wait...you're leaving?" She leaned away and looked at her friend, glanced at Shorr, who was still talking earnestly with Kinra. "Both of you are leaving."

Sim nodded, smiling. "It's what we've been working for."

Long nights, after the hard work of surviving and learning Draigon skills was done, Simmini and Shorr drummed and danced for all of them. Practicing, and playing with passion at their chosen arts, until they could learn no more from the histories stored in the Library, or the skills of those living in Cyunant. Pentryp beckoned, one of the dozen other Draigon villages scattered throughout Arnan, the one home to the greatest artists among them, the most determined learners and teachers. The ones who kept old traditions and skills alive, and celebrated the new ones being created. To be welcomed into such a place was an honor that demanded joyous laughter. Their dream. Realization struck. To be other than what was expected for those who chose to remain in Cyunant was also a mighty thing. Leiel smiled. "Old gods, I'll miss you both! But I'm so happy for you!"

"Oh, but not for long. Once you take the Great Shape, you can visit!"

"It'll be a few days flight, but what a way to stretch your wings," Shorr said.

Leiel blinked at the idea. Yes. One day visiting across great distances would be easy for her. Not simple, not safe, but easily managed in the physical sense.

"Well-earned!" Gahree said. "Enough work for the day. This calls for a celebration."

"And a swim!" Wynt grabbed Shorr's hand. "Come on!"

Shorr grinned, leaned close and gave Simmini a fast kiss, and took her hand. "Swim!"

"See you below!" Sim let herself be dragged away along with Shorr. Shouts of anticipated pleasure came from the trio as they raced down the trail toward the pond.

"That leaves us to get things started," Kinra said. "I'll set up the bonfire." She waved and headed down the trail as well.

"We'll take care of food and fine wine." Gahree said. "Never things to be argued with or disappointed in being able to provide."

Leiel studied the other woman, the smile on her face, the pure happiness in the relaxation of her shoulders and the lift of her chin. "Or a chance for people to live their dreams."

Gahree shifted her gaze, looked at Leiel out of the corners of her eyes. "A chance for as many as possible."

Leiel was quiet. As many as possible. As many as wanted to. And not just here. Simmini and Shorr had found more than than their art here, they had found each other. They had found acceptance and love. Everyone deserved the chance at that. The wilted grass at her feet —might she really be, at last, learning what she needed to make her dreams come true? "That's what I want," she said.

"A chance to live your dreams?"

"Yes, my dream of becoming a Draigon. My dream that everyone can live their own. That I can make that happen."

Gahree smiled. "You have always had the strength you needed, wild daughter, to achieve the first. You think I have not known your doubts? You prove your worth every day, just as you did as a child. You are worthy of what you wish to become. And your other dream—that is not one we offered you. That is one you created for yourself. And it might matter most of all."

"Was that your plan for me? Yours and my mother's, when you decided to bring me here?"

Gahree threw back her head and laughed. "Oh, daughter of wings, we planned only that you discover the best of yourself, and the freedom to decide on your own purpose." She smiled. "I think you are well on your way. It's now not the what you have to discover, but the how of making it so."

Chapter 18

Leiel - 26 years

The afternoon light slanted into the small workshop. The clutter of well-used tools, and the scent of worked metal were sure signs that Wynt had been spending more time working than sleeping.

Leiel's eyes crinkled as she watched the Draigon pull the soft cloth through the inside of the ring. Wynt turned it in her hand, buffing the inset stone with aggressive care.

Since Cleod had given Leiel the stone, she had kept it close, but hidden. The knot that formed in Leiel's chest when she had handed it over to the copper-haired Draigon had not loosened until this morning when Wynt had greeted her on the trail to the Library and told her the ring was complete.

Set at an angle in a wrap of yellow gold and mounted on a band as wide as the nail on her smallest finger, the smoky-brown stone glinted in the morning light. Not bright flashing, like mica, the stone reflected with a subtle sheen that forced a second glance of true appreciation. Wynt had suggested cutting the stone, shaping it for a more striking flash, but had acquiesced to Leiel's request that it be left in nearly its natural shape, with only a strong buffing to bring out the shine.

"It's beautiful," Leiel said as Wynt took the base of the band between her thumb and forefinger and raised the ring for closer inspection. The somehow ideal contrast of the smoke-dark crystal with the gold was both more elegant, and more striking, than she had imagined it would be. This stone...so much of her heart tied itself to this simple rock and the memories it brought close to the surface. And now this ring. A decade, a century, ten centuries—it would endure, unlike the man who had gifted her the heart of it.

"This will be awkward to wear in a fight. Try it on." Wynt dropped the ring into Leiel's palm.

"Do you think of everything in terms of battle?"

"Battle? No. But potential necessary action—what else is there to consider?" The wink that accompanied the question put a smile on Leiel's lips.

"You and Kinra," Leiel said and slipped the ring onto the middle finger of her left hand. It settled into place with a comfortable snugness.

Wynt chuckled. "Kinra dreams in battle plans. Looks like it fits."

Never had Leiel possessed any jewelry, and the look of it against her skin was strange to her eyes. She turned her hand, flexed her fingers. No slip. No pinch. "It's perfect."

"Don't romanticize the thing. I know how to measure."

"If appreciation of things fitting is romantic, I'm guilty today."

"Just remember to take it off before you take the Great Shape."

With a shake of her head, Leiel raised her gaze from the ring and met Wynt's. "I'm a while from worrying about that. I haven't even found my full expression of Gweld, yet."

"That might help." Wynt tapped a finger on the stone. "Owast, we call it. Some find having it nearby makes seeing with Gweld easier."

Leiel canted her head and frowned. "Cleod told me the Ehlewer call it Wild Stone."

The sound that rose from the huntress was a mix of amusement and contempt. "The Enclaves say many things. What's wild about a rock?"

"I never thought about it."

"I doubt the Enclaves have either."

Leiel twisted the ring on her finger. "There had to be a reason at some point."

"If you find it, tell me." Wynt shrugged. "It might be useful."

"You think there isn't one?"

"I think they figured out Owast was useful for their needs, and someone decided it needed a better name."

"That's not a reason?"

Wynt laughed. "Maybe it's the actual reason."

Walking down the path toward the common cabin, the new weight on her left hand drew her attention time and again. She rolled the ring band with her thumb, and flexed her fingers, seeking balance. Time would tell whether this had been the best choice—not just to have something created with the stone, but to have such a thing as this made, all flash and impracticality.

She smiled, stopped, and raised her hand. Fall light drifted crisp and gold over the stone, moved from shadow as the breeze shifted the leaves. Something in the back of her mind tingled, and for an instant the stone took on a gilded light, rimmed in a rainbow of tone. A blink, and it was gone. Her thumb rocked the ring again, and she grinned. Illusion, imagination, it hardly mattered. Beauty was beauty. *Cleod reached out and set the dusky quartz on the table before her...* And the caring that came with a true gift remained.

"I remember," she said, and opened her heart to the warmth contained in that memory.

Golden light bloomed around her, shifted, and expanded into sheeting waves of red and green and lavender. Her breath locked in her throat and her eyes widened. A series of heartbeats pressed up into her throat. Then realization claimed her, followed by laughter, and every note of it rang gold through the air. Color. For her, Gweld was color. Every sound, from words to wind, flashed with vibrant shades, newly layered in glowing tones. The canopy above her shimmered green and amber with the movement of the breeze. The water of the stream moved silver, then indigo, as it twisted over rocks in more nuanced shades of blue, and swirled darker into eddies. It was starlight and rainbows and it tumbled toward the pond below.

She stepped forward, and the rustle of undergrowth against her legs sent an earthy ribbon of browns and greens rippling around her.

Leiel stopped again, breath light in her throat, absorbing the trembling swirl that charged her senses—opened to a dozen interlocked levels a vision of the world she had never imagined, she could not stop the joy that flared through her.

Her legs trembled, and she pulled in her laughter, let it shake the rest of her and vibrate gilded tones against the trees and rocks around her.

Never in a thousand days of lessons and seeking, had she imagined an end result such as this. *For every person Gweld is different.* Was the magic she was experiencing shared by no one else? Was she the only one to see the world this way? It was impossible to imagine anything to compare with what she saw and knew in this moment. Wild dreams! What must others feel? Could there be anything to equal this? How could she ever explain what she experienced enough to compare it to others?

A calming breath, two, and the intensity of the expanded color sense began to fade. For a moment, she was afraid that if she lost touch with it, she would not know how to regain it. But she glanced at the ring again and relaxed. The feeling remained, of warmth and true caring. As long as she had access to that, she would never lose the wonder she had just touched.

The world settled into its usual spectrum, and Leiel sank to the ground at the edge of the trail. She smiled a little, and looked out through a break in the trees. Below, a glimmer of light on the surface of the pond was just visible, as was the roof of the central cabin. She saw Gemda walking toward the water. Did she know? Did the Draigon going about their work and studies across Cyunant know what Leiel had just achieved? She wanted to climb to the top of the mountain and shout her victory down the length of the ravine, let the entire Northern Range know what had happened within her today. She shivered a little, visualized the vibrating colors that had claimed her expanded vision. Not just colors she could see every day, but colors that were more tasted and heard than seen. Was that possible? What wasn't? Oh yes. That much she had learned—never count anything as impossible.

Alone on this mountain trail she had encountered, without ceremony or struggle, an entry into magnificence that would forever change and guide her life. So much to be explored now—the layers she had sensed in her few moments touching Gweld—finding a way to move within the abstract beauty without losing herself in its allure. She hardly dared to consider how vast the knowledge was that she must absorb to make full use of her new-found skill.

She cupped her right hand over her left, pressed the stone into her palm. Had Cleod felt like this? Had he held down elation and awe? Had he looked ahead and wondered at all he might accomplish with the knowledge? Or had the way he was forced to access the Gweld so marred the experience that it was only a moment of shock and pain? She hoped that was not the case, but based on what both he and Gahree had told her of Draighil training, her chest tightened to think of what he must have felt.

Through the wavering leaves, she watched Gemda wade into the pond and glide into strong strokes that sent her swimming across the water and out of sight. How did Gemda know Gweld? Was it sound or scent or movement or light? Gahree had said the Draigon could communicate within Gweld. Could they, perhaps, share each other's experience? Was that possible?

If she saw Cleod again someday, could her understanding of Gweld touch his? She shook her head at the thought. Even after all these years, when she learned something new, discovered something she wanted to share, her first desire was to share it with him. Especially today, when his gift had become a touchstone for her awareness. But when could such a thing ever happen? Could the Draighil and the Draigon share Gweld?

Footsteps on the trail drew her attention. Gahree. Leiel knew it before she looked up and met the Draigon's gaze. Silence and understanding filled the space between them, and Leiel hesitated, unwilling to shift the energy of the moment. But the question pressed.

She spoke softly. "The way the Draighil use Gweld, and the way you spoke to me as Shaa—"

"Yes," Gahree said. "Yes, wild daughter, we can connect with the Draighil."

"But you don't."

Gahree tipped her head, silent a moment. "We don't. If we did, they would know what we are—more than they might already guess. And that is more danger than we are yet ready to bear."

Something in the tone of the words pulled at the back of Leiel's mind, something unspoken, like a question half- formed. It shivered, faded away. What had she missed? She frowned and asked, "But you think someday we will be ready?"

"Someday, yes."

Leiel's frown deepened, then she caught a flicker of color and shine at the corner of her sight. Relief rocked through her. At last, the path to her becoming Draigon lay fully open before her. Tears filled her eyes. She closed them, drew in a slow breath, and when she opened them again, the world was once again aglow and vibrating with a myriad of prismatic bands.

Someday. Perhaps there was a way for all the people of Arnan to have a chance to see the world gleaming with brightness. Perhaps, *someday*, anything. Perhaps someday this for everyone.

Chapter 19

Leiel - 29 years

It took her like a sudden rising of wind before a storm. Her skin rippled like the surface of water under a hard breeze, and she froze, her step half completed, on the boulder-strewn cirque that filled the bowl above Cyunant. Not halfway home from her astronomy lesson with Gydron, her mind full of the sky and the taste of the wind, a shaking began. Accompanied by a rising heat that started in her gut, it erupted across the rest of her body with the force of a geyser.

For a few seconds, she could make no sense of what was happening. Her bones went fluid in her limbs, and she shuddered, folded to the ground without even a cry. Knowledge squelched panic. *Change.* All the years of study, the culmination of her studies—the first shift happened in the seconds she had to absorb the first layer of transformation. She grabbed the ring from her hand and dropped it to the ground, just in time.

Change cracked her apart like a glacier calving, exploded her into something molten—a mountain being born. Gweld burned through her, shredded the parts that doubted and carried them away on a wind wild with the smell of the first frost and the crackle of fallen leaves. To be afire and edged in chill in the same moment, to be split asunder and drawn tight in the finest detail—every bit of her cried out, expanding, grasping, until something more than what she had been reached back and caught the best of her, as though to yank her upright and offer her the finest view.

She tried to contain fear with logic. *The physical change was only a manifestation of the accumulation of knowledge.* But knowledge, for all its power, fell short in the actual moment. Sight burst into flares, waves of color and light, rippling and ripping through multiple spectra. The very structure of the air opened, spinning across a field of vision grown wide and strange with depth and clarity.

Leiel cried out as she shattered and became.

Legs and arms, powerful and formed to purpose. Wings unfurled. Wings! She had wings—she had WINGS!— snapped taut, arched, trembling with newness and wonder and anticipation. She turned her head...and a neck long and muscled moved in concert. Shaking overtook her, electric through her system. She would have collapsed, but her new body knew, better than her astonished mind, how to balance and control.

The world swam with brilliant color, and it bled over and off her in sheets of magnificent glory. Could she...? The mountains echoed with energy around her, and the sky—oh, the sky—it beckoned, bright with starlight and dashed with fast moving clouds. They swept through the night, racing the stars themselves. Could she match them? Dance with them? Surpass them? Thought was left behind as she leaped—and the mighty wings beat down, caught air, lifted—*lifted her!*

That air could carry this giant new form was a mystery—yet she stretched and caught a gust sweeping over the ridge. It filled the space beneath her, buoyed and propelled her out over the valley below. She cast shadow over shadow, sweeping over the earth with a precise control that made no sense. Her mind skipped and trembled, even as her body followed a half-formed whim and banked a turn that set the world on edge and split her sight between mountains and sky. Recollection expanded, moments, fleeting and bright, songs she had once known, games played in childhood, old rhymes and lessons, all long forgotten, filled her with each stroke of her wings. She had wings! New thoughts and old flooded her, none overtaking another, each vital and part of her. In this new shape, she had room for them all.

She flexed shoulders crossed by new muscle, sent wings into a new rhythm that launched her out of the turn and higher into the sky. Color streamed over the land below as everything she had learned found space inside her, settled, took root in the soil of a mind so vast and willing that truth could not help but grow. So much room inside her! Like the space between the stars toward which she soared, and no more empty than the dusting of stars forming the pale sweeping cluster that banded the dark of the sky from horizon to horizon.

Silver and black and gray, the normality of night was the base over which her Gweld sense laid a multi-spectrum rainbow of color. Every beat of her wings sheeted light, pushed her through air awash and full as a rushing river with life and color and the texture of things in motion. Uncontained. Unmeasurable. What in her human form could ever compare to this? Laughter bubbled through her mind, and she changed direction and followed the sweep of the mountain range, and all questions dropped away as wonder consumed her.

CHAPTER 20

Leiel

Music rolled up the valley, out of the edges of the great bowl, and echoed across the ridge tops as though calling every living thing within hearing to dance. The circle of women swayed in the firelight. Leiel's ears filled with the rising notes and the happy sounds of their voices. So crisp, so vibrant, every sound and sight and scent. The world was fresh and new, and gleamed across planes Leiel had previously only read about, but never touched. Her laughter danced as she raised her glass for Gydron to refill with wine.

Leiel had long since run out of words trying to describe the joy of what she had experienced in her first flight, when everything she had ever learned found a home inside her, and the ability to seek whatever the world had to offer was laid bare before her. All day and night she had flown, driven and carried by an amazement that grew each moment and an unbounded freedom like nothing she had dreamed possible. Mountains and plains, rivers and lakes, clouds and sun and moonlight and rain... Why did the Draigon not hold the Great Shape? Why move among humans at all? Why care?

But care was the thing, she realized as dawn broke the next morning, that made her mortal shape matter. Leiel, the girl at the pond, the woman who had climbed the mountain, and who cried when returned to her mother's arms. Leiel was *her*, and whatever this glorious bronze-scaled form could offer her, it could never be all that she was. Human was sipping tea on a chill evening, and the pleasure of soaking in a tub at the end of a hard day's work. Human could grasp old books and turn their pages and smell the musty dream of time trapped between them. Draigon shape could hold every memory of all that, but it could not grasp the joy. So she had turned toward home, and dropped herself sobbing with gratitude before Ilora where she waited atop the mountain bowl.

Now, among those with whom she belonged, beyond words or the need to explain, Leiel let her laughter speak for her, let the thrum of the instruments carry her onto her feet as she joined the other women in dance. Was she more drunk on the fine wine or on her victory-induced euphoria? After all the years of study, her dreams had found harmony and blended and lifted her until the Great Shape took hold of her and allowed her the uncanny exhilaration of pure understanding...and flight. Oh, that flight!

"Dance with me!" Ilora grabbed her hands, spun her about. Leiel threw back her head and laughed, whirled on bare feet over the damp earth. The ground seemed to press up against her feet, offering to spin and carry her, as though the mountain, too, wished to join the celebration.

"So quickly! So quickly you learned!" Ilora gasped.

"Five years, mother." Leiel squeezed her fingers. The days and nights of near-constant study, the work, the questions, the riddles of new languages and the challenges of new ideas and art and stories and manners of thinking—and so many doubts. So many fears. And yet she had done it. Now, to be worthy of the miraculous accomplishment and find a way to birth her other dream into being.

"It took me twelve." Ilora hugged her close a moment, then backed away, grinning. "Gydron said you are the best student she's had in a century. Only Wynt learned the change sooner, and she was born to it! Leiel, I am so proud of you!"

Only Wynt? Had all her years of uncertainty been for nothing? Leiel blinked back tears. And Ilora was proud of her! How many years had she gone thinking she would never hear those words again? Despite being with Ilora every day, sometimes it was the simplest statements and moments that went deepest, tugged hardest at her soul. "I'm so glad to be here. I'm so grateful for all of this."

"As am I, to have you here and watch you earn all this!"

Leiel laughed again. All her work, so many dreams—this is what it had all been for, this feeling of completeness inside her, becoming all she had ever sought to be. And another thought whisked through her mind, a question. Was this what Cleod felt when he had reached the goal he had spent his life striving toward? When he had earned the title of Draighil and the right to face Shaa on the Spur? No wonder I couldn't talk you out of your fight, old friend.

"Oh, smell that!" Ilora laughed, leaning close to be heard over the music. They had danced across the circle. The sweet sent of roasted corn filled the air. Fresh corn this late in the year—like Gahree's peppers, the best things were never out of season for the Draigon. Not something from the greenhouse, this. Where had someone been to bring back such a treat? The south coast this time? Or the southern Nis? Those were places she wanted to see one day. The more stories Gydron told her of her old home in Sowd, the more Leiel read about it, the more she wanted to know. Someday she would get there.

And Sibora—the city of Delhar's birth. The gardens, the flowers, and the shining stone. One of a dozen places she had explored only through the tales of those born there. The varied and mysterious pasts of the Draigon—she was part of that now. Already she had been in Cyunant long enough to take for granted the look on the faces of the newest arrivals, fresh from their brushes with death and the terrifying fire of Sacrifice.

At least no other Draigon had been lost since Shaa had wounded Cleod on the Spur. Even Trayor, the remaining Draighil, had run from his last encounter with Kinra—run and told a tale to cover his cowardice that was so far- fetched only desperation among its hearers could make it believable. But some, as always, heard only what they needed to hear to get them through the day. Without something to fear and to hate, they might have to face something else entirely. Perhaps even themselves. And what would they find? Who would they be then?

She knew the terror of that moment—looking into the mirror of her own heart and seeing all the things lacking. The only way to survive it was to find the holes and fill them with better things than the ones she feared— knowledge and understanding and respect and love. She glanced at Ilora. And forgiveness. That most of all. For herself and the things she had done, and those *she* had abandoned to get here and earn the happiness she had found.

"Let's eat!" Leiel grabbed Ilora's hand and pulled her toward the roasting pit on the edge of the circle. They filled plates with ears of sweet corn and settled by the fire.

Juice dribbled down Leiel's chin as she sank her teeth into the hot, crisp kernels and felt them catch between her teeth. She giggled, the small annoyance a pleasure she would miss if she had held forever to her Great Shape.

But oh, the temptation of that form... The lands she had glimpsed beneath her as she carved through the sky sewed a bright patchwork of mountain and rivers. Did they have names? Peoples who lived among and loved them?

"Mother, you said you don't travel. Have you never left here and explored the world?"

Ilora took a sip of wine, shook her head, and poked a long stick into the fire to stir the coals. "Not often. I've been to the northern villages and once to the port of Bajor. A very pretty town. It smells like fish."

Leiel laughed. "Fish smell pretty?"

"The two things are notable, but not necessarily linked." Ilora smiled and leaned forward to toss another log on the fire. Bright against the sky, sparks jumped into the air as it landed. "Are you thinking of all the places you want to see?"

"What else?" Leiel smiled. "Half of what I heard tonight have been suggestions of all the places I can go now that I have my wings."

"And what will you do in all those places?"

Leiel sat back, considered. What would she do? Breathe deep. Listen. Taste the air and take in the scents on the wind, of things cooking, like the corn, of the messages of nature, like whatever fish smelled of as the scent of it carried in from the sea. She would learn, all she could, the form of the land and the voices of those who walked it. She would take a bite of it, however strange or burnt or bitter, however sweet or spicy, to savor on her soul. She chuckled to herself.

"I think," she said at last, through a smile pushing against her lips, "that I will find all the best things to eat and devour them." She laughed, looked at Ilora and winked. "You should come."

Ilora waved down the shouts, and finally nodded. "I'll tell it." She laughed. "I'll tell it."

The shouts shifted to cheers and drifted into silence as the women gathered close around the fire. Leiel settled next to Wynt for the telling. As fine as Gahree's stories were, Leiel had always preferred her mother's way of speaking the old tales.

Ilora took a breath and began, her smoky voice weaving images of light in the gloom.

"The Spur country has always been known for its storms. Even, it is said, in Desga Hiage's day. The mountain offered her shelter from the weather with the stones it cast down to build Adfen Tower. And she built the city to outlast weather and time. In fact, to outlast all things except the foolishness of the people living there.

"And the weather raged through the decades, sun and wind and rain and snow and hail. And no foundation ever cracked, neither did any wall or casement. Every roof was as Desga had built it, so stable that people painted them on the inside. They covered ceilings in happy scenes, or ones that told their stories and praised their faith.

"The ceiling in the library was especially beautiful. It showed the building of the Tower. The art was based on the old tales. Though they were not properly remembered, they still held enough of the truth to make the newest residents of Adfen nervous."

"Oh, come now Ilora," Wynt called out. "They were scared thoughtless!"

Leiel elbowed Wynt as laughter broke over the gathering.

Tossing back her hair, Wynt winked. "Why else would there be a story at all?"

"None of them make such admission in my tale," Ilora called over shouts and chuckles. "So I'll get on with it, if you please."

Leiel raised her voice. "We please!" The others added agreement.

Ilora continued, "The *nervous* newcomers did not like the story on the library ceiling, especially once they converted the space into their Sanctuary. They painted over the art. They did not even paint a new story, just whitewashed it, as thick as they could spread it. They called themselves clever—" She waved a hand at Wynt, and Leiel laughed as the woman beside her shut her mouth without comment. "And whether they were or not, they convinced many people that it was so.

"The next week a storm blew up. It brought rain in a season the Spur usually saw only sun and hot winds. And hail fell. The storm was huge. The fury of it cracked the library roof around the edges and sent water down the interior walls and flooded the floors."

"But not over the books," Leiel shouted, unable to resist adding her favorite bit of the story. Ilora's face scrunched in exasperation, but she just gave Leiel a wry look and continued.

"The librarians panicked. They sent for the priests—yes, Wynt, the *priests*—who had painted over the ceiling. Because nothing like this had ever happened in the entire history of Adfen.

"Of course the priests sent for the carpenters, and the carpenters sent for the stone masons, and none of them could stop the leaks any more than they could stop the rain.

"But on the other side of town, above an old, forgotten bookshop, lived two women who loved and read old books, and loved fairy tales more than nearly anything. They heard about the leaking roof and one remembered an old story, something that sounded mad-but-oh-so-much-fun to two old women."

Leiel's laughter bubbled along with everyone else's. She remembered the first time she had heard the story, as a little girl in the warm kitchen back at the farm, with Elda humming by the stove, while Ilora embellished it with silly voices and wild gestures of panic made by priests. And she remembered Gial's violent reaction when she had repeated the tale as Ilora told it... Now here it was again, the same tale, but this time repeated in the open, appreciated by all, and edged with joyful laughter.

"The women found the old book they remembered, and carried it with them through the rain to the library. The doors had been left open to let the water drain over the threshold, and the two women walked right in. Inside, they lit candles. They opened their book and found a poem there, or maybe it was a song, and they sang every word as though it were the most important poem ever written.

"They sang high, and they sang low, and they laughed, and they danced and splashed in the water. They were happy—happy to sing and dance. They were happy with the idea that the story *might* work. They would even have been happy if it did not."

"But it did!" Kinra shouted. A cheer went up.

Ilora laughed and agreed. "But it did. The cracks mended themselves and the leaks sealed, and the whitewash on the ceiling peeled and flaked until the original painting shown through again. And when their song and work was done, the women went home, satisfied that their story had kept other stories safe."

Another cheer echoed up the mountain. Leiel raised her wine glass with the others, and with a great inhale of breath, they all began to sing. The old language rolled and lilted, not a beautiful harmony or a glorious chorus, but a wild, jubilant, broken-toned ensemble that would make even the most tone-deaf of choral leaders cringe. Leiel's heart was light, and her head seemed to float on her shoulders, and the words of the song rose and rose until she was practically shouting them.

Strong are the voices of ancients.
The stories they tell will live on.
Forgotten by all of the recent
Fools who wish deep wisdom gone.

But voices will rise up in chorus,
Harmonic and vibrant and strong.
Hearts will recall the old ways,
And change shall arise before long.

Bright sun and bright moon and bright music,
We open up hearts with our song.
That which is hidden and lonesome,
Is revealed when we rise as one.

Half-drunk on the old poem and half-drunk on fine wine, Leiel collapsed back laughing on the ground. She rolled on her side, propped her head on her hand and looked at her mother. Leiel grinned, her eyes crinkling her whole face, joy so resonant in her expression that it pulsed through every part of her. If she tried to contain it, it would burst though her and spill over the ground and into the fire and blow up the world in a glorious whirlwind of color and warmth. Somehow, that seemed like a less-then-perfect tribute to the happiness she felt.

Leiel winked at Wynt, scrambled to her feet, and began to dance before the musicians recognized her intent. For a few seconds, she had the space to herself, moving in time to the chatter of voices, crackle of fire, and the rush of the wind in the low-bent trees. She opened her arms and spun in place, dancing to her own heartbeat, just as she had on that day in the Tower, an act of defiance, an act of joy, of faith in herself. The music swelled again, caught up with her, and others gathered around her, joined her, lifted her, and she knew she was wrong—that moment in the Tower had been only the first turn toward freedom—this was what she had been moving toward all along. Finding her strength had been glorious, but true happiness was found here among those who loved her, and found joy in her joy, and who would dance with her to far past the morning light.

Leiel tore another chunk of the still-warm piece of bread and popped it into her mouth. The crust crunched as she chewed to the rhythm of the drums still ringing the air. Across the fire, Wynt and Ilora were leaning on each other, laughing. Gydron came round with a pitcher of wine, and they both held up glasses for a generous refill.

The vibrant thrash and hum of the fiddle, the pip of a reed flute should have clashed with the heavy whining blow from the pipes, but somehow the music melded. A tingling, fretless lute bent tones among the stronger rhythms and carried a trembling melody into the night. Leiel waved away Gydron's offer of more wine and leaned back against the tree and let herself drift on the sound.

She watched the dancing, the different styles and steps, all finding their own place among the music. Women with black hair and brown, or red, or even an occasional rare hint of gold, from far-flung parts of Arnan, and even different eras, all here laughing and sharing and celebrating her success. Never had she imagined that such a thing could be.

A hand brushed her hair, and she looked up into Gahree's smiling face. "The best of all things," she said.

Leiel smiled, turned her gaze back to the party. "Women laughing."

"Women *being*."

Leiel laughed. "The most dangerous thing in the world."

Gahree folded herself down beside Leiel. "Oh, yes," she agreed. "That and fine wine. And when the two come together—" She tipped her head toward the laughter and dancing. "Such happiness should never be hidden from the world."

Leiel sighed. "And yet it is. Why, Gahree?"

"It is what has been called for, all these years. But nothing holds. Change will come. One will find the other—us the world, or it, us. As the wind will blow."

"You can't just choose it?"

Gahree laughed. "There is always choice. One day, it might be mine to make." She canted her eyebrows, raised her glass, and waited.

With a smile, Leiel did the same, laughed at the clink the glasses made as they touched. "When we met, this is not a scene I could ever have envisioned."

Gahree sipped her wine. "It's better that the worst that comes to us, comes as a surprise. So, too, the best of things."

"Leiel! Come dance! It's Lista's favorite song!" Wynt was on her feet, beckoning.

Leiel glanced at Gahree and grinned. "I'll stay with the best, for now." She set her drink aside and stood, let the music and her friends' shouts of laughter carry her across the ground into the heart of the music.

CHAPTER 21

Cleod - 28 years

Balancing the tin plate in one hand, Cleod leaned back against the fallen tree and watched meadow grass tilt around him. The air held the scent of old stone and damp pine, and carried the summer stickiness that was ever-present even this far north. Crickets chirped in anticipation of nightfall, and a few distant peeps rose from frogs at the creek beyond their encampment. To his right, Kilras sat finishing his coffee, his long hair still damp from their dunk in the river after their evening spar.

Cleod sighed. As well as he knew Kilras, certain things reminded him that the Dorn was a man more complex than he seemed. The slice of cake on his plate was one of them. Year after year, their stops outside Adfen meant this treat appeared with the late meal. Flavored with vanilla, and backed with a faint citrus scent that Cleod had never managed to identify, the body of the cake was thick, rich without being creamy, and heavy on his tongue in a way that made him close his eyes and sigh. The texture never failed to surprise and delight.

With the edge of his fork, he cut another bit and popped it into his mouth. He turned his gaze to the distant city as he chewed. They were camped just far enough beyond the walls that only the top of Adfen Tower was visible, a dark T-shaped shadow against the outline of the Spur. Deliberate, the attention Cleod gave the scene, the rolling clouds over the grey-green peaks, and the way the fading sun back-lit everything with purple and gold.

How many years, how many visits, had it taken him to be able to gaze at this view and not break into a shaking, half-contained rage? So many times Kilras and Nae had restrained his fits, his ravings, until exhaustion forced calm. Then, this cake. Always this cake, always carried back from Adfen and offered by Kilras's hand like a reward for sanity and survival. And it worked. Somewhere, with the passage of years, this absurdly delicious dessert had become the thing he associated with this campsite, as though it formed a sweet barrier between him and the reality of the city itself.

"Some trick, Kil."

The Dorn laughed. "Trick?"

"Making me love this damn cake more than I hate Adfen."

Kilras leaned back against the log, grinned over his mug without shifting his gaze from the horizon. "It wasn't easy."

Cleod fell silent, nodded. No, it had not been. Even now, seated quiet and comfortable within sight of the parked wagons that made up his home, memory clawed at the back of his skull. The smells of the market, the crack of the ax splitting wood, the buzz of summer insects at the pond, the chatter of an irritated squirrel, all wended through his thoughts. And the darker recollection of bright laughter and fire, screams and smoke. He shivered.

"Easy," Kilras said. "Cake conquers only so much."

A blink, then laughter pushed aside darker thoughts. "Cake conquers?"

Kilras glanced at Cleod's empty plate. "So far."

Cleod shook his head, smiling. "Where do you get this?" Far from the first time the question had been asked, and if the previous lack of response held true, it would not be the last. "I was raised here, and I never tasted this until you shared it." The old argument, that home-town secrets should not be so well kept by those not born and bred in a place.

"Your lack of thorough exploration still isn't my fault."

"I was a boy when I left."

"Maybe one day you'll settle yourself enough to come into town with me and learn."

Cleod drew a breath, sighed it out. As far as his control had come, the idea of riding through the city gates flipped his gut and tipped his mind toward spiraling unease. Senses flared, awareness seeking to leap out and press through the narrow streets, seeking, seeking—what, he did not wish to acknowledge. He swallowed and shook his head again. "Not yet."

A nod of agreement was Kilras's reply. He beckoned with his fingers, and Cleod handed over his plate and fork. Kilras pulled his knees in and rose to his feet with a contained swiftness that spoke of something besides years in the saddle. "I'll bring back more."

"You're going in again tonight?"

Kilras looked down at Cleod, took another sip of coffee. "Nae knows where to find me if I'm needed."

Rare as it was that Kilras spent a night away from the caravan, it was another thing Cleod had come to expect from their stops at Adfen. Family? Friends? A lover? The Dorn never said, any more than he revealed the origin of the cake.

Cleod nodded. "See you in the morning."

Kilras winked, stepped over the log, and walked toward the cook wagon. Cleod shook his head and turned his attention back to the skyline. He swept his gaze over the ridge of the Spur, then north, toward the notch beyond which the Ehlewer compound perched just below the top of another glacier-rounded peak. A shiver gripped his shoulders. Almost, he could hear the clang of swords and the shouted orders of the Elders.

You leave me no choice but to count you as an enemy. Was Soibel still alive? Did his anger still burn as hot and deep as Cleod's? He swallowed and got to his feet as a tug that was part fury, and part unmitigated need, yanked at his gut. Turning away from the sunset-wrapped Spur range, he headed back to camp.

"Cleod." Firm fingers gripped his shoulder and shook him awake.

He blinked and pulled a hand from under his blanket to wipe sleep from his eyes. "Trouble?"

Sehina shook her head. "Nae's on guard. A man approached. Says he knows you and wants to see you."

Cleod sat up as sleep fled completely. A man to see him? The limited list of possible visitors left him cold. "Who?"

She shook her head. "Refused to say. Nae's got him stalled."

Trust the old guard to be good for at least that. "Arm everyone," he said as he sat up. He reached for his boots. "There's no one left in Adfen who'd wish me well." Except Klem Councilman. The thought came unbidden. But the chance that the stranger was Leiel's bitter brother was more than slim. More likely, the waiting visitor had ties to the Ehlewer. A tremor went through Cleod as he tugged on, and tied, his boots. Gweld swirled the edges of his vision. He gritted his teeth, shoved it back. But as he stood and settled his sword harness over his shoulders, he acknowledged that the twist in his chest was nearly as much anticipation as it was unease.

Sehina moved away, and soon faint sounds drifted to him, as she roused others and brought them to quiet alert. Moments later, she was back at his side with a set to her jaw that told him argument was pointless. She tossed her braid over her shoulder and dropped a hand to rest it on the handle of the knife sheathed on her hip.

He nodded, and she led the way. The night was luminous with moonlight. The stars overhead blazed crisp, their motion through the heavens pressing into his bones with each step he took toward the unknown visitor. Dew had formed in the night and it left his pants wet to the knee as he made his way through the swaying grass. Sehina's walk held determined purpose, each step firmly planted. Cleod pulled in every breath with like intensity, let it fill him and press back rising nerves.

At last, two dark shapes blotted themselves against the landscape. Sehina stopped. Cleod stepped past her, already taking in the height and stance of the man with Nae, and naming the stranger before his face was visible in the starlight.

Trayor.

Cleod waited for the catch in the back of his throat that signaled surprise, but it did not come. Who else would it be? None of the Elders would stoop to ride through the night to seek audience in a field. Hoyd was not perverse enough to enjoy the effects showing up in the middle of the night would generate. Bonniri was dead.

Nae offered a grunt of greeting and backed away to wait with Sehina.

Cleod stopped a few arm lengths from the Draighil. Trayor's pale hair was a strange, bright splash in the low light, and the familiar sing-song contempt in his voice was unmistakable. "You've got yourself a contingent of guardians. And you're sober. How things change."

A chill crawled up Cleod's scalp. He sucked moisture into his mouth, forced a swallow. "You asked for me?"

Trayor laughed. "Asked? I suppose." Trayor waved a hand toward the waiting scouts. "I'd rather we speak alone."

Cleod looked into the other man's face, gray-white in the moonlight, and nodded. "Nae. Sehina. Give us a moment."

"Not the best idea," Nae said.

"I know. But I'm asking anyway." He had lived ten years in the Enclave with the man before him and whatever had brought Trayor through the night to find him would not be expressed within earshot of others. "I'm all right."

Nae muttered something unintelligible, and Sehina offered a soft curse, but he heard them move away, footsteps soft in the wet grass. Cleod waited until he could no longer hear them, then turned his full attention to the Draighil in front of him. Violence had been the last word between them, and where that left them this moment was not something he dared to guess.

"You've done what you wanted and woken me, and half this camp, from a well-earned rest. I'd know the reason."

Trayor lifted his hands, the motion shadow in shadow. "Soibel sent me."

Cleod straightened and set a hand on the hilt of his sword. "Why?"

Trayor grunted. "I've been keeping track of you. Soibel appreciates what I've told him. He sent me to offer you another chance to come back where you belong."

Cleod did not relax his grip. Keeping track of? What did that mean? Spies? Here in Adfen, or throughout Arnan? He shoved aside the thought. "I am surprised you gave attention to the activities of a man as disgraced as me."

Trayor smiled and his teeth showed briefly with the same sharpness that marked his hair. "I tracked you in case the Elders decided to send me to kill you."

The chill raced over Cleod again. Always, retribution had been a possibility, but the passing years had dimmed his concerns. "All this time, the Ehlewer are still watching me?"

"You chose interesting company when you left us."

Cleod shook his head. "I chose to be a drunk."

"And you were. Until a certain caravan leader chose you. Do you think you could ride with Kilras Dorn and be long outside our attention?"

Of course. Of course they would have tracked him once Kilras hired him. The Dorn was known across Arnan, respected or feared in turn. "Why do you care, Trayor?" he asked. "Any of you? I am not Draighil anymore."

"No. Not for some time." Trayor's gaze narrowed, took on an edge that hinted at a glare suppressed. "But you've been known to forget what you are, or aren't. Do you think we'd take chances, as many secrets as you know?

Cleod tipped his head and studied the Draighil. What was this really about? Too much, even for Trayor, the half-threats and the barely contained disgust.

Something tripped in Cleod's chest. "This isn't just about Soibel wanting me to come back to the Ehlewer," he said. "This is *you*, Tray. You've tracked me for your own reasons. I wonder, do you know what they are?"

Trayor's grin turned vicious. "Your plan was to drink yourself to death. It must have taken an impressive change of circumstances to shift that."

"I asked you why."

With a shrug, Trayor stepped closer. "Why? The last time we met, you were raging drunk. I was never able get the stains out of that uniform. I thought seeing you sober might deaden that memory. And that of your stench."

Cleod held back a flinch. "I am too familiar with it. Nothing in this meeting will remove that from your mind. The lingering effects of ercew are not easy to escape."

"You went from having the best taste in wine of any cefreid alive, to drinking the cheapest brew cooked up in the foulest vats ever conceived."

At the last insult, a smile crossed Cleod's face before he could stop it. "I was without paying work. Ercew was the least costly way to achieve my goal."

Trayor grinned, shook his head. "When you talk like that, I could think you actually cared about the Draigon-damned consequences of your actions."

"I might," Cleod said, then frowned. Just like that, so easy, to fall back into rapport with a man he had not seen in years. Every one of his memories of Trayor was tied to the boldest and most disastrous time of his life. And yet, a few phrases and an old private joke turned back the years, and the vast differences in their lives drifted away. For a heartbeat, they were friends again, rivals in a game that had never been a game, and warriors in a centuries-old battle that neither of them truly understood. His belly flipped, and he took a step back.

Trayor shook his head. "You're not drunk this time. I'm here for a real answer not clouded by that damned drink."

In the middle of the night? A strange time for a real conversation."

"Since when does something so trivial matter to you? We received word of your arrival near Adfen, and I rode."

Late night talks. Running the mountain before dawn. Training with swords at night on the practice field, in rain, in snow, in sucking heat, until light and weather and time of day would mean nothing when battle engaged. "Talking to me is that important?"

"You were an *Ehlewer Draighil*. What has ever been more important than that?" Trayor shook his head, and he spoke stiffly, the words like thrown rocks. "The things you know... What you're throwing away riding with for that half-cefreid Dorn... Soibel has lost his mind thinking you're worth my time, but he wants you back."

"You once thought it was worth your time." The memory of that snowy day in the alley still woke Cleod at night, restless, belly churning. "My answer is the same as it was then, Tray."

"Why? Answer me, sober. Give me something besides puke and nonsense. You earned your title. You can earn another chance to kill Shaa."

The name speared through Cleod like a shot bolt. Superheated, like the memory of the flames that had scarred his body, the name ripped his thoughts apart and set him reeling. He stepped back to regain an equilibrium Trayor had known just how to disrupt.

"Fire and rot," Cleod said. A chance to kill Shaa and have true revenge for everything... What was cake or kind company compared to that? As Trayor had offered him cold water on the Tower on the day of Leiel's choosing, the promise just laid before him was a thing, unexpected, he had not even known he needed.

But something else tugged, half-known, at the back of his mind. Damn the years of drink that had clouded so much... And damn the fact that he was not drunk now. If he had been, he would not have to deal with any of this. "After all these years." Cleod shook his head. "Why this offer now?"

"You're a day's ride from home, in the shadow Adfen Tower. What better place could Soibel pick? If you'd ever come into the city, he would have met you himself."

Into the city, even deeper into the shade of the Tower. Cleod had been carried from Adfen to the healers in Sibora, and he had never come back through Adfen's gates. And he had no desire to do so now.

Cleod drew a quick breath, stepped back. "No," he said again. "I owe you nothing. I owe Soibel nothing."

Trayor frowned, shook his head. "It's not an offer you'll get again."

"The next one will be of my death?" Cleod's fingers tightened around the leather wrapped hilt of his sword.

"Your death has been my right from the day you renounced the Ehlewer," Trayor said. "And that will be true whether you come back or not. As least, if you return, you'll live long enough to kill more monsters and find a way to die with honor."

Cleod blew air through his nose, shook his head. "You didn't dare face me when I was half-drunk. You won't fight me now. Go back to the Enclave. Tell them I've no use for their offer. And they've nothing to fear from me."

"You think the Enclave fears you?"

As much as you do. The words formed, unspoken, and Cleod just looked back at the Draighil. Night sounds filled the quiet, the skittering of small animals and the cheep of crickets and the whisk of breeze through damp grass. A buzzing started at the top of his skull, and his belly cramped a little. "Go," Cleod said.

"Your last chance," Trayor said as he took a step back.

Cleod shook his head.

"Cefreid traitor." The sneer that turned the Draighil's face was mottled into greater bitterness by moonlight and shadow. He turned and stalked away toward the city, and a moment later disappeared against the tree line.

Cleod released breath as Trayor moved out of sight. He waited, listening, but the other man was gone. At last, relief allowed him to relax the grip on his sword, and he turned back toward the caravan encampment. He passed Sehina and Nae without word, heard a few comments pass between them, but he kept walking.

"Cleod—" She caught up with him at the edge of camp.

"We're clear," he said, the words rough against his throat. More conversation was the thing he wanted least in the world. "Stand everyone down. I'm sorry for the trouble."

She caught his arm and turned him around. "Who was that?"

Pure will stopped him from yanking free, but a tremor went through him and she released him when she felt it. "Cleod? Who?"

"A Draighil named Trayor. We—we trained together."

"Trayor?" Sehina's gaze narrowed. "A name as famous as yours was." She raised her chin. "He wanted, what?"

"Me. To return to the Enclave."

She folded her arms, studied him. "I take your return to us as refusal."

The shaking in his limbs increased and heat pushed at his belly. "I need sleep," he said, voice tight.

Sehina pressed her lips together, but she nodded. "Morning is soon enough for explanations."

He turned and worked his way down the line toward his bedroll. The night darkened in the shadows of the wagons as their bulk blocked the moonlight, and something stumbled deep inside him as he passed the herb smuggler's cart. Before he let thought form to consider the action, he pulled himself up on a wheel, lifted the hinged seat and pulled out a nearly full bottle of ercew. Panic beat hard wings on the inside of his skull, but he ignored it.

Turning away from the camp, he yanked the cork free. The bottle was to his lips before he had taken three steps. He half-choked as the liquor burned down his throat, then it hit his belly, and the winged thing struggling in his mind died.

He awoke in the back of a rolling wagon with his eyes stuck shut with grime and his shoulders bouncing off a pile of grain bags. Nausea boiled, and he groaned. Flinging out a hand, he sought instinctively for the cure of a fresh bottle. He found, instead, a canvas-clad leg. With a grunt, he rolled onto his side and opened his eyes.

Expecting Kilras's heavy black boots before his face, he instead stared at a much smaller brown pair. Sehina? No, still too small. He tilted his head up and stared into the face of one of the merchant's daughters. What was her name? Ten or twelve years old, she stared back at him with an expression so flat she had no need to speak how unimpressed she was with him.

She pursed her lips and, before he could say a word, scrambled across him to the front of the wagon. "Ledi Sehina! He's woke up!"

The sharp impact of her shout struck harder than her knees as she clambered on top of him. He groaned and wrapped his arms over his head as the consequences of last night's decisions echoed through the entirety of his being.

The girl—Tres, was that her name?—plopped down by his head and leaned over him. "Wake up Sere Cleod. Sehina's yelling mad."

He flinched, but forced himself to uncurl and meet the child's gaze. "Seems you're yelling, too."

She giggled. "Woke you good." Then she popped to her feet and hopped over him as the wagon stuttered to a halt. A fearless vault sent Tres over the tailgate and out of sight, just as Sehina's head appeared through the flap at the front of the wagon.

"You can thank Kilras I didn't just throw you in the creek and let you drown."

"Sehina, I—"

"You damn fool, we broke camp two days early because of this stunt. You'll have to be worth your weight in gems and fine wine to make up for the lost cash."

"How did—"

"Shut your mouth and get out." She shook her head. "You're an idiot. Kilras saved you some cake, back at the cook wagon. But you've got the next two weeks of riding rear guard. Maybe sucking dust will dry you out." She sat back and yanked the flap closed, leaving him only a few unsteady seconds to pull the pins and kick down the tailgate. He managed to hop down just as the wagon rolled out from under him.

Raising his hand against the glare of the sun, he tried to swallow, though his mouth felt stuffed with cotton. He tried a step, but had to fling out an arm to hold his balance. Trayor and ercew—a more horrific combination had not graced his night for years. He put his hands to his head and did not bother to look up as hoofbeats sounded and a blowing horse stopped beside him.

"Kil, I—"

"I know. Luckily, I'm wise enough to not think you were past this. Sehina told me what happened."

Cleod lifted a palm from his eye and blinked up at the Dorn. Sunlight blazed through to the back of his skull, and he winced. Then Kilras shifted in the saddle and put himself enough in front of the offending orb that focus became possible. Damn Trayor and his temptation.

"Is this ercew or Overlash?"

"Mostly drink," Cleod managed to say.

"Then walk it off. And enjoy your slice of cake. We won't be stopping at Adfen for the foreseeable future." Kilras turned his horse away and the sun blazed over Cleod again. Blinking hard, he stared after the Dorn. An offer from the Enclaves. A plunge back into the bottle. And the result was calm acceptance and cake? The knot in his belly unwound a fraction. The day he understood Kilras would be the day he stopped being grateful for being alive.

CHAPTER 22

Leiel - 32 years

I could wish to remain a witch issuing orders," Leiel said. She shook her head, looked over at Gahree where she sat in the rocking chair next to her on the porch of the community cabin.

"I know this is not the role you wish to play in the world, not the final dream of your heart. But to be Draigon you must recognize all that it now means, not just to the memory of what we were, or the dream of what we hope to become again. If you are to be completely Draigon, then your skill and control must be trained in all things. And your confidence must be certain.

"You already speak well to the councils, but this final thing that you must be mistress of, matters just as much."

Leiel looked over at Ilora where she leaned her hips against the porch rail. A flicker of recollection beckoned, of Ilora leaning into rising heat and a darkening sky. So long ago. And now Leiel was not simply to witness the rise of Draigon Weather, but to fly into the world and cause it.

"You did all this?" Leiel asked.

"On a smaller scale. I trained in the Northwest, in the smallest villages." Her lips twitched into a smile. "And I was not sent alone. Gydron came with me."

"Because of what you told me—that you were tempted to come back to Adfen."

"Always."

"And you don't fly anymore, to set Draigon Weather."

Ilora shook her head. "I am content and most useful here, with my histories and my teaching. I had enough of the Sacrifice on the day mine was made."

Leiel reached out a hand, and Ilora grasped it.

"All that you have learned, Leiel, comes to this task," Gahree said.

"It's a test, then." Leiel squeezed her mother's hand, but looked at Gahree.

"You may think of it as such, if you wish. It is a taste of the power you now hold—to be used with care and skill. A test only if you consider it to be one. We try things and fail, all the time. We learn more, and try again."

"And how do I try again at Draigon Weather if I fail in this? If the storm does not take hold—"

"Then you try again. Tahnis is large, but its population is not. The people are used to storms sweeping in from the sea. If the weather you set raises only hard rain and waves, they will take it as natural. And you will try again, until the heat you seek to create claims the land—and you claim the one they will choose as Sacrifice."

"And we're certain of that choice?"

"Shorr sent word that this Ellisa is the only one they will choose. She is bright and feared."

"Any artist that talented seems to make people uncomfortable," Leiel agreed. The young woman's drawings were heart-stoppingly raw—of life on the island, for the women and the poor sailors and farmers who worked the harsh volcanic soil. The few nobles and clergy who ruled the place did not care for being presented with the reality that supported their easier lifestyles. They would welcome the opportunity to silence her. But Leiel's heart thudded hard. "And the Draighil will not come? The Tahnisi hate them that much? More than they hate Draigon?"

"It's hard to believe, but it's true," Ilora said.

Gahree laughed. "The Tahnisi hate cowards. When the Draighil abandoned the Nys Enclave a century ago out of fear of the volcano, they lost the respect of the island. They would rather see a Draigon take one of their own, than owe anything to the Enclaves."

Leiel gave a shake of her head, withdrew her hand from her mother's grasp and ran her fingers back though her hair. "I need to do this," she said in agreement. "I need to know *how* to do this. And know that I can." She needed to take the responsibility, the weight of this action that so defined the Draigon in the eyes of all of Arnan.

"Strength you've never lacked, Leiel. Once a decision is made."

"It's the deciding that's hard," Ilora said. "Not accepting the consequences."

There would be those, whether or not she accomplished the task ahead. Learning new things always brought new weight to those who truly took them in. Failure she had feared. She feared it still. But never knowledge. She was not about to start now.

Naked on the mountaintop, Leiel stood motionless in the orange light of the setting sun. No goosebumps rose on her skin, despite the chill she tasted in the air. The constant flicker of heat at the base of her spine saw to her comfort, a ward against chill, and a balancing force, even when heat was the norm. Regulated, measured, it marked the comforting reality of her changed body. Unleashed—it would soon scour the land.

She turned to face the semi-circle of three Draigfen standing behind her: Gydron, with a sheaf of maps tucked under her arm, ready to answer any last questions that might arise in the face of true commitment to what lay ahead. Gahree, still and straight with a smile on her face that turned her lips and crinkled her eyes into laughing gems. Ilora, holding Leiel's folded clothing in her arms, her jaw tense in an expression marked half by concern and half by pride. It was an expression Leiel had come to understand as a mark of motherhood.

"I'm ready." Leiel said the words, but they did not match the flip in her belly or the dryness in her throat. Was she really? How could she be certain? Did she really have the skill? The control? Did she have the *wisdom*? So many lives soon to be held under the power she was about to wield over the land...

"And you have doubts," Ilora said. "As any wise woman would."

"Am I wise?"

"You are closer than you were last year."

A smile pulled at Leiel's lips. "I'm glad you didn't say yes."

"You're too smart to believe me, anyway."

Leiel laughed a little. "Ah, mother, I hope I am at least that smart." She turned the ring on her finger. Cleod had assumed such a level of action once, to change the world. His outcome had been brutal and bitter. If he now led a life far from that pain, she could not imagine that his past had not etched itself deep inside him, just as had hers. She slipped the ring from her finger and handed it to Ilora. "Keep it safe."

Ilora nodded.

Leiel faced Gydron, shook her head. She had no more questions. The route south was clear in her mind.

To Gahree, she offered a small smile. "You believe me ready."

"I believe you have never been anything else. Go, wild daughter. Claim this part of you, with all your heart."

Leiel turned away, lifted her eyes and her arms, spread her hands wide and let the change take her, lift her. Responsibility such as this could not be abdicated. She had received a chance rare in the world, to choose her own path. The gift of that required acknowledgment. If freedom had any price, it was that of accountability.

She dove on mighty wings into the sky.

Chapter 23

Leiel - 39 years

The summer sun angled through the window and warmed Leiel's back, but there was little comfort in it. Gydron's news was too disturbing, it was too soon, the pain too raw, for her to simply accept the need for another Sacrifice. Leiel frowned as she looked around the table at the other Draigon. "Melbis?" She glanced at Gahree where she stood by the hearth. "We were there just five years ago. What's happened?"

Gydron leaned forward, placed a journal in the center of the table. "Nortu Healer has passed." She ran her hands over the open pages of the book, a simple reverence in the gesture.

Kinra drew a sharp breath. "That's unwelcome news."

"It's too soon," Leiel said.

Kinra shook her head. "Losing Nortu is a solid reason to violate the agreement."

"Especially since it seems the Draighil have already done so," Gahree said, and Leiel closed her eyes in the silence that followed. The empty seat at the table, Wynt's space, was a cold, deep hole. Too soon, after Wynt's death. And too soon after the last Sacrifice in Melbis. What about the natural death of one woman in the eastern reaches could demand yet another potential loss?

"A worthy risk," Ilora said. Leiel looked at her mother. Tension pulled at the skin around her eyes, signaling a level of worry Leiel had not witnessed since she was a child. A new scent filled the air, sweet and tangy at the same time. Leiel sat up straighter.

From where she stood behind Ilora, Gahree nodded. "And far from the first such we've accepted."

"Who was Nortu?" Leiel reached out and pulled the journal toward her. She read the first few paragraphs. Could this be right? A healer of this skill? Leiel looked up, around the group. "Why did you never bring this woman here?"

Gydron smiled. "She refused. Even when she angered the Council of Melbis so greatly we thought they would kill her outright. But she wanted to stay and protect her granddaughter, and teach her. Nortu faced the Council and pointed out, quite rightly, that she was too skilled a healer for them to murder her without risking a city-wide outcry."

"She was a woman we would have brought among us, with joy. But her pride was great. And she did not need us to find her way in the world," Gahree said.

"Can her granddaughter do this, too?" Leiel put her hand on the journal. "Use Gweld to enhance healing?"

Gahree nodded. "Not just enhance—expand, empower. We seek talent. We mark potential. Some, like you, wild daughter, learn to enter Gweld easily. A few, the rarest, match the rhythm of Gweld without even knowing what they seek. Perhaps once, before the Farlan came, such people were more common in the world. But most people never hear a song before they are taught to sing it. Nortu was born hearing it. As was her grandchild, Teska."

Ilora sighed. "There isn't much room for those who can see great things in the every day."

"This skill is that special?" Leiel asked. Healers in Cyunant used Gweld every day. "More special than anyone here?"

"In a thousand years, we've never seen one who could do what Nortu could—what her granddaughter can do," Gahree said. "Teska Healer has her mentor's knowledge. She dances with Gweld as though it is music in her blood. Her skills, enhanced by the Great Shape, could lead to the physical healing of entire regions—plague, blight. Teska holds possibility to heal such things on a scale Arnan has never known."

Leiel considered. The potential of the idea... The thudding of her heart filled her awareness. The ability to stop plagues, or cleanse crops...if the Draigon became known for those things as they were known for destruction and drought—such a thing could lead to peace, free the Draigon to move through the world again—the Draigon and all their knowledge. Leiel met Gahree's gaze in sudden understanding, and Gahree smiled, nodded once.

Kinra pushed back her chair, rose, and paced the room. "Teska is without Nortu's protection now. Does she know about us?"

Gahree shifted her attention to the fight trainer and smiled. "It was her Grandmother's way, to share all vital knowledge."

"The Draighil won't be pleased. They will send their best." Ilora shook her head. "Maybe more than *just* their best."

"If their frustration has, as we fear, led them to seek a more certain outcome, then we should match that intent." Gahree looked to Leiel. "We will need an envoy, to carry our expectations to the council ahead of my arrival."

Leiel straightened her shoulders. Not so long ago, she would have questioned why she was being chosen when there were so many more experienced Draigon to chose from. But that was, she had come to understand, the very thing that made her valuable in these situations; she remembered most clearly what it was like to face a cadre of fanatical men, and how to triumph in the face of their self-assured power. She simply nodded.

Gahree smiled. "This time will be a bit different, wild daughter. This time you will have to claim your full power. And this time you will be staying for the battle."

Leiel caught her breath, glanced at her mother. Ilora pressed her lips together hard, her desire to protest written in the sudden paleness of her face and the way her jaw muscles tightened. Ilora breathed in hard through her nose, blew it out. "So soon," she said quietly.

"Past time," Gahree said. "She has the spirit for it, Ilora. And I may have need of her flexible mind."

Leiel's belly rippled with unease. Flexible mind. Flexible. That meant Gahree assumed anything might happen. And *anything* left open entirely too many unpleasant options. Over the last few years, Leiel had traveled much of Arnan, sought out women and girls, taught them as Gahree had once taught her. But never had she been the one to accept the Sacrifice face-to-face with a Draighil, and make decisions that meant life or death for all. But that possibility now opened before her. Memory beckoned. The uncanny speed of Cleod's actions that long ago day on the mountain. The terrible beauty of his skill and determination.

The day might come when she would face a battle like that.

Leiel let her chest expand with a slow breath, nodded. "So soon," she agreed. Though, had a hundred years passed, she doubted she would feel any more ready than she did in this moment.

CHAPTER 24

Leiel

Leiel's hair brushed strange over her bare arms as she lifted it off her neck, twisted and wrapped it around a silver hairstick, and pinned it atop her head. Her nerves tingled, still filtering energy from the Great Shape out of her human form. An extra heat accompanied the settling, residual intensity pulling through her being. Holding Draigon Weather in balance was the most trying thing she had ever managed.

Gahree handed her a loose-fitting linen shirt and pants, dyed in earth tones to match the prairie surroundings. Leiel pulled them on, letting the touch of the cloth resettle her mind into her human form. The burn of her nerves eased. She relaxed, took in where she stood.

Below her, slivers of silver water formed bright paths along the wide riverbed, and Leiel shook her head at the sight. Slivers only, not the powerful rush of water that usually formed the Seebo. She straightened, swallowed. "I didn't think there could be so much damage this soon." The withered brush on the bank and the thin trees behind her were all dry, stressed.

"You're powerful, Leiel, but this is more than Draigon influence." Gahree shook her head. "The farms west of here have drawn too much water from the Seebo for years now. Draigon Weather has emphasized the problem. Unfortunately, Teska's need has drawn us back to this region too soon."

"So, people will die?"

"I sent word to Gydron. The villages will send aid as needed. We'll make sure the suffering is minimized."

Leiel glanced at the sky. Light was fading, and the last of the dust kicked up by her landing in the Great Shape had settled. "Then we should get to Melbis quickly." She bent to pull on her socks and boots.

Gahree did not reply, and her silence drew Leiel's attention. Gahree was stripping off her clothing, folding it neatly and tucking it into her pack. Leiel glanced around. Gahree had not set a camp.

Leiel straightened. "You're taking the Great Shape?"

"More rumors have come from the Oryok. Such stories as have reached me these weeks, about Wynt's death, have raised new concerns. Before we call for a Sacrifice in Melbis, I must be sure what we are facing." She tucked her shoes into her pack, turned down the top flap and fastened the straps. A quick reach into a side pocket brought out small bundle of cotton fabric. She handed it to Leiel.

With a smile, Leiel accepted the twist of cloth and unwrapped it to reveal her ring. She slipped it on, but unease muddled the comfort it usually brought. If Gahree took the Great Shape now, burned energy to fly south to gather information, it would mean that by the time she transformed to claim Sacrifice, she would have made three changes in only a few weeks. "Let me go instead," Leiel said.

Gahree unwound her braid, freeing her hair over her bare, brown shoulders. "The Weather is your responsibility. You are needed here."

"But so many transitions—"

"Are necessary in the coming weeks. Make your way to Melbis, wild daughter. I will meet you there with what news I may find."

"Gahree—"

"A hug, daughter of wings, then I must go. Rest well, and I will see you in a few days."

Frowning, Leiel stepped up and returned Garee's embrace. Heat flowed through the touch, amplified by Leiel's recent work, and Gahree laughed in her arms.

"Oh, you've learned so much, so well." Gahree pulled back, hands on Leiel's shoulders, and grinned. "I will meet you in Melbis."

Leiel nodded, smiled in return. Be careful. An unspoken thought. But Gahree winked, as though she heard it, then turned and made her way down the embankment into the riverbed. Her bare feet left deep prints in the mud as she walked to the center of the river, her form a slender shadow in the fading light.

Gahree stopped near the fullest of the remaining channels of water. She lifted her chin, and stood quiet, motionless, for several heartbeats. Soft at first, crimson light bloomed around her head, draped over her shoulders, and flowed down her back. Even without reaching into Gweld, Leiel watched the color glow vivid, reflected off the narrow trails of flowing water. Then with a burst like a rising aurora, change erupted in an explosion of light and wind, and Gahree's Great Shape unfurled. Fast and elegant, Gahree's transformation claimed the twilight. Shaa, her form impossibly large, expanded and filled the riverbed, born of darkness and fire, knowledge and heat. Black-leather wings arched shadow against the sky. Green-gold eyes blinked, glittering.

Tears burned Leiel's vision, as they did every time she watched Gahree claim her role as Shaa. The control, the grace of the shift, the power unveiled, each time raised a shaking tension in Leiel's chest. This creature, this being, so powerful, was the same who laughed by the fire, blended teas that smelled of place, and worked in the greenhouse for endless hours, sharing stories and knowledge that spanned centuries. The humble and the mighty, alive in one creature Leiel knew as mentor and friend.

Leiel lifted a hand in farewell as Shaa raised her head, gathered herself, and launched into the night. Wing wind flattened grasses and shrubs, rippled water and sent it streaming, whipping Leiel's clothing and tugging tendrils loose from the twist atop her head. Fanning streaks, like the feather prints of a grouse left in the snow, imprinted on the river bottom, and the water splashed back to fill into giant clawed tracks. Overhead, the Draigon swept away, a living stamp moving south against the darkening sky.

Leiel stared across the remains of the Seebo as long moments passed before the sound of Gahree's flight faded into the distance. The marks in the riverbed became invisible as the sky darkened and the moonless night took hold. She blinked, shifted her awareness a half-degree into Gweld, and watched the shimmering red and green-golds that lingered along the edges of the wing prints flicker and dance. She never witnessed Gahree's transformation without a thrill pulling through her gut.

As the light faded, she closed her eyes. The earthy scent of rot mingled with the starkness of dust, opposing and uneven in the enveloping night. No breeze moved to ease the hot weight of the air, the density of odor crowding her senses.

She reached out with Gweld, following Gahree's flight...and something rippled, a tremor on the edge of her senses. Her eyes snapped open, and she stared west through the last glimmer of dying light, as though she could will the distant presence into visible range. Somehow, impossibly, she had missed it while crossing the land. Missed *him*. How? The answer came, a whisper in her mind. Because your connection to him is human, not Draigon.

Now in her born form, his presence burned a pinprick light, far off. A day's ride a least. But moving steadily toward her. She whispered his name, unable to hold it inside. "Cleod?"

Chapter 25

Leiel

Leiel sheltered in the minimal shade of the dead shrub and watched the slow progress of the caravan. Her throat, drier than even the parched air of the plains could account for, ached, and she raised her canteen for a sip of tepid water, even being Draigon did not lessen the comfort of such human action.

It was needed. Since the Seebo, a steady buzzing lodged in back of her skull. Gahree's transformation at the river had branded the land with her presence. And Cleod's reaction to the tracks and patterns left behind—the violence of his collapse, the shaking that overcame him—had cut her to watch. The steady rise of unease in Leiel's mind had, ever since, kept her close to the caravan.

Watching Kilras's response to Cleod's near-breakdown at the river had left a lump of emotion lodged like a rock between her throat and her heart. She had not bothered to decipher the details of what she was feeling. Her body's too-raw reaction, yet to dissipate, told her enough. Sleep was restless and fleeting, and she was unable to turn her full focus to the tasks ahead of her.

Why this caravan, on this route? The thought refused dismissal. Yes, it was the most direct way from Sibora to Melbis, but it was known for bandits, and it missed the smaller trading posts that dotted the south-central grasslands, and that meant lost opportunities to add clients to the group.

Memory rose on the tide of her thoughts—a warm summer day tucked into her favorite shady copse of wind-bent trees, with the birds singing above her and a hand-stitched book in her lap—Kilras's story of finding Cleod in a dank tavern, of the years of patient friendship on the trail, that led first to trust, and then sobriety, for her old friend.

And other stories, of Kilras's competence, the steadfast fierceness with which he backed his people, and the sharp- minded decisions bolstered by his veiled adeptness with Gweld. What must it have been like for him, all these years, to travel the length and breadth of Arnan, never able to acknowledge the truth of his past? What it must have taken to have spent the past thirteen years in Cleod's company, and never once have suffered a revealing slip? Such isolation was daunting. And yet, by the truth of his actions, and the straightforward clarity of the words she had read in the safety of Cyunant, he accepted the self-imposed limitations of his life with a grace she could never have managed.

Was it luckless coincidence that had brought them this way, or something more? Would that Gahree were near enough to ask an opinion, but she was by now in Oryok, in search of a truth Leiel feared even more than the answer to the question she had just posed.

She sighed. The train of wagons rolled closer, rolled past, distant through the dust—dust that hung thick in the air, and settled only slowly as the train passed. No wind moved, and so it clung to the swaying wagons, coating hardware, people, and stock in a silt that blended all colors into one. Amorphous shapes wavered within the distant cloud, but Leiel's glittering eyes picked out Cleod's form. Still graceful. Still proud, if less imperious in his mannerisms.

"You've ever been one to command respect," she said. "Old friend—I did not expect to see you here." Damn that he had ended up on this road. Stories had come to Cyunant through the years, and through them she had observed the friendship build between Cleod and Kilras. She had come to appreciate the older man's impulsive efficiency. He was never careless and rarely acted without reason, but the choices he made were not predictable, and his reasoning, as often as not, was based on instinct as much as fact. She was grateful for his willingness to take risks—that part of his nature, and his understanding of who the Draigon really were, had led him to Cleod, and to gamble on the former Draighil's value. But if simple instinct had led the caravan this way, she could find reason to wish he was less ready to trust it.

Cleod. The one regret that she had in all the years that had passed. She had bargained for his life, and the fact that he had retained it had somewhat tempered her guilt at the lies that she had told him, and the harm done to him. Cleod, who she had watched draw his sword night after night by firelight, as though compelled. Cleod, the memory of whose laughter still sometimes woke her in the night. Cleod, who possessed the skill to back a desire for vengeance that, she could see now, had never quite died.

She raised a hand and ran a finger through the air, tracing it down the tiny shape of Cleod's outline. A frown twitched down her lips as he halted the horse he rode and swung the mount around to face her.

Connection. A blessing. A hindrance. Had he sensed her so easily, even after all this time. Was he fully aware of what he noticed? Did he suspect? No. He could not know. If he did, he would be riding toward her at full speed, all caution and control thrown to the wind.

As she watched, he turned the gelding and spurred away through the yellow dust. She adjusted the dull scarf that covered her hair. Questions lingered, like the dust, and she could only hope watching would reveal answers to ease the disquiet in her gut. Melbis was still a week away, and the work she had to do there could not be put off, even for the risk of Cleod's proximity.

CHAPTER 26

Leiel

She stopped in the street with a curse poised on her lips as Cleod crossed in front of her on the way into The Nest. Old Gods and damnation! How had she missed that he had come into the town? You're distracted, Leiel. Breath held, she waited as he walked up the steps of the inn and the door shut behind him, then she turned quickly to cross the street. Better to take the long way, than risk him spotting her. The dust hung like haze, pale and sour in the too- bright air. Behind her, The Nest loomed, but the sun was high, and the building cast only scant shade, leaving the heat unrelieved.

A wagon rattled toward her, and she stopped to let it pass, tension slanting down her back at the delay. She should have just backtracked.

She felt him see her—a shock between her shoulder blades. A half turn of her head brought the front windows of The Nest into her peripheral vision, but light bouncing off the glass kept her from seeing through them. She had only seconds. Turning back to the street, she shifted her pack on her shoulder and stepped to the far side of a crossing wagon. It rattled behind her, kicking dust high. She lengthened her stride, reached up and pulled her scarf over her hair and turned over her left shoulder to go back the way she had come. She moved around the back of the wagon, where the dust was thickest and walked up the wide alley along the side of The Nest.

The front door of the inn banged open just as she stepped out of sight and stopped in the shade of the building. She leaned against the stone wall and watched Cleod step out into the street, his head turning slowly as he searched for her in the passing crowd.

Three steps and she could be beside him. She had forgotten how tall he was, forgotten the lean strength and purpose with which he moved. When had she last been this close to him? That terrible day on the mountain more than fifteen years ago...

He stood between her and the Draigon, straight-backed, chin down, strength in the tense lines of his legs. She called his name, but he did not turn, made no sign that he had heard her as he stepped forward.

No years could change what had shaped him, created the crispness of his actions and the sharpness of his gaze. Another moment and the old training that underpinned his awareness would notice her.

Turning in the scarce cover of The Nest's shadow, she moved down the alley, pressed close to the building.

I am not here for you, Cleod. She told herself that—and it was true. Her trip here had been planned for weeks. But not this. Not Kilras's choice of route, or Cleod's response to what he had seen at the Seebo. And certainly not her own reaction. *He turned the sword in the firelight, and the reflected gleam of the flames seemed to arrow along the steel.* What was this tightness in her belly at the thought of how near she was to him?

Her one regret.

She shook her head. She had a task to complete, one that could not wait. Lives depended on her actions, as they so often had in the last few years. No time now for distraction, even one she herself had created.

The Council's meeting place was not in a tower, but in a sturdy, wooden building beside the Trademaster's station. Always, she made this comparison when she met with a new group of city leaders. Her time in the Council chamber in Adfen had forever set her expectations of what she would encounter. Only in Sibora had the grandeur of the space and the callousness of the men in the room come close to what she had met that day in Adfen Tower.

She knew more now, about the history of that building. The thought of the desecration it underwent daily as the home of such a group as the Council brought a tightness to her chest every time she considered it. But time would rectify that. And time was something she now had.

She stepped into the room, took off her pack and leaned it against the wall, then turned and closed the door behind her. Only then did she give her attention to the men standing in nervous clusters on the far side of the room. Copper and vinegar, the scent of their unease filled her nose.

Sunlight graced the space through broad windows, and the air was hot. There were no shadows in which anyone could skulk in hope that she might not take note of them. Not that it would matter. Even had the room been black- dark, she would know each of them forever by the taste of their breath on the air and the unique rhythms of their hearts. But she had insisted, as she always did for these meetings, on a brightly lit space. What had they thought when they had received her message—a directive that a messenger of the Draigon would be coming to meet with them—and the conditions of that meeting?

"It is well that light fills this space in this moment. It touches so few of your decisions." She pushed back her dusty scarf and stepped into the center of the room. "I have come to tell you what your decision will be."

"You come to *tell us?*" The words came from an old man standing as far as possible from the windows.

She flicked her gaze at him and let the *otherness* that she had once wondered at in Gahree's eyes burn in her own. She did not even pretend that his flinch was not satisfying. "I come to give you an *order*," she said, and scanned the entire assemblage, noting which men tensed their shoulders and which dropped their gazes. One even found the ferocity to outright glare at her. She smiled. "But you will not begrudge it when you hear it."

She turned and walked to the windows, looked out onto the dusty street. Melbis was a good size town, its buildings weathered with age, but still solid. And somewhere in those buildings, or traveling those streets, were women and girls who these men feared so much that they wanted to see them dead. Leiel faced the Council again. "I've come to save you days of squabbling. You have spent too much time undecided, so the Draigon have decided for you. The name you will call is Teska Healer."

They erupted in protest, as they always did, speaking ill of her looks, and heritage, and the imagined manner of her birth. How many such meetings had she endured in the last decade? Nearly a dozen. Always the same. The men who formed the Councils did not appreciate having even the smallest decision stripped from them. Much less a large decision such as this one. Much less by a woman. Most especially by a woman who spoke for the Draigon. Had they ever guessed who the women were, who acted as occasional messengers between the towns and the creatures they most despised? Perhaps a few had. They could not all be completely without imagination.

She folded her arms and waited. The shouts calmed at last. Finally, the old man spoke again, loud enough to silence the others. "Ours is the decision of who will make the Sacrifice to protect our people from the beasts you have chosen to serve. You will give us no orders, witch."

Leiel scoffed. "If protection for your people was what you actually sought, you would choose from among *yourselves* who would be staked out to greet the Draigon."

The old man went white.

She smiled at him. "You cannot pretend with me," she said. "I am a witch, remember? The bargain made long ago to stop the Great War could be altered for the benefit of all, if you were ever to become willing to do so."

"Altered?"

She looked at the man who spoke. He was young, clearly a newer member. This was likely his first time participating in a negotiation for Sacrifice. "It never occurred to you that the way things are, is not they way they have always been? Or they way they must always be?"

The young man's brows scrunched together and he frowned.

Leiel swung her gaze the rest of the council. "You would all do well to consider such things."

"This woman you name—we may decide on another instead."

Gahree's words flashed through Leiel's mind. *Teska is a mind and spirit that can under no circumstances be abandoned.*

Leiel sought the gaze of the speaker in the back of the room. He was short, with the pale hair and skin of a true Farlan. "You may decide on another," she said. "In which event you will find yourselves explaining that decision to the people of Melbis as the drought deepens. I am certain that you can do so, but perhaps you will not wish to have to make that effort. Because the Draigon *will have* Teska. That much of any decision is no longer yours. Resign yourselves."

The pale man stared at her, his eyes wide. She did not have to look at anyone else to know they all wore similar expressions. It never failed to amuse her, how shocked they were that she would dare speak to them so.

She remembered the moment before the Council of Adfen, after her selection, when she had realized how little power those men actually had over her. And how much they truly feared what she stood for. That lightness of spirit came back to her at times like this. It was all she could do not to let loose the laugh that bubbled up in her chest. The unease of the men before her was a subtle perfume in the air, their frustration a bitter whiff mingled beneath it.

Leiel stood a moment longer, then turned and retrieved her pack, swung it onto her back.

"You have not been given leave to go." The old man had found his voice again.

She shook her head. "I have not," she agreed, pulled open the door and left it standing wide behind her as she exited the Council chamber. Behind her, the silence crackled with rage, like static before a building thunderstorm. If such anger were combustible, all Melbis might go up in flames.

CHAPTER 27

Leiel

Leiel stood with her back to the town as the sky shifted toward twilight. The brittle-dry plains stretched before her, and the air smelled of dust and sweat. Behind her, Melbis was settling for the evening. Fewer wagons rattled the streets, and the voices carried on the air were not those of bartering merchants, but rather of tavern patrons, looser and more inclined to laughter. Human sounds, full of human emotions and desires, and the need for human camaraderie. There were similar sounds to be found in her life, but they were more shared and less self-conscious—the mixed blessing of a life among those who were unable to keep secrets from one another.

The wilderness beckoned as the sun slid toward the horizon. Leiel adjusted the pack over her shoulders, and turned back toward Melbis. She stepped close to the buildings and made her way toward the tavern district, keeping to side streets and the narrow alleys between buildings. Cleod's presence pushed through the city, a pulse like the blood in her veins, a hot scent on the air, and *something* turned within her sense of him, the same *something* that had drawn her to keep watch on him since the crossing at the Seebo. *The flash of firelight over steel as he drew the*

Draighil sword. The focus in his expression as he raised his arm to cant the blade in the flickering light.

She spotted him outside Masharuh Tavern, standing nose to nose with a flamboyantly dressed man his own height. She drew back into the shadows and climbed the steps that ran up the outside of the hotel across from the tavern. A smile flickered over her lips. The better to stumble up while drunk. Thanks to Kilras, it was unlikely she would ever again have to worry about that with Cleod. What she had learned of the years he spent trying to drink himself to death still lurked as a deep ache in the pit of her stomach and churned through her entire awareness.

She paused just at the top of the stairs and took a seat with her back against the wall of the hotel. The growing shadows of twilight enveloped her, and she willed herself to be unnoticeable. Cleod, despite the passing of the years and all his struggles, was still a trained master of the sensory planes. Damnable Enclave teachings.

Leiel looked down at him through the slats of the balcony railing and listened. He was relaxed, poised, the lines of his body revealing no tension as he spoke to the other man—but she knew him even after all these years. His energy shifted between annoyance and amusement, marked by the small muscles along his jaw tightening and releasing as he fought first a scowl, then a smile.

"You would be wise, to remember where you *aren't*, Glassman," Cleod said. He shook his head. "Kittown's weeks behind you. Melbis has its own laws. Some aren't even written. But *don't insult the locals* would be at the top."

"Pffha!" The other man scoffed. "When the locals need lessons in proper deportment of business, I'll insult them as needed. If you will, Ruhlern, I must see to this matter. I will do them the honor of letting them correct their errors."

Leiel put a hand over her mouth to stifle a laugh.

Cleod stepped aside and the man strode past him. Cleod shook his head, then looked over his shoulder as another man addressed him from the Masharuh's doorway. Leiel recognized him as one of the older members of the caravan team; Nae was his name. Kilras's stories of the older man skipped through her mind, and she smiled a little more.

"Wasn't lurking," the old man said. He yawned and came to join Cleod on the boardwalk. "Was taking care to not be found by that one."

"Nae, you have moments of wisdom." Cleod shook his head. "I'd rather face another Draigon than work with that man after this trip." He paused, and in the heartbeat of silence that followed, his words rippled over Leiel's skin. There it was. The thing she had been feeling for weeks, the thing deep inside that whispered its way out of the silence of his mind. He was actually considering it—considering taking up his sword again—against the Draigon! She held her breath. Was it her? Her presence? Would such a thought have occurred to him if she had not been near? Or had the sight of Shaa's marks at the Seebo—so huge and distinctive—been enough to awaken the idea? No way to know, or change either thing now. Ancient wisdom! She could not let him take such a course.

"If this weather holds, you'll get your chance," the old man said.

"I might at that," Cleod gathered himself, shifting his shoulders and facing old Nae. "Where's Jordin?" he asked.

Nae shrugged. "Dorein's place. Found him a runaway Farlan girl. Seems she thinks she's having an adventure working that place. Pasty thing. But Jordin's not picky."

"Go back," Cleod said. "I'll bring him."

Nae sighed. "Draigon-damned guard duty." He walked away.

Cleod stood still—she had never seen another human who could be as still—and watched Nae go. After a moment, Cleod gave a shake of his head, then a low laugh. Had she imagined what she had felt in him, the dangerous determination? The poise was back, the ease.

He stepped down into the street, moving with purpose. But after only a few steps, she saw tension rise along his spine and into his shoulders, a ripple—red-gold—shearing the air. The scent of him grew smoky rich. His steps did not slow, but something *skipped* in her sense of him—a hint of awareness rising out of his controlled consciousness, reaching, searching before it was yanked back.

Leiel held herself quiet, in action and spirit and form, as she heard him curse. He looked over his shoulder, eyes bright, seeking—her.

Holding, blending, she thought of air and darkness and casual patterns of light and shadow. Willed herself among such things. To be such things. His gaze swept the place she sat, moved on without pause.

As she watched, his shoulders relaxed, but he spoke, his tone hard in the dry air and fading light. "Stay gone," he said. "I have neither the patience nor the desire to play your games." He stood a moment longer, listening, then turned and continued away.

Rising gods, the *will* in him! The strength of his perception even after all these years! If he set his mind to take on a Draigon again...she couldn't let that happen.

When he was out of sight, she rose to her feet, gaze still fixed in the direction he had gone. The bent of his thoughts had been growing clear for weeks. He would choose to fight, to face old demons, rather than let his failure stand. Winged lady, she had to stop him. But how?

She shook her head. How had she influenced anything these last years? Face to face, speaking truth. The air around her hung heavy with woodsmoke and liquor and unwashed bodies, but for a moment she could smell again the clean-stone air of the Tower room. Her skin quivered with the remembered tension of that conversation with Cleod. She had failed then, with words and pleas. Could she make any difference now? Fifteen years...so much had changed for both of them. Enough? No way to know until she tried.

"Oh, Mother—Oh, Gahree—should I even give attention to this idea?" She let her words ride the air as though either could hear her and offer wisdom. Whatever they would do, or say, this choice was hers. And so too, the consequences of making it.

CHAPTER 28

Leiel

At a distance, she kept pace with Cleod, paralleling his trip back to the caravan camp. Watching, she pulled her heightened senses close, containing the expansion of her presence with the same care she maintained when she confronted Councils. The trail to Melbis and the recent near-encounter in town had shown her how bright her connection with Cleod remained.

His ride back to the caravan was slowed by the horse he led. The air hung flat and unmoving, even the dust kicked up by the mounts fell straight back to the ground. A still night, moonlit, dry and heavy. She was too far away to hear the complaints lofted by the young scout, now slung belly-down across the second horse's saddle, whom Cleod had retrieved from Dorein's brothel. Periodically, Cleod turned in his saddle to speak to the other man.

What was she doing? What good could rise from placing herself this close to the caravan, to Cleod? His presence beat, moth wings against lamp glass, at the surface of her awareness. The churning disquiet within him was a beacon to the too-sure worry in her heart. Each passing hour intensified her certainty—Shaa's presence had pierced the time-forged barrier inside him. Old anger, old promises called. Shaa. Leiel herself. He would step back into a fight he could never win.

Unless she stopped him.

Old gods, was it arrogance to think she could? She shook her head.

When he rode into the camp, she slipped south into the forest bordering the small, vital springs that had likely drawn Kilras to this location. Moonlight cast cold shadows through the trees, the chill tone of the light a stark contrast to the dry burn of the air.

The undergrowth waved and cracked, brittle around her as she moved among the trees. At the edge of the woods, she stopped, her gaze on the far circle of wagons, and waited. Each of her heartbeats was a drum in her chest, calling forth, marking time. How many times through the years had she considered what it would be like to meet him again? How many times had she rolled in her head the words that she would speak—explanations to draw forth understanding and reconciliation? But such fancies had always been just and only that. This moment before her was real.

What could she gain by speaking to him? Was trust even possible after what had happened on the Spur, after the loss and pain she had wrought in his life? Knowledge, not pride, drove that last thought. She had mattered to Cleod, and she mattered still. She had Kilras's written words through the years to assure her of that. And she had Cleod's response to her presence on the trail, and just this day in the city. The caring that had been born between them so many years ago in a sunlit schoolyard lingered. What possibility lived in that connection? The idea that he would again take up his sword against a Draigon stopped her cold.

She shivered as though she stood in savage wind atop Cyunant's mountain. Cleod would face Shaa. That truth, so beyond doubt that she had followed him without hesitation, tore through her. She could leave this place now and let him do as he would—or she could step forward and offer him knowledge—and with it a different choice.

Too soon for the decision that needed making, three men on horseback left the camp to ride sentry. Their circuit brought them close to where she waited, a still-carved shadow under the spreading boughs of an oak.

The half-drunk young scout passed, and even the awkward shying of his horse did not alert him to her presence. Kilras must not be expecting any trouble. Such slack attention was not something she expected he usually allowed. Or else he counted overly on Cleod's presence in the trio.

She assessed her old friend as he rode slowly toward the treeline and nodded to herself. In that reliance on Cleod, Kilras's judgement was clearly sound—except perhaps this night. This night, *her* choice—long since made if she were honest—tested all certainties.

The grey gelding carried Cleod close, then tensed and took a shortened pace, bringing his rider to alertness. Options remained for a moment more: to stay and follow through, try to reach him—or to walk away and let *his* choices unfold, unconfronted.

The look on his face at the Seebo. His cries as the memory of his battle with Shaa pulled him under. The scars buried beneath his clothing that stiffened both his movements and his will. The hollow sense of him as he turned his sword in the firelight. Yes, she had a choice. And it was made, this night, *to try.* Despite the odds, and the turmoil in her belly, she must.

He halted the big grey horse and scanned the woods. Like a blow, his gaze landed on her shape in the low light. He drew a breath and swung his leg over the saddle horn and dropped to the ground, sliding his sword from its scabbard as his feet touched the earth.

Color rippled at the edges of her senses as Gweld flickered at the edge of *his* mind, demanding he call it into action. Gweld and the unnecessary pain it brought him. Anger rippled across her belly at the thought of what had been done to him by the Enclaves—and what that might mean this night.

He stepped forward again, then stopped and spoke into the night. "Let yourself be seen."

A heartbeat more, indecision lingered, then she braced her mind and stepped into the silver moonlight.

The struggle that erupted through every part of him flared across her senses. Her stomach roiled to see the wild flurry of emotions that crossed his face and blazed into her Gweld-tinted vision.

"No," he said, his voice hoarse and thick in her ears. "She's dead."

The pain of his tone seared her mind, and she surrendered to a yearning that she had not admitted, until this moment, gnawed at her heart—to touch, to reassure. She reached forward the hand that bore her ring and placed a finger upon his lips.

His skin was cool under her touch. How was that possible in all this heat? Or was it her, the Draigon heat so much a part of her now that every human contact seemed chill by comparison?

Wide-eyed, he stared at her, every line of his body alive with the tension of disbelief. A dozen explanations might be offered, a hundred words be spoken. She chose the simplest. "Hello, Cleod."

"*Leiel?*" A tremor ran through his body, then another, so violent the force of it shimmered pale light into her awareness. His voice broke. "You...you can't be here."

She wanted to pull him into her arms and prove to him that she was real, breathing, alive before him. But the stiffness of his jaw spoke of more than shock. It marked a level of rage she had no way to measure—had never dreamed to encounter in him.

"How could you do this?" he demanded. "How—you died on that mountain. I nearly died on that mountain. Part of me—old gods defend—*most of me did.*"

What could she say to that? "Old gods, in truth." She tried a smile, saw the familiarity of the expression awaken something in him that she recognized from their youth. Humor, kindness—then a shudder racked him and washed any trace of comfort under, drowned in a rising column of anger.

She started to speak, but he cut her off. "Why aren't you a ghost?"

Despite the ache burning through her, his question tugged amusement into her heart. She pressed a smile into her voice. "I am a ghost, Cleod." The flatness of his expression announced that the tactic failed utterly. A chill slipped up her spine. Was she so wrong about him?

He took a step back, shaking his head, and stared at her. "Riddles? You offer me riddles? After all these years—"

His face twisted, dark and menacing in a way she had never seen. Wind on high, how could she reach him? "There is so much you don't know." The words seemed frail, useless as soon as they left her lips.

"You survived?" His face shifted again, a tangle of emotions rolling across it as he struggled to make sense of her presence. Her chest ached at the confusion, the pain.

"Was it Tray?" he demanded. "Did he save you?"

That caught her aback. Tray? The other Draighil? Cleod feared she had been saved—but by another—and that Trayor had never told the truth? Her heart jerked in her chest as he demanded, "*Where have you been*?"

She shook her head, tears gathering in her eyes. Because the reality... What had she done this night by stepping out of the shadows? "No," she said, and raised a hand to touch him again, but stopped short of contact. "No, Cleod, no one saved me. I told you then—that was not what I was in need of." Tears gathered in her throat. She swallowed them. "Old gods—I am so sorry."

"*Where have you been?*"

She met his gaze, spoke truth she knew would shatter. "With the Draigon."

He caught her shoulder, shaking his head, words of denial and fury spilling forth as though with them he could hold back the fact of her survival and all that it meant. As though through will alone he could force a new truth into being, something wrong and dire, but not so vile it would further feed the rage building within him.

She spoke softly, touched him, half in attempt to comfort and half in pleading.

But he recoiled, this time, from contact, as though all she now was transferred through her hand and into a hard reality he would do anything to deny. "What are you?"

How she answered that, how she tried to explain would be everything, shape all. "I'm a myth" she said, and more words came, hot and pitched for comfort. She reached—spoke to all of him—the boy she had known, the Draighil she had watched him become, the man in Kilras's many stories who healed and grew and cared again. But each phrase she uttered struck hollow, found no hold within him. The shock of her standing still before him rocked loose too many moorings, battered at a foundation of self so fractured by pain and loss that determination alone held it together.

And he was Draighil. Draighil still, despite time and friendship and new vocation. As some part of her had become Draigon the moment she met Gahree at the old mill, he had encompassed the soul of a Draigon slayer the day he joined the Ehlewer Enclave. She smelled it, like heady wine, the blooded determination within him. The soul-forged focus and hate. And the skill to back all the violence that such indoctrination called forth. Draighil to the bone. Memory seared through her, of the idea that came to her that long-ago day at the pond when he told her of his plans for his life: *Being a Draighil was being something different for always.*

She had known it then. But she had grown up, gained knowledge, sought to become wise. And in doing so, unlearned the thing the child she had been had understood completely. Had she held to that youthful awareness of truth, would she have assessed him differently this night?

"What are *you,* Leiel?" he demanded, the battle within him etched in the stiffness of his stance. "What did you choose all those years ago that you can stand here now as the girl I knew?"

"Not that girl," she said. "It has been so long since I was the girl you knew. And that day on the mountain—you never knew the person I was in that moment. No one did. You could never have imagined it. If you had, you would have cut me down as you intended to cut down the one you named enemy for my sake."

"*What are you?*" he shouted.

She took in the reflexive tightening of his fingers on the hilt of his sword. "What I chose to be," she replied, looking up at him. "Draigfen, Cleod. I am Draigfen." And watched as Gweld erupted and claimed him.

No thought drove the action that flooded him. Violence bloomed beyond control, hot and vile, into the space between them. She snapped into Gweld and moved the way only Draigfen moved, with scorching speed that outpaced human response, left behind heat and ash and burnt air. He followed, screaming his anger, half entranced, sword in motion. Gweld spiraled around him in a riot of color, into the space her mind occupied until it threatened to merge completely with her senses. She sucked breath, retreating. Old gods, how unprepared she was for the reach and depth of his trained skill! His lack of recent practice saved her. That and her own knowledge. He advanced, seeking her death, and she cried out against the very thought of it, "*Idodben, Cleod!*"

He stumbled to a halt as the old command ripped into his mind, quenched the fury and unfurling violence, and dropped him to his knees.

Trembling, she looked down at him, her breath heaving in her chest as though she were the one who had just attacked. As though the very air were elixir enough to squelch the fire blazing through every nerve. The scent of ground charred by her motion chased each indrawn breath, and she stared down at him, horror billowing inside her like the smoke of a newly lit fire.

He raised his head and met her gaze and she saw that he *knew*. His awareness flickered, tested, then reached out and batted against hers. And he recoiled as the truth poured into him, pooling behind his eyes. She trembled to watch it take hold, crack open inside him, and sunder everything he had built of himself, everything that had come to matter.

He closed his eyes against it, against her.

What had she done? Every moment with him awakened new danger, new pain. "I must go," she said. "The truth is too dangerous—for both of us. You know it already. It's in the very air. Don't look for me, Cleod. As you loved me once, you cannot seek me out—as you cannot seek out the Draigon now marking the land. You would not survive it. Not this time. Please. I know you are Draighil still, whether you bear the title or not. No years will change that. But I have come to ask you—you abandoned that life—*don't seek it again.*"

His gaze found hers again, and he shook his head, over and over, short, quick, desperate. "No," he said.

"Please, Cleod," she said again. "You were never meant to see me again. Or ever guess I lived. But I had to come—to ask you to put away these ideas. I am so sorry. You were my friend once. Please don't go after the Draigon."

He shook his head, the battle within him rattling the barrier of his contained will until she could almost hear it. "What are you?" he whispered.

One last chance. One last moment to reach him. "Let it be, Cleod. Nothing can now change what I have become." As she spoke, something flicked the edge of her mind, too fleeting and faint for her to bring into focus. "There can be nothing between us but what there has already been."

The failure was utter. Like blood and shattered bone, the colors of battle erupted again across her vision, swirling like a cyclone around them and hurling hope into the night.

She took a step back, then another. Too late, too much, all the long-suppressed hate and self-loathing within him. Like a red sunrise signaled storms to sailors, Gweld ripped apart the air between them, reaching, demanding, snatching at her as though it held intent to snare her soul.

The struggle to even draw breath racked his body as his fingers twisted tight against the hilt of the sword and he pushed to his feet. "*Tell me.*"

Truth then. Only brutal truth. And all the raw damage it would lay at their feet. "*Draigfen,*" she said, the words soft as she could utter them. "Just *Draigon*, Cleod." The gentle tone reached nothing within him. She stared into his twisting face. Red light spilled across her senses as the force of his anger triggered a reaction so fierce that it hurled her into full Gweld vision, a firestorm of color and emotion that threatened to strip all focus from her mind. Wind and wings, what had the Ehlewer wrought across his soul to awaken such violence as this? The question flashed through her mind in the space of a heartbeat.

His gaze was fire. Torn from the depths of his rage, a single word escaped him. "*Run.*"

Fight or flee? Kill or hold to hope? She pivoted and bolted into the forest.

CHAPTER 29

Leiel

Part of her wanted to make the transition and be gone. But the time for that choice had passed. She ran, her nerves burning. But true escape was not an option.

She could not undo her decision to seek out Cleod.

At first she heard him behind her, sensed the touch of his awareness as he searched for and tracked her. She was glad for the darkness, and glad that disuse had softened his skills. Had they been fully honed and practiced, she would have been much more pressed. As it was, she needed cleverness and care in her flight. But she was more than human, even in human form, and she outpaced him. She stopped only to strip off her skirt, tuck it into her pack, and pull on loose-fitting pants.

She moved even faster then. The woods fell away behind her and she found herself back on the open plains, moving west through brittle grass. It crackled as she touched it, and she took care that she did not burn it with her passing. A trail like that, no one could miss. Luckily, she was south of the trade road, and far enough from town that only someone actually looking for her would note her passage.

How long would Cleod follow? Had he still been drinking, she could have counted on alcohol to cloud his memory, make him doubt what he had seen and heard.

"You're wishing he was still a drunk?" she said aloud to the land and sky and air. "Fool that you are these days, why not? What were you thinking, Leiel?" Had she truly believed she could reason with him? Had she herself not reacted wildly, fighting painful fact, after learning that her mother lived? And that was after Gahree prepared her, taught her, and planted the willingness to accept and understand the truth about Sacrifice and the Draigon.

Leiel shook her head. Why had she expected Cleod, so damaged by his time in the Enclaves and his encounter with Shaa, so torn over what he had supposed was her death, to simply accept her reappearance and all that it meant?

She slowed, stopped on a low rise of land, and turned her gaze back the way she had come. The forest was a low smudge on the horizon, the sky just brightening behind it. Nothing moved, not even a breeze. She stared, letting her heart slow in her chest and her breathing settle. Would he follow? How far? For how long?

He would be missed—had long since been missed. And Kilras, what would he do? Cleod was vital, a partner and a friend. The best kind of friend anyone could hope to have. She knew. Even now it was true. Kilras would follow—worried and determined. He would follow and he would help.

"It won't be enough," she said. The sun broke over the horizon and she blinked against the blaze of light. She had started something, or fed fuel to the smoldering ashes of whatever had sparked in Cleod at the Seebo. And Cleod, focused, was a force like Draigon Weather—intense, dangerous, unalterable by anything but the most dire of actions. She stared at the treeline far behind her.

The light changed yet again.

Something shifted low among the trees. She dropped her chin and gave the area her full attention. Yes. He still followed. Through the night, the maze of trees, and whatever he must be feeling, he still sought her.

No time to rest, then. She pivoted and made her way down the west side of the rise. Only when she could glance behind her and see only the slope of the hill, did she stretch her legs into a run. Whatever it took, she must break his sense of her, his ability to notice where she had been and follow at all cost. Only two things that could do that now—distance or wearing him to exhaustion. She must keep moving, until one or the other was achieved.

CHAPTER 30

Cleod

Gweld possessed him and he let it. Beyond control or caution or fear, he pursued the unpursuable through a maze of senses beyond rationalizing.

She was gone.

He ran.

Tree branches slapped against his arms. Briars slashed his legs and hands and face, and the light changed as clouds moved across the moon and the canopy thinned above him. The breeze created by the motion of his body sang in his ears. No destination lay ahead, only something that he must destroy. He slashed at the brambles, the Draighil sword cleaving like lightning through clouds.

He ran.

He fell.

And climbed back to his feet and continued.

The world echoed and warped around him, every leaf and blade of grass and flight of breeze alive in his mind and calling him forward. Thought became something that rolled like wind over the land. Shifts in the air as he passed, flickers of color, and dusty sharp scents, led him forward. Time slipped, waved, swept on.

Starlight burned between dancing leaves and pierced the night. His breath came hot as his heartbeat, and he drove forward, seeking.

He fell again. Again, got to his feet. The sword seemed a silver arrow leading him on through the trees as he raised it and chose a direction. No stopping. He had to find—catch—Leiel. What was she? No! He moved on, sweeping aside the ache that rose in his gut as Gweld stuttered and logic tried once again to take hold.

He ran. And ran, until moonlight waned, and the air around him took on a twisted silver-blue hue.

New brightness slipped between the thinning trees and added an edge to the heat. Night faded into day. Was that sweat puddling along his spine, stinging his eyes, slicking salt over his lips? Yes. And pain, cutting his side, burning his legs as misused muscles and old wounds sent their complaints screaming into his brain. Was that thirst? And in his chest, tightening, wrapping his heart and ripping deep, was that grief? Or rage? Or hatred?

His right hip locked and collapsed his forward stride into a lurch. He cursed, sought the control of the Gweld trance, but it was gone. Through the long night, he had never governed it, only ridden it, carried along by chaotic energies possessed of their own inclinations.

Strength fled, along with any semblance of control, and his knees collided with the leaf-covered ground. This time, the sword left his grasp and cartwheeled away, skittered through the underbrush. He lay still, bruised all over, the side of his face pressed into the humus and dirt.

Across his hips, spearing through his legs and spine, needles of pain traced his once-mangled nerves. Cleod closed his eyes and clamped tight his jaw. He sucked air through his nose, forcing himself to breathe through the unrelenting assault on his battered body. He shuddered, rolled onto his back. Need released his clenched teeth and he stared up through the dawn-touched leaves and screamed his fury to the sky.

Thirst woke him. Had sand been packed into his mouth, he could not have needed water more. He could not even dredge up enough moisture to groan. Canteen. Did he have his canteen? Where was he? What had he done?

He rolled onto his side, and his lips curled into a snarl as his abused hip took his full weight. His vision clouded, slipped, and he fought to stay conscious. Seconds passed, and the pain ebbed. He pushed against the earth with a trembling hand and levered upright, forcing himself to his feet through the scream of muscles and a woeful lack of balance. Gods of old! *Gods...*

It came back—the run through the forest. The creature he had chased. A creature. Leiel.

Gweld erupted, spiraling, and he choked, bent over, heaving, but nothing remained in him to disgorge. Fight the Gweld and accept the agony of Overlash, or use the state and push on? He could not avoid, only put off, the inevitable price. The trance would carry him, beyond physical need, beyond wellbeing. Either choice brought a cost.

As his body rebelled, he chose.

The uncontained trance washed him under, and his senses struggled, fought to categorize the world around him and his body. The sword. Water. Those two things were vital. The first he sought, gathered into a hand that seemed distant and strange. The latter would be found, or he would die. He bent himself to necessity and plunged forward again.

Gweld streamed his awareness forth, until, far off, a hint of something cool and liquid, trembling at the base of a cluster of boulders, drew him forward. The remaining trees fell away. He emerged from the forest onto the open roll of the prairie. Distant, toward the dim line of hills to the north was something that might be water. Beyond that, dimmer still, but in the same line, was the presence that tripped fury inside him. His lungs on fire, his heart rammed his ribs as he ignored the needs of his body and struck out through the brittle grass at a run.

CHAPTER 31

Leiel

The brightest heat of the day burned the land when Leiel stopped and looked back. Still coming. Still in motion.

Had he eaten? Had he taken water? Where could he have, once he reached the plains? No streams or springs graced the route she had chosen. And it was she who he followed, unerring.

He's dying. The thought tripped the rhythm of her heart. He was using Gweld to sustain himself past normal limits. Was that to be the price for her choice to seek him out? His death? Had she broken loose so much hatred inside him, that he would destroy himself in pursuit of it?

She stood stiller than silence, forced emotion deep, focused her senses and measured his passage. He was following her, yes, but the angle of his travel had turned slightly. Obliquely parallel to the way she had come, it veered slightly westward. Her attention shifted, seeking.

There. In a cluster of rocks. Water. So it was not purely rage that drove him now. Some part of him was aware of his danger. Some part of him was planning, seeking to survive.

Could she use that? She would have to, or simply stand her ground and force a confrontation. Nothing in that option gave her hope. Maybe, if he survived this, she could find a way to approach him again... If she could stop him now, before he did himself irreparable damage. *If.* But to halt now and wait for him, was to beg a fight she did not want.

She bent her head. There was a way. But it was dangerous. As dangerous to Cleod as his continued pursuance of her.

Destroy the spring.

Where was Kilras?

She reached out again, pushed her senses to their distant limit. Her decision depended on him, the most infamous Dorn in Arnan. Leiel had never met him, but she knew the stories. And his letters, his books, spoke his character into her heart through her years of learning among the Draigon. He would be out there. He would be following Cleod. But was he near enough? Would he reach Cleod in time if she burned away the only water source that could keep him alive?

She closed her eyes, let other livened perceptions fill the space sight had abandoned. Distant, but not so far as to make her plan unworkable, a line-straight sense of purpose, bright as Cleod's, marked the man she sought. Kilras Dorn. She bowed her head, her breath easing in her chest for the first time since she had stepped out of the trees and faced Cleod. As he had been for so many years, Kilras was the key to Cleod's safety and sanity. Someday, she would find a way to thank him. But today, she was simply grateful for the tenacity of his friendship.

She drew a breath, opened her eyes and turned southwest, sprinted into motion toward the water source. She had been reborn of heat. It was life or devastation, as need be. Today, she asked forgiveness of the water and all the creatures who depended on it for the destruction she was about to commit to save one man.

CHAPTER 32

Cleod

Cleod awoke to the sound of a crackling fire, and to an ache that pounded through him, body and mind. He had no strength to even moan, but he managed a sucking breath that expressed both pain and confusion.

"This is familiar." Kilras's voice eased Cleod's senses like the poit eased sore muscles. Every bit of him settled.

Cleod cracked eyes crusted from dust and hard sleep. He pushed air to speak, but breath caught in his throat and set him hacking. Wracked by the harsh action, his body twisted in on itself, and he rolled a little away from the fire. He was sore all over, deep into his bones, his joints loose in their sockets. His skin twitched like a cat's under a breeze. There was no spit in his mouth, but he forced his lips to move.

"Water," he managed to say.

A strong hand slid under his shoulders and lifted him a little. Cool water touched his lips, a brief offering, barely a swallow. Cleod gasped as the liquid filled his mouth, washed down into his belly. His lips parted and he nodded, accepted another few sips. At last, his mouth was washed clean enough for him to speak clearly. "How? Where are we?" He managed to get his eyes to focus and looked up into Kilras's face.

Kilras shook his head, tipped the cup to Cleod's lips again. Another few swallows of water and Kilras sat back and set the cup aside. "At what appears to be the remains of a spring. From the plant growth, I would say it has not been dry long."

Cleod lay back, closed his eyes again. Memory returned.

Fire. Heat. A pillar of steam rising into the distant air as the spring toward which he traveled burned away in a violent fountain of forced evaporation.

"It flowed until I came looking for it," he said.

A white pillar lined into the blue sky, and cut through Cleod's Gweld-turned senses. The message the steam sent was unmistakable, as the water he sought streaked skyward into oblivion.

He stumbled to a stop, staring at it. Gweld vision lineated the rising vapor with a myriad of color, turning, and refracted in sunlight. The creature had burned away the water. The beast. Leiel. *The horizon tipped, swayed. No. He was swaying.*

He took a staggering step. Leiel. Pressed to exhaustion, the trance slipped as he did, fell away. He took the impact on his shoulder as the ground rushed up to meet him. No water. No hope of catching her now. No hope at all. She would kill him here, in the brittle-dry hills, one way or another.

A shudder racked him as the pressure of Overlash began behind his eyes. Soon his body would surrender to the weight of what he had demanded of it. No chance, now, of avoiding it...

"She did it," he said. Leiel's face floated against his closed eyelids. "She burned it away. To stop me."

Silence held a moment. "Who did?"

"Leiel," Cleod said, her name bitten out with quiet tension. How impossible the words sounded.

"Leiel," Kilras repeated. Cleod could identify no emotion in Kilras's voice. The careful neutrality of the Dorn's tone was familiar from so many past, delicate moments. The pressure in Cleod's chest eased a bit. Kilras would hear him out, reserve judgment.

Cleod turned his head, opened his eyes. Firelight flickered over Kilras's features, sharpening them against the darkness. "I am not mad, Kil. Leiel. I saw her."

"You told me. In Melbis. A woman who looked like her."

"No." Cleod coughed a little as he rolled to his side and forced himself to sit up. His vision blurred, the dim light speckling before his eyes. He braced his hands against the ground, held on until the dizziness passed.

Kilras picked up the cup and offered it.

After a moment, Cleod lifted a shaking arm and took it. He sipped. Breathed, and sipped again. "No," he repeated. "Not someone who looked like Leiel. It was her." He met Kilras's gaze. "She came to me, when I was on guard. She came to me and spoke to me and—" He choked a little, on the words, on the reality they represented. "She's alive," he whispered. "Alive, and not who she was."

Brittle and uneasy, silence held in the hot air. A log popped in the fire, broke the moment like a pulled wishbone. "If I told you this wasn't the strangest thing I've heard this week, it's not likely you would believe me," Kilras said at last. "You've had Draigon on your mind since the Seebo. Whatever you sensed or saw in the forest—"

"It was Leiel," Cleod snapped. His grip on the cup tightened until water shook from it, spilled onto his lap and the thirsty ground. The cup fell from his grasp.

"Easy, my friend," Kilras said. "I never said it wasn't."

Cleod frowned, shook his head, stared down at hands clenched into fists. He breathed deep once, again, to settle his rising nerves. "Don't mock me, Kil. I know what I saw."

Kilras said nothing, and after several seconds, Cleod raised his gaze and looked at his friend. A frown creased Cleod's brow. "You weren't mocking me."

A shake of Kilras's head was his answer. "Never."

"You believe me."

"I'm afraid to, but yes."

"Afraid to?"

Kilras frowned. A few seconds passed, then he spoke softly. "If your Leiel came to you... I don't like where that leads."

Cleod sighed. "After the chase she led me out here...I don't like it either. I was out of control, Kil. I am not in control now."

"But you're too worn down for it to matter."

Cleod smiled a little. Kilras's knack for judging the danger he might be in had always served their friendship. "If I was anything but barely conscious, you wouldn't be anywhere near me after what just happened."

"True enough," Kilras said. "But you're as battered as I've seen you since we met. The question becomes, what now?"

Cleod dropped his gaze into the fire, let the dance of low flames focus his still-scattered thoughts. A fire in this heat. Trust Kilras to understand that the need to comfort the mind outweighed everything else. Cleod sighed. What now? Leiel was out there—somewhere. She had come to him...why? To warn him, she said. To warn him away from the idea that had been turning in the depths of his mind since he had looked down on the Seebo and known what the devastation meant—that only one creature could cause such destruction, one creature he hated and desired to kill. What now indeed? Did he return to Melbis, try to pick up his life and pretend he had never seen her? Impossible. As was continuing his pursuit of her. Of whatever she was now—something else, something other, something *them.*

He shuddered. No. He could no more chase her than he could abandon the knowledge that now turned in his gut— that Leiel *lived.* And that she must have some purpose in being here, in this place, now, with Draigon-sign more brutal and deadly than it had been in decades. "Melbis," he said at last. "Back to Melbis. But Kil—" Cleod again met the Dorn's gaze.

"No need to say it," Kilras sat back. "I'll get you back. You can make up your mind what to do next." He reached behind him and picked up a few sticks, added them to the fire. "Decide who you are, after all this time."

Decide who you are. Not decide what to do. But decide who he was. Cleod met Kilras's gaze. "I thought I knew."

A grunt, and Kilras's lips twitched with the hint of a smile that faded quickly. "That's easy to do. We think we know, when we get comfortable. But life doesn't like us to be comfortable. It prefers the twists time brings, and to bring time around to meet us."

Leiel's face flashed in Cleod's mind. *Time.* It seemed little had passed for her. And yet...her expression had not been young. Gweld trembled the edges of his senses, but he pushed it aside. He was too tired to sustain the trance, too weak to keep it entirely at bay. Heat flickered in his belly. Why? After all this time? Why had she come to him and smashed his hard-won security into chaos? The heat was rage, deep and pressing. His jaw clenched, exacerbating the pounding in his skull. Even his lips were tense, pulled against his teeth.

"What did they do to her?" he whispered.

"Who?"

"The Draigon. They took her. They *changed* her."

Kilras was silent a few seconds. "All these years and you're still assuming women don't know their own minds? I'll let Sehina know." He sat back. "You think she had no choice whatever she is? That doesn't sound like the woman you've told me about all these years."

Cleod choked a little at the thought. He pressed clenched fists to his eyes, trembled. Kill her. Make her pay. The eager awareness trained into his soul by the Enclaves clawed his mind. He was Draighil, blooded and bound, even after all these years. And yet...the quiet sounds of the man across from him, adding wood to the fire, stirring a pot, echoed with a promise Cleod had made himself—that nothing could be allowed to destroy the life he had built.

He was thirsty. Need ripped through him as though it were another form of Gweld. He could almost smell ercew on the air, the way he had once scented cuila burned to combat Overlash. His stomach churned and he rolled onto his hip, heaved bile into the sand behind him.

A few seconds passed, then Kilras's hand landed on Cleod's shoulder. Whatever came, the strength of the Dorn's support was constant.

"Always pull—" Cleod's voice creaked, and he licked his lips, tried again. "Always pulling me out of my own filth."

Kilras chuckled. "I thought I was past needing to."

"No," Cleod pushed himself up a little, stopped as the arm he braced himself on spasmed.

"No?" Kilras said. "Twelve years, and the best you come back with is 'no'?"

Cleod took a breath and shoved himself upright again. "A least I'm not naked this time." Needles shot through his hips and across his lower back, and he hissed out his breath. "Blinding damnation, I could—" The oath was swallowed by a groan.

"You've wracked yourself to paroxysm for three days," Kilras said. "Take it easy."

"Three days?" Cleod dropped his head into hands. Leiel's face flickered in his mind. To believe what had happened was simply a nightmare, that he had slipped and delved into ercew, would be a blessing. But the scream of abused muscles and the hollow burning in his mind marked the strain of Overlash. He ran his hands back through his hair, then examined his arms. Cut and bruised, his chest, too. It had not been nightmare. He shuddered. "And before you found me?" he asked, his voice low and hoarse and hollow.

"Almost a day."

"You came after me."

Kilras just looked at him for a long moment. "Sehina knows what to do. And we've been training Rimm to handle the unexpected. They're fine."

"But we never planned that I would be the crisis."

"My plan for crisis has always included you." Kilras laughed.

Again Cleod shook his head. A pulsing pressure began behind his eyes, one he could not blink away. "The unexpected," he said. "She's *not dead*, Kilras." Saying the words made it real, etched truth into his gut and set his head reeling. "She's alive. And she's— She's a *Draigon*." Barely a whisper.

Kilras straightened, stared back at Cleod.

"I'm not crazy, Kil."

"Not this moment," Kilras said. "But you can't tell me the trance you experience is not a kind of madness."

"I saw *Leiel*," Cleod said sharply. He sighed, pulling his frayed nerves back into control. "I talked to her. She *touched* me." His jaw clenched. His hands bunched into fists. He stared at them, forced his fingers to uncurl, though the rest of his tension refused to ease. "All the gods forgive—Kilras, she burned the *air*. Just as they do. She said it. She told me. She burned away the spring—tried to kill me. She's a *monster—one of them.*" His hands shook as the tremors crept through his body. His perception slipped. A split instant, he nearly allowed it to bleed into that place of painless focus. But he caught himself, yanked back his mind and emotions, and deposited them firmly within the boundaries of the moment.

His vision normalized, the infinite instant of transition contained by pure will as he bent his head and sucked breath through clenched teeth. He must face the truth of that encounter. No matter the desire to bury himself in anything else—ercew, Gweld, even the desperate simplicity of sleep—no space remained within him now to continue that descent; it led only to madness. He had spent enough time there, so many years ago, and in the last few days. Whatever the knowledge he now held meant, he would not allow it to mean *that*. If Kilras did not believe him? Old gods! What would he do if he could not convince Kilras of the reality of Leiel's existence—of whatever her existence was now? He focused on his friend, spoke low, forced down the tremor that wanted to shake his voice."She was real. As real as you, and this fire. *She is alive and she is something else.*"

Kilras's didn't look away. "I know," he said. "I believe you. I have reason to."

Cleod stared. "You have reason to?"

A smile creased Kilras's expression. "I know you. Your flaws have never included lying—or hallucination."

Cleod sat forward, caught his head in his hands, shook it as he ran his fingers back through his hair. "You chased me for three days and never once thought my mind had foundered?"

"That would have happened years ago if it was going to," Kilras said. "When Nae told me you'd taken off through the woods like a wild creature, I knew a Draigon was involved." He poured another cup of water, handed it across the fire to Cleod. "I didn't expect it would be your Leiel."

The grass moved around their horses's knees, brittle and brown and broken by their passage. Kicce's stride was familiar and comfortable. If not for the dense ache in Cleod's head and hips, it might have been any day on the trail—if not for those pains, and the churn of new knowledge inside him. Though he must have passed this way days ago, he remembered none of the journey.

"What did you tell the others?"

"I told them we'd be back," Kilras said.

Cleod shook his head. "You couldn't know that."

"I'm an optimist."

The start of a smile twitched Cleod's lips, but it faded quickly. The state he had been in...the rage and itching desire to drive a blade through a heart—"I could have killed you."

"We've had this conversation."

They had, a dozen times or more through the years. Cleod looked over at Kilras. The subject had been broached often in the early days of their acquaintance, when Cleod had faltered and roused to find himself wrapped around a mug of ercew, or half-frozen in a gutter. Each time, the hands that pried him back to his feet and the voice that drew him back toward life—both unwavering despite the danger—had belonged to Kilras. He had never flinched from Cleod's worst moments. "All too often."

"And probably not for the last time."

A grunt that was part laugh jolted Cleod's battered body. He sucked a breath and held still a moment. Beneath him, Kicce shifted. Cleod managed a word of ease, and the grey flicked an ear back at him, but relaxed. "You knew it was a Draigon that had drawn me."

"You weren't drunk when you came back from Melbis," Kilras said.

A faint smile touched Cleod's lips. "Simpler if I had been."

Kilras laughed a little and shook his head. "You're a bigger ass when you're drunk than when you're caught up in that Enclave trance."

"Gweld."

Kilras tipped his head, met Cleod's gaze in silence for a long moment. "They did you no favors." A hint of careful restraint in his tone drew Cleod's gaze to the Dorn.

"I'm alive because of what the Ehlewer taught me, Kil. So are many people. You among them."

"I don't argue the usefulness of what they taught. I disagree with the cost."

"Overlash is something to be endured." Cleod turned his attention back to the trail. "It won't kill me."

"I didn't say Overlash," Kilras said.

Cleod glanced at him. "You're not usually cryptic."

"You're not usually half-insane and following Draigon-sign through a forest at night."

Heat washed Cleod's face and he looked away. "No," he agreed, and swallowed down a sudden bitterness that coated the back of his throat. His stomach did an unwelcome turn and flared to heat. He had failed in the duty he owed Kilras, and those he rode with, failed to contain the heart of his old training, failed again to win a battle against the darkest thing he knew. Somewhere between shame and rage, he shook, fought rising violence.

"There's no depth of embarrassment you can drown yourself in that I haven't seen already."

Despite a strange stiffness in his lips, Cleod smiled a little. "I'm not sure," he said. "This round of half-madness is based in something I never imagined."

The Dorn shook his head. "Never?"

Cleod looked at him. "Why is that a question?"

"You've never imagined Leiel alive?"

Cleod grunted, closed his eyes. "Of course I did. I dreamed it. I wished it. But I never—"

"What? You imagined her somehow escaped, and growing fat and old in a kitchen somewhere, hidden from view? Happily cooking stew, and regretting all the things she did that got her noticed by the Adfen Council?"

Cleod winced, and he shook his head slowly. He looked out past Kicce's ears and studied the trees ahead as his mind drifted through all the possibilities he had considered through the years—all the ways he had imagined Leiel surviving, and the things he thought of her doing. He had dreamed of her hidden in a mountain cabin somewhere, raising rabbits. Or working as a Healer's helper in some warren of a coastal city. In his wildest imaginings, she rode beside him in the caravan and taught every stranger who traveled with them to read and write and sing. Nothing he had imagined Leiel doing involved a kitchen. His lips twitched. And one more thing was consistent in his dreams. "I never envisioned Leiel regretting much."

Kilras did not reply. Cleod flicked his gaze at the Dorn. Kilras stared straight ahead, a smile on his face that held at the edge of a smirk. What, in this situation, warranted that particular expression? Cleod frowned. "You think she might regret something?"

"She must. After all these years, she showed herself to you."

Cleod sat up a little straighter in the saddle. Kicce flicked his ears at the change, but Cleod did not spare breath to comfort him. What would Leiel regret? The choices she made that set her in chains on the Spur all those years ago? The battle that followed? The passing years based on lies? Those seemed unlikely. She had her life, her freedom, and her youth. She had escaped her brother and her life in Adfen—

A jolt crossed his gut. When had he begun to think of Leiel's life as something she needed to escape? To consider that was too trying a prospect, required too much aware thought. Anything *he* might regret, beyond what he had allowed himself to face through the years, was caught up in the answer. He bowed his head, acknowledged that he was too weak in spirit and mind, this moment, to face such thoughts.

She had showed herself to him. And he had tried to kill her. How could she not regret stepping from the shadows? He turned the knowledge he now held—of her existence—of what she was, and therefore, what all Draigon must be—and something twisted inside him. It churned dark and cold, wrought of chilled laughter and bitter drink and the scent of unsheathed steel in cold, mountain air.

The Draigon were human.

They were human, and that meant they were mortal.

He said it out loud, to make it real, to judge Kilras's response. "The Draigon are human."

Silence held a moment, then Kilras said, with an ease that tingled something deep in Cleod's mind, "I'd say they're more than human."

Cleod drew Kicce to a halt. A stride later, Kilras stopped his mare and turned her a little to look back. Cleod stared at him, glad that Kilras's calm nature meant that even the most unexpected events were simply to be accepted, and dealt with as needed. Yes, the Draigon were human—*and* they were the monsters that had spun drought and fear across Arnan for centuries. They were more than human or beast. They were more dangerous, and suddenly more vulnerable, than he had ever dreamed. What would the Councils and the King and the people of Arnan give for such knowledge? What would be the cost of them having it? "Who pays?" Cleod asked. "Who pays for this knowledge? Me? Leiel? The Enclaves? The King?"

Kilras made a sharp, disgusted noise. "Pays?" he asked. "In coin? Or in life? Who'd die to possess it? And who'll die because *you* possess it? Will you sell it? Use it? Kill with it?"

Cleod started. What was he going to do with it? What was it worth, in changed perception and fear? He held Kilras's gaze. "What about you, Kilras? You know now, too."

Kilras grinned and shook his head. "What the Draigon are, they were this morning and last week. They'll be what they are tomorrow, and next year, and long after I'm dead. What *I know* changes nothing for me. What affects me, is only how much this knowledge changes *you*." He turned the mare and rode on. A few strides brought him to the edge of the forest, then under the shadows of the trees.

How this knowledge changes you...

Cleod watched Kilras blend into patterned light cast through the canopy. Suddenly breath would not fill Cleod's lungs and he caught hard at the pommel to steady himself as the world tipped a little. Because he *was* changed, irrevocably. Just as he had been after the fight on the Spur when he realized that the Ehlewer Enclave had sent him to face Shaa without what he needed to even survive, much less triumph. Memory tripped truth inside him, a truth long suspected—that *the Ehlewer already knew*. Maybe not the *humanity* of the creatures they trained their followers to kill—but at least the beyond-animal intelligence of them.

He bent his head a moment, drew a breath and let it out. A heartbeat, two, then he spoke to Kicce and followed Kilras into the forest.

The Dorn waited among the trees, at the edge of a beaten stretch of earth that might be a trail. It was narrow and overgrown, but not low-hung with branches. More than a deer path, then. "You found a way?" Cleod asked.

"I found it following you. You took the rougher route."

Cleod grunted. "You are implying I like to do things the hard way?"

"I'm noting that you tend to find the most difficult way to your goal. The amount of pleasure you derive from it is your business."

Cleod shook his head. There was a level of truth to that. He had always chosen the things that took work and required striving to master. But was that preference, or happenstance? When he had chosen the Enclaves, he had done so with purpose and intent. When he had chosen ercew, he had believed it a fitting escape. But the choice to master that addiction...that had been the hardest choice of his life. And now, another choice lay before him—what do to with his knowledge of the true nature of the Draigon? Could he hold it? Contain it? No. The answer was an unwelcome blow.

He was Draighil.

"All these years," he said. "And I am still...*Draighil.*" No matter the pains he had taken to bury that part of himself, to avoid all contact with the Enclaves and others of his ilk, he had been turned and molded, bent and forged.

Kilras shook his head. "You are," he said. "You think I don't know what's been rattling in your head since the Seebo?"

Cleod's jaw clenched, and he turned his full attention to Kilras.

"Don't waste your glare," Kilras said.

Cleod forced his shoulders to relax. Of course Kilras had guessed. All the dark thoughts and sleepless nights on the trail, the tension not quite contained. Kilras would not have missed all that, or failed to guess its meaning. "I should not be surprised."

"No," Kilras agreed. "And you shouldn't be surprised that you're still what you were, despite what you've become."

Cleod frowned. What did that mean? He let the words settle inside him until an answer came. What Kilras had said of the Draigon was true for more than just the beasts. What Cleod had been yesterday, he was today and would be tomorrow. Nothing had changed. And yet, seeing Leiel had shifted *everything.*

Memory rolled through him. Her laughter when her name was called. Her face that day on the Spur. He heard, again, her voice, ringing through the smoldering air, begging for life. Begging him and begging *for him*. The way he had felt in that moment—the surety and power within him, the pride and confidence. So much of that based on lies... Why had the Enclaves never used what they already knew of the Draigon's intelligence to truly vanquish the creatures? The Draigon demanded so many Sacrifices of Arnan—the loss of its daughters across generations, the deaths of its sons...

"What have I made myself part of, Kil?" Cleod asked. Sacrifice. Was that truly the Draigon's choice? Because the Draigon did not in fact demand death. He knew that now. But did the Councils know it? "The Councils choose," he said. "The Councils and the Farlan and their Priests and the Enclaves with their secret training." Had his life always been a feather blown in a wind of ambition and greed?

"We all choosc," Kilras said. "Sometimes we're wrong. Our lives change because of it. Sometimes we're right and things change again."

Cleod half-smiled. How many times had he watched Kilras act as the catalyst for such change? And never had those acts been for power or based in ambition. "You've made more right choices than wrong."

"As have you, since you met me," Kilras said. "Before that, you lacked perspective."

"Ha." Cleod shook his head. "Is that all I lacked?"

"It's a dangerous thing to be without," Kilras said. He reined the mare around and led the way down the narrow, twisting track through the trees and underbrush.

Cleod ducked his head to the side to avoid a low-hanging branch. Perspective. Twelve years criss-crossing Arnan had at least earned him that. Kilras had offered him that, along with the most important friendship he had ever known. As important as the one that had shaped his youth. Leiel. The bright ring of her laughter cut through his mind.

"And you haven't asked the right question," Kilras said.

"What question?" Cleod demanded.

"If the Draigon-sign at the Seebo belonged to Shaa, and Leiel's what you say—" Kilras looked over his shoulder at Cleod. "Why are there two Draigon in Melbis?"

CHAPTER 33

Leiel

Leiel twisted her ring a little, then let go, flexed her fingers instead. Her voice was rusty metal and hard wind, creaking out of her body, reluctant and stiff. "There's a Draighil in Melbis."

"Already?" The air was thick with the scent of herbs and steam. Gahree held out a cup of tea, and the fire before them reflected off the waxed wood.

Leiel shook her head as she accepted the mug. "Yes—but not as we expected. Gahree—it's Cleod."

Gahree sat back a little. "Your friend has returned to the Enclaves?"

A faint smile crossed Leiel's face. "No. Kilras's caravan crossed the Seebo a week ago. They found the place of your Shape taking. And Cleod—his old training awoke. His thoughts turned to killing you."

Gahree stretched out a hand and picked up the kettle to fill her own mug. "He is not the one I was expecting. Trayor is on his way, if he's not arrived already."

Leiel sucked a breath and could not find a way to let it out again for several seconds. At last, she blew out air. "Trayor..." She closed her eyes. "He's the one—the one who killed Wynt."

"The one who held the sword," Gahree said.

The air in Leiel's chest took on a new density and she forced a long breath to relieve the pressure. "You found proof, then."

"Yes," Gahree said. "The songs in Giddor and Waymete are consistent with those from Oryok." Gahree lifted her mug and the sweet steam that rose from it rolled with the rhythm of her breath. "Wynt faced two Draighil, against all precedent. Only Hoyd Draighil was officially listed in the records, but the bards sing Trayor's praises. They tell a tale of cunning, a plot that assured her death."

"Deception."

A tip of Gahree's head acknowledged the truth of the word.

"Why?" Leiel sighed, closed her eyes. "Hundreds of years —"

"Yes," Gahree said. "We have kept the pact, all of us."

"But if Trayor struck the killing blow, Hoyd was never the threat we thought," Leiel said. "Has it been Trayor, all these years? Even when the records named another?"

"Bonniri was alone. But perhaps, sometimes, Trayor has been there as well," Gahree said. "Or perhaps it was simply that Wynt was powerful and they knew they could not defeat her honestly."

Leiel fell silent. Moisture gathered on her lower eyelids. Her most difficult lesson in winter survival had been guided by Wynt's fearless competence. The smile that split the copper-haired Draigon's face when Leiel emerged from the snowy forest after a week on her own, had rung the mountains like a bell. Three years after Wynt's death the rumor had reached Cyunant—that the Sacrifice had seen the participation of more than one Draighil. "Why would the Enclaves risk it? They had to know we would learn the truth."

"The Enclaves have priorities all their own, wild daughter. The question remains—was this their doing? Or did Trayor Draighil act on his own? Since your Cleod turned his back on the Enclaves, Trayor has grown vicious in his hatred of us."

"Gahree—" Leiel blinked back tears. "Trayor is strong. He could kill you."

"Any Draighil could kill any of us." The old warning, often repeated. But for the first time in years, a jolt twisted Leiel's belly at the words.

Gahree sipped her tea. "Change. Fate. Inattention. A strong breeze. We have no control over our deaths. We have only knowledge that they will come, and a hope to make a difference before they do."

Leiel smiled despite the knot in her throat. "Still trying to teach me philosophy, Gahree?"

"You'll never speak in riddles, or ring odd tones from the air. You're far too forthright for that. But you can still benefit from me baffling you on occasion."

At that, Leiel laughed outright. "I never could argue with you. I'm still not sure how you manage to be both wise and absurd." Even after all these years, Leiel could rarely predict what the woman would say.

Gahree shrugged as she sat back and sipped at her tea. The wind buffeted the tent around them; the scent of dust filtered into the cloth-wrapped space. *The look on Cleod's face as she stepped from the shadows...* The weight of their encounter balanced on Leiel's spirit like a rock on the edge of a cliff.

Trayor and Cleod in Melbis, and a Sacrifice in motion. The possibilities rebounded, ricocheted in her mind. No matter the pattern of interaction she envisioned, the prospective futures unleashed by the reunion of Cleod and his old compatriot were all brutal, and dangerous, and unbearable. What potential outcomes, made reality by their meeting, would lead to anything wise and good? She could see nothing.

"Gahree..." Leiel whispered, head bent over her cup. "I can see no clear way through what I have started."

"What you have started?"

Leiel nodded, raised her eyes and met Gahree's green-gold gaze. "All this time, and I still know Cleod like I know my own heart." She sighed. "I saw it in him—that old need—to be what he hoped to be. To finish what he began. He was ready to face the Draigon—face you. Whether or not a Draighil was sanctioned by the Enclaves, he was planning to declare himself."

Gahree held a rare silence, waiting.

"I went to him. *I spoke to him,*" Leiel said. A shiver ran through her. "Did I really think I could stop him? I must be half insane to have done this. Whatever happens now—*What was I thinking?*"

"You were thinking that you care for him," Gahree said, her voice rang notes across more than Leiel's hearing, bells and hammer strikes combined. "You could have trusted Kilras to guide Cleod away from Melbis, had his mind truly turned toward his old ways." She raised a hand, stopped the angry words forming in Leiel's throat. "But I think you know Cleod best—and such a decision as you made was not based on your human memories alone. Whatever comes, if created in love and knowledge, will not be wrong. It will be a pattern woven through the world, wider than what any of us can see."

Leiel stared at her. "But Cleod and Trayor, together in Melbis, both preparing to destroy you. How is that a possibility born of anything I might feel?"

Gahree's laughter filled the small space. "Ahhh, Leiel, that is a mystery we must solve, because the ties spun between you and Cleod Draighil hold the potential to be the binding, or unbinding, of all Arnan."

The words pushed through Leiel's senses, rebounded, and caught her breath in her throat. "Promise me there is nothing so foolish as *prophecy* involved here. Nothing *fated* about Cleod and me. No insane notion that our friendship will change the world."

A chuckle shook through Gahree. "No, nothing so dramatic as that." She tipped her head toward her pack, with its dancing embroidery that spoke of countless intertwined lives. "But what do Draigon do? We study the world. We seek knowledge. We watch connections form, and seek to nurture those who expand freedom. You and Cleod Woodcutter—you were always a joy to see together. To see him choose the Enclaves, the path to the Draighil, that could have made us weep. But then I met you, and learned why the boy would have done anything to help you heal. His choices were only ever for you—twisted though they became. Whatever happens, the potential of your relationship—then, and now, and in whatever future arrives—is founded on the caring between you. I can see only hope in that, if you can see it, too."

Hope and caring. What more had sustained her through the cruel years of her growing up? How much more had she learned to value that among the Draigon, in becoming Draigon? Leiel smiled, slight and wistful, the curl of her lips just creasing her cheeks. "You really think this story has a joyous ending?"

"No," Gahree said. "But I think I can hope for one." She lifted her mug in toast.

The answer did not untangle the knot in Leiel's belly, but she returned Gahree's gesture, though she could think of no clever words to accompany it. For all the comfort she had always found in hope, something, this time, seemed lacking.

CHAPTER 34

Cleod

The years of his friendship with Leiel seemed so far away. And based in an innocence he had long since lost, in a simple certainty that the world was built one way, shadeless, and drawn with conviction. But the taut lines of surety he had once envisioned strung through every aspect of life, did not, in fact, exist. They never had. Ercew had obliterated any thought that he was in control. A life on the trail had burned away the idea only one truth existed.

More than one truth. More than one Draigon in Melbis.

Kilras's question lingered as they rode side-by-side, a silence that would normally have been easy, pulled strange between them.

"Two Draigon," Cleod said. His vision trembled as he spoke the word, but he checked all response. Kicce's stride did not falter or skip. A small victory at the very moment he most needed one.

"Twice the struggle," Kilras said.

"Twice the chance to make things right with the world."

"Spoken like a Draighil. What's the Ruhlern say?"

A hitch marred Cleod's inhalation. He turned the question in his mind. "It's still my job to protect," he said at last.

"Not your job. Your nature. Or do you still not know why I dug you out of that hole of a tavern?"

The trail narrowed, and Kilras eased his mare up.

Cleod urged Kicce into the lead. He raised a hand to lift a low branch, ducked a little to slip beneath it. "You have an affinity for broken things."

"I know when a scarred edge and a lot of corrosion mask a fine blade forged to safeguard others. I was there that day, you know, in Adfen, when Leiel's name was called."

The Dorn's words struck like hailstones, stinging and cold and startling. Cleod reined Kicce to a halt. Kilras had been in Adfen for the Sacrifice? The words pulled and twisted between them, woven like the path through the woods, caught between shadow and light. A heartbeat, two, Cleod sat stiff and motionless, pulling everything in, straining against every instinct. Well, why wouldn't Kilras have been there? Half of the Spur had been there. At last he looked over his shoulder. "Why did you never tell me? Why are you telling me now?"

"Because you never needed to know before. And now you do." Kilras's gaze was as direct as sunlight in the desert. "I sought you out because I saw what you were that day. And I saw why you couldn't be that, afterward. You'd have killed yourself with ercew before you returned to the Enclave. Whatever you are feeling now, and whatever you've been thinking is the right action to take, is not about anything you were trained to do or think or feel. It's about who you are, Cleod. So decide what happens next. Because it matters. And to more people than just yourself."

"Why?" Cleod asked.

Kilras grunted. "That's not a question you have to ask if you think about it."

"Kil—"

"Do you think friends are plucked from trees like apples? Don't insult me by pretending you don't know your worth."

Cleod stared, then smiled before he realized he was doing it. Had his own thoughts not a few moments ago walked the same path? Friendship. Loyalty. Things that had both cut him to the soul, and healed that same damage. "I have not yet begun to insult you."

Kilras laughed. "I await your crack wit."

Cleod shook his head. The way he was feeling, Kilras would have a long wait. Humor faded as the question posed rose again in his mind.

Why were there two Draigon in Melbis?

In all the years that the Draigon had made their demands of the cities of Arnan, had two ever come to take a Sacrifice? How would anyone know? If only one of the beasts came for the Sacrifice, would anyone ever know how many others lurked out of sight? Unlikely. Especially if the others were in human form. "There could always have been more than one."

"Why would there need to be?" Kilras asked.

"But there's a need now?"

Kilras shook his head. "Maybe something's changed. Something important enough for your friend to have decided to make herself known to you."

"You sound like you admire her."

"Why shouldn't I?" Kilras asked. "You've talked about her for years."

Cleod frowned. He had spoken of Leiel on cold, lonely nights, and when a good book touched his heart, or a finely crafted bard's tale crossed his ears. Years of missing her, shaping her in his mind, until she glowed like phantom-light in a foggy swamp—earthy, wild, and beckoning.

And now this.

"She knows you're Draighil," Kilras said. "She chose to come to you. There's courage in that. Maybe not wisdom, but courage."

Cleod set his jaw and blew out a breath through his nose. Why had she shown herself to him? Why? She had to know what his reaction would be. Why? To save Shaa from his sword? Or had she based the decision in something else, some need he did not understand? Or was it simpler than that?

They had been friends, once.

They had shared caring and good humor and trust. And that day on the Spur... She had begged him. And begged for him. Whatever she had done to earn herself that place, chained to the rock, whatever she had since become, she had acted, in that moment, to save his life. Death had been his other option, looming and certain. Shaa had needed but a single instant more to wipe him from the mountain, from existence...

Had Leiel *saved* him?

"Kil," he said, "What if she really is trying to protect me from something?" He paused, considered the bent of his thoughts over the last weeks. "Or from myself."

"Then she should queue behind me. I have been trying to save you from yourself since I met you. Have I succeeded?"

Cleod laughed, a real laugh that eased tension from his chest and loosened his jaw. He shook his head.

"Then your Leiel's taken a dangerous step for no purpose. Perhaps she doesn't know you as well as she hoped."

Cleod blinked, swallowed. How could she think she knew him at all, after all these years? Did she expect him to just accept her sudden appearance? No. Whatever she was, she was too smart to have expected a simple reaction from him.

Sweat broke along his brow and, for a moment, his mind was once again ablaze with heat and memory. Perception snapped wide and the world around him suddenly trembled with light and fire—

"Cleod!" Kilras's voice *pushed* through the expanding field of Gweld perception like a spear thrown toward the heart. Cleod yanked his awareness back, fought, trembling on the edge of control, as the ingrained response tripped the violent triggers deep within him. His strength was returning for the reaction to be so strong. He grasped the thought and turned it on itself. He gasped, gathered will, and slammed his rushing senses back into containment with a determination that reeled him in the saddle.

Kilras was beside him, hand steady on his shoulder, holding him upright.

"How did you—?" Cleod said.

"You've been with me as long as you were with the Enclave. Long enough for you to pay attention when I yell."

But it had been more than Kilras's voice that pierced the Gweld. Cleod's mind tried to form thought to consider that, but a renewed roil of nausea contracted his stomach. He bent double, one hand twisted hard through Kicce's mane. Kilras's firm grasp stabilized him in the saddle. Cleod spilled what little was in his stomach along the grey gelding's shoulder, then closed his eyes and pressed his face into Kicce's neck. "Damn and fire," Cleod said, wheezing.

"You were feeling better," Kilras said.

Cleod choked out a laugh. "Too much so. I can't stop it, Kil," he said.

"You've stopped it for ten years," Kilras said, his voice a blunt object. "Quit thinking you can't, and get hold of yourself."

Cleod raised his head and met the Dorn's gaze. "You're right too damn often."

"And you're stronger than this." Kilras looked back, his dark eyes set hard in a face that had resolve written over its every plane. "Sit up. Your Gweld won't serve you here. There's nothing to fight but yourself."

Cleod flushed, nodded, and straightened in the saddle. "I feel like the broken thing I was when we met."

Kilras grunted. "You're not. Remember that, and you'll work through this."

A rough laugh jerked from Cleod's throat. The papery emptiness behind his eyes echoed with his breath. Was he really the same person he had been a few days ago, when he had felt easy in his skin and in his life? He closed his eyes and tried to pull his breath back into his body, to fill the strange hollow space in his mind. The sounds of the forest settled over him, bird song and leaf rustle, twig snap and the sweep of branches through the canopy. The brittleness in the noises spoke to the ongoing drought, but life rode through them as well, a wave that rose and fell with the breeze. Understory to canopy, every level of the woodland was *alive.*

He blinked and looked around. Signs of stress marred the leaves. Streaks of brown and curled edges, the beginnings of autumn colors were fragile, drifting toward withered faster than the season would normally dictate. One hard wind would lay the trees bare, strip the shrubs, bury the ground in a litter of dying waste. Such was the pattern of life. Was it so different for the particular hardships of this one year? The forest was always shaped by rain and wind, heat and snow, the changes wrought each day, and with the turning of the seasons. Draigon Weather was a blow that rocked the woods to the roots, bent the birds and boars and the smallest bugs under the desperate weight of survival. But the forest always continued.

And the events of the past weeks had bent him, just the same way, awakened dark needs and dormant instincts. What remained? He was Ruhelrn of the finest caravan in Arnan. He had friends. He had the reliable horse beneath him, and the ongoing victory of sobriety. Kilras was still at his side. Everything. Everything that mattered.

Cleod nodded.

Kilras eased his grip and sat back into his saddle. "We're nearly back."

Sehina. Nae. Rimm. "What do I tell the others?"

Kilras grinned. "What we always tell them. The truth."

What else would Kilras say? Despite a new roll of nausea through his belly, a smile found Cleod's lips. "Tell them the Draigon are human and everything we've all been taught is a lie?"

Kilras actually laughed. "Why not?"

"By all the—! Kil—"

"The truth is that you reacted to Draigon sign. And to the sight of an old friend tied to the worst of your past. We'll answer their questions honestly, and make sense of where that takes us, together."

Together. The friendships Cleod had forged through the years were strong. The others would listen. They would work through the emotions sure to arise with the revelations to come, and find a solid path forward, he had no doubt. The idea should have brought relief, but in the back of his skull, a low pressure remained.

Everything that mattered. Was everything enough?

CHAPTER 35

Cleod

The trees gave way to the grasslands surrounding Melbis. Caravan groups dotted the plains, expanding the bustle of the city on the horizon. How many had arrived in the time they had been away? How many knew the depth of the drought they faced? The danger?

Cleod looked at Kilras. What else was there to be said? It settled his heart to know that Kilras's trust was unshaken. But tough choices loomed.

The circled wagons that had been his home for more than a decade, the rise and geometry of Melbis's buildings with the low hills rolling away behind them, seemed odd and unfamiliar.

His vision vibrated, and his hearing was bordered by a constant echo. He had experienced such disconnection before, in the determined days of his youth. Emerging from Gweld trance the first time, the world had twisted the same way. What distorted the familiar, burned it brighter and changed it until once known places and people seemed odd as an exotic country visited for the first time? Only one thing, for good or ill. The one thing that had ever bent his perception was *knowledge*. With each new thing he learned or understood, the shape of his existence changed. Knowledge, and how it blended with history to tremble the foundations of his life.

The truth about Leiel, her aliveness, the nature of that life—that was understanding he could not turn from, and yet he still had to decide what to do with it.

The wagons were as he had last seen them, circled for organization and the unlikely need for defense. Cleod glanced at the sky. There was no defense against what could come. What walked unnoticed among them all these years… He shook himself.

Sehina and Rimm waited at the circle's edge. Rimm stood a little braced, as though he could not decide whether to be worried or angry.

Sehina exhibited no such conflict. "In the blessed name of every god who ever lived and died, have you lost your mind?" Arms folded, she glared up at Cleod as he drew Kicce to a halt beside her.

Cleod blinked and started to speak.

"Snap your mouth closed." Sehina's face flushed, and her normally neat braid, sparked with fly-away hairs, hung scraggly over one shoulder. "You've some nerve! Ruhelrn my ass! What in flaming chaos possessed you? You just—"

"Sehina—" Kilras halted his mare beside Kicce. "It's been a long ride back."

"A long *ride*? Melbis is half boiling over with rumor and speculation. I've been fending off as many questions as groping hands in the taverns these last days." Her words pounded, small rocks thrown at Cleod's skull

"You're a damnable ass when you're drunk, no lie in that," Rimm said. "Here I thought you were the only one to go on duty sober the other night."

Cleod stared at his friends as they voiced pure irritation and normal concerns—as though nothing more trying had occurred than a simple lapse of judgment on his part. Nothing else could calm so quickly the ache in his belly, or quench the fire burning along his spine. They knew nothing of what had transpired, of the gutting truths loosed upon him these last days. Their naïveté was a balm to his soul, and he took his first unhindered breath since the moment Leiel had stepped from the shadows.

"Ease off," Kilras said. "This isn't ercew. This is Enclave training. Leave him be." He swung down and handed Rimm the mare's reins. "Take her. Tell everyone there'll be a meeting with supper tonight."

Rimm hesitated, glanced at Sehina, then Cleod.

"No, damn it," Sehina snapped. Her stance had not eased one bit, and she turned her glare on Kilras. "Where in all the burning nights of the Anyaluft Rayyat have you two been? Our Ruhelrn takes off as a mad fool in the night, and you follow like a hound dog mindless on a scent trail. If there is an explanation, I would love to hear it."

"It'll sound like a tall tale." Kilras chuckled. "It'd be better entertainment if it were."

Sehina folded her arms and waited.

Despite the tumble of thoughts cluttering Cleod's head, and the ache that seemed determined to bore through his body and turn him to useless mush, Cleod grinned. Rarely had he seen Sehina so irritated. She was ready to throttle both him and Kilras. And Rimm—the scout waited, one hand grasping the mare's lead, the other gripped around his belt, his fingers wrapped so tightly his knuckles were white—holding it together, despite confusion. Just what Cleod had come to expect from the youngest member of their band. The *normality* of their behavior was far afield from the churn and ricochet of thoughts crowding his mind the last several days. Cleod shook his head, and his smile grew.

Sehina turned her iron gaze on him. "Rotten. Both of you."

"Sehina. Rimm." The crisp edge of Kilras's words cut the moment. Rimm straightened a bit, and Sehina's shoulders lost some of their stiffness.

"Tonight is soon enough." Kilras's tone lifted. "It's a story best told over a good meal. It'll be easier to hear how rotten I am when I've a full stomach."

Sehina's scowl deepened, then shifted and ended with the flash of a smile. "I never can stay angry with you." She glanced at Cleod, fought down a wider smile. "*You*, though—I can hold a grudge." She turned on a heel and walked away.

Rimm hesitated, glanced between them. "You're both all right?" he asked.

Kilras nodded. "Take the mare."

Watching the exchange in silence, Cleod let his gaze linger on Rimm as the scout followed Sehina. The familiar rough banter and humor meant Cleod was back where he belonged, but the old comfort failed to settle over him. He looked at Kilras and shook his head. "They are not going to understand."

"Not at first." Kilras stepped up beside Kicce, patted the big grey's neck and looked up at Cleod. "It's a lot to make sense of. Give them truth and time, and they'll take it in."

Cleod shuddered, and the motion wrung through him as though his bones were jellied. He sighed. "I need to get clean."

Kilras nodded. "I made sure The Nest held your room. Go melt yourself in that poit. We'll save you a plate."

A smile crossed Cleod's lips. Leave it Kilras to get to the heart of the matter. Cleansing heat and good food. Those were exactly the needs to be filled. Cleod gave a shake of his head. "Tell Jahmess not to burn the beans."

"When has he ever succeeded with that?"

Cleod smiled, and it felt real. Kilras backed away, and Cleod turned Kicce for town.

Cleod let the gelding set the pace toward the city. He blinked to ease a sudden burning behind his eyes. A shimmer at the edge of his sight blurred, shifted like the dance of stars in a crystal sky.

A glance back toward the camp summoned dark thoughts. Did they think he had broken? Or abandoned them? Would they find a way to trust him again? How could he explain to the others? Would they believe him, or think him mad? Could he convince them of his truth? Did he want to?

And Leiel. Somehow, she was part of his future again. The idea struck heat through his mind, and he fought vertigo, swayed a little in the saddle. Leiel and *her* truth were not to be settled lightly or soon. Gods of old! His stomach churned. Part of him was unspun, adrift. The dangerous part. The part that did not want to understand. The past had leapt up and led him to strike at her with all the startling viciousness of a coiled snake. Now, did he strike again to kill, or step away? Could he return to the life he had lived these past years, do as Leiel asked and back away, despite what he now knew? Either way, would his friends forgive him?

Kicce's hooves struck the hard-rutted surface of the main road as Cleod joined other riders and wagons making their way toward Melbis. The grey, stone roofline of The Nest stood out among the wooden buildings. For the first time, the granite did not offer easy comfort, but awakened the twists of dark memory. Was it just days ago that he had seen the strange woman through the inn's dusty windows? Seen Leiel and convinced himself that it was a simple trick of mind wrought from his recent encounter with Draigon sign?

Hooves and wheels kicked dust into air that grew thicker the closer he rode to town. By the time he passed the first buildings, the noise and chatter and clattering motion made him pull his hat low and concentrate on Kicce's ears.

In the livery, he stowed his gear in the lockroom, then took extra time to assure the grey gelding was curried smooth, every speck of sweat and dust wiped away, hooves picked clean, and tail and mane untangled. By the time he was done, he acknowledged the attention to detail was as much about his own need to focus on simple things as it was for the comfort of the horse.

Through the dusty air, The Nest loomed solid and comforting. Every bit of him ached for the poit. Cleod let out a sigh as he reached the steps to the porch. A few hours to pull himself back together, then a warm meal and, he hoped, the support of true friends awaited him.

"They told me there was another Spurman in Melbis. I never imagined it was you." The voice rang into the darkest corners of Cleod's mind, against the already cracked foundation of self.

He stopped in mid-stride and looked up. A pale man, dressed in black, rose from his seat on the porch and walked to the top of the steps. He sipped from the cup in his hand, looked down at Cleod.

Cleod met crinkled eyes in a weathered face marred down one side by a thin scar. Trayor's short, pale hair was thinner and laced through with grey, but he was still whip-thin-strong, and the ease of his stance was unchanged. Of course. After all that happened these last few days, why should any surprise exist that this man, of all men, was waiting for him?

CHAPTER 36

Cleod

A decade had passed since their last meeting. Before any words came a biting thought: If Trayor is here, someone is going to die. Draigon. Draighil. One, or both, would burn. So, the Sacrifice was to be in Melbis. Not one of the smaller towns of the region, but here. Soon.

The edges of Cleod's vision trembled. Something pushed at him, tested the boundaries of his senses, a cold mist crawling through his mind. Instinct braced reaction and locked down, pushed back. Old Gods, of all people, why Trayor? Why now?

The Draighil smiled, the scar twisting the expression. "You're out of practice, but you haven't forgotten."

"Circumstances have awakened old habits," Cleod said. He steeled his mind, then climbed the steps and joined Trayor on the porch. The Nest loomed above them, sat firm stone under their feet. The mineral scent of granite soaked the air. They might have been back in the Spur country, in Adfen, or even the Enclave. They might, for an instant, have been young again—confidants and rivals, and cocksure of their own worth and skills. Then a dry breeze blew dust along the crowded street, and the world and all the years between swept over them.

"Circumstances like Draigon Weather."

Lights danced at the edges of Cleod's vision. He blinked them back. "You're far from home, Tray." Cleod drew a breath. "What else would bring you here but a call for Sacrifice—and for someone to defend against it?"

"And what brings you here?" Trayor leaned against one of the beams that held up the porch roof and folded his arms. "Chasing old dreams of glory?"

Too close to the truth. Despite the heat, a chill traced up his spine. Impossible, that Tray could know anything of what had transpired the last few days. He could not know anything about Leiel. Cleod's teeth ached from the strain in his jaw. He shook his head. "My work brings me to Melbis this time most years."

"So, it's coincidence that both you and Shaa are here."

Cleod pulled in a breath through his nose, let it out. "An unpleasant one."

"Huh." Trayor straightened and stepped up before Cleod. He held out a hand. "It's been a long time."

Cleod made no move to accept the offered greeting. "You weren't waiting here for a Spurman," he said. "You knew I was in Melbis. You knew I would come here."

A gruff sound of amusement escaped Trayor. He lowered his hand and pressed his lips together a moment, then smiled.

Cleod pulled off his gloves, slapped them together in one hand. "You're here for the Draigon," Cleod said, forced his voice to remain steady as he spoke the last word. "What do you want with me?"

"It's not enough to greet an old friend?"

"We did not part as friends. It's been ten years. Why are you here?"

"To kill a Draigon. As you have already surmised. Why here?" He gestured to The Nest. "The look and feel of home."

Cleod met the other man's gaze. "You've been waiting for me."

"I have. Join me. Have some wine. We'll talk about old times, and this time, maybe we won't beat the breath out of each other."

With a shake of his head, Cleod declined. "I've had many long days in a row."

"You have to eat. Join me for a meal. We can wipe away some of the stains of our last meeting."

Cleod bent his head a moment, then raised his eyes and met Trayor's gaze again. Anger had been the last word between them, and through the years and silence that had gathered since, the only thoughts Cleod had spared for the man before him were wonder that the two of them had ever been friends. Had they really shared worry and work and thoughts of glory? Had they conspired, and plotted mischief, turned their freshly-learned skills to gibes at the newer Draigre? Had they truly dreamed of a life of blood and battle, where victory meant all, and glory for the Enclaves was the highest honor? Cleod shook his head. How had he ever been a man who had thought such things were important? "That seems an endeavor unlikely to succeed," he said.

Trayor grinned, but a tightness around his eyes lent the expression more malevolence than amusement. "Like so many of your endeavors."

Cleod's shoulder and neck muscles pulled in opposition as he straightened. "And no few of your own, I'm sure."

Trayor took a sip from his cup. "As though you know anything of that."

"What do you want, Tray?"

"Time with an old friend."

The last word vibrated between them, and Cleod's re-sharpened senses discerned just how much effort it had taken Trayor to speak it at all. Their last meeting had been filled with too-easy banter. But it compared not at all with the homey irritation of the people who waited him back at the caravan camp. Truer emotions had been conveyed by their expressions than filled Trayor's words.

And suddenly the decision Cleod had been struggling with the entire ride back to Melbis was no decision at all. Did he call a man like *this* friend, or a man like Kilras? Whatever Cleod decided he needed to do about Leiel, the choice of who *he* wanted to be was clear. Something inside him settled, clicked back into place.

"Whatever your real reason for seeking me out, consider it a pointless undertaking." Almost, he wished the Draighil luck, but what outcome was he truly wishing the man, in the face of the knowledge he now held? Leiel was a Draigon. How was that possible? He turned for the door. Stopped. What would it mean to the Ehlewer to possess that information? What would it mean to Trayor, of all the Ehlewer?

Cleod pivoted to face the other man. "You're here because you think I owe you something."

Trayor scoffed. "Me? Why concern yourself with *me*, when you betrayed *everything*?"

"Because you're standing here. And you're one of the few people with the ability to seek an accounting."

Trayor laughed, his shoulders shaking with amusement. "If I'd been waiting for a chance to kill you, it's unlikely I'd do it on the porch of an inn in full day."

"No," Cleod said. "That's not your way. You would demand a bigger audience."

Trayor grinned. "Maybe one day we'll have one."

Cleod shook his head. "No. I'm done, Tray."

Was he? Leiel's face, full of such human emotion despite the power coursing in her... No.

He took a step back, turned away again.

"Hoyd's dead."

Cleod paused, a hand on the door knob, and for a moment the pale, smug face of the boy he had mentored was clear in his mind. How? When? He swallowed back the questions. But it did not matter. Draighil died. They killed, and were killed.

"He killed one," Trayor said, "after his investiture. And then Wynt, the young beast, broke Hoyd's back in Giddor, before I killed it."

That brought Cleod back around. The news had reached them in Bajor, years before, of the copper Draigon's demise. He remembered the cheers from bars and store fronts, sitting with Kilras while the Dorn, in a rare moment of slipped control, drank to the beast's end. Cleod frowned. "That kill was Hoyd's, by record."

"By record," Trayor said in agreement.

Kilras's question became vital. Why are there two Draigon in Melbis? Cleod pitched his voice low. "Who is with you?"

Trayor smiled, but the turn of his lips did not crinkle the flesh around his eyes. He raised his cup and drained it, stepped close to Cleod—moved forward until Cleod had to turn his shoulder to let his old colleague pass.

Trayor turned the handle and stepped into The Nest. Cleod stood, staring at the black varnished door as it shut in his face. A tingle at the base of his spine offered a warning he did not know how to measure. Trayor had walked away without claiming the last word. Dark possibility wove through Cleod's perception. Whatever purpose drew Trayor to greet him remained. Well, he would be back at the caravan before the other man pressed the issue.

Cleod pushed open the door and stepped inside. Trayor was nowhere in sight. Released breath diminished tension. He looked toward the desk, and a nod from

Lorrel confirmed that the solitary relaxation of the poit shed awaited him. Gods, he needed that as much as he needed air.

Chapter 37

Cleod

Heat soaked deep, pressed through his muscles into his bones. Sweat ran off his shoulders and down his sides and back in thick lines. Eyes closed, he tipped his head back against the wall and breathed deep.

Trayor. Not enough to have encountered Leiel and her terrible truth. Trayor had to be here as well. But who else would the Ehlewer send? Trayor was the best the Enclaves had—had been for nearly two decades. Cleod's lips twitched with the hint of a smile. At least the best since *he* had left them. The things he could teach them all...

Where had that thought come from? He blinked open his eyes. The air in the room shifted slightly. Old gods, was he so tired that Gweld bent his mind even here, where he should be most at peace?

He sat up and reached to crack the small window on the wall beside him. No wider than his hand and only the length of his forearm, the pane opened just a finger-width to let in a hint of fresh air, though the heat outside was so great it did nothing to affect the temperature of the poit. Cleod sighed and settled back again.

Only days ago, he had relaxed in this space, his mind heavy with thoughts of past failures, hard truths, and pointless wishes. What had he called up since then? Something old and dark within himself. Had he awakened it when he stood in the dying Seebo, gazing at wing-prints that could only belong to Shaa? When he drew his sword and envisioned glory?

Honor. Victory.

He sighed, breathed deep. How good it had felt to be known for great deeds, recognized wherever he went, to be honored and respected and renowned.

How far removed from that he was now.

How long it had been since strangers had called him by name with quiet awe in their voices. Moving quietly through the world, in Kilras's shadow, he was just another hired swordsman. Was that *all* he was now? A paid hand? A mercenary? Just another simple man, in a land of simple men?

No.

Cleod sat up.

The walls swayed and shifted, and he shook his head.

No.

Years ago, such proud thoughts had guided his every action. Years ago. Not now. He pushed to his feet and the poit-room tilted around him. He reached out, braced a hand against the wall, took another ragged breath.

Sharp, biting, the scent of rotten sage over-laid with burnt greens filled his nose. He gasped, recognized the danger even as he drew cuila deeper into his lungs.

No!

The thought ripped his mind as his senses spiraled and the air exploded with the hues of power and rage.

The cleansing heat of the poit erupted with bleeding color, sheets of red and bronze, refractions of black, and a continuously falling rain of dancing light. The fevered lightfall wrapped him, took his breath and reeled him away from himself. Gweld broke over him, not a spiraling of senses born from anger or necessity, but a manufactured release, familiar and horrifying.

The stove. Cuila. Trayor.

Decades fell away and the stone walls of the poit trembled, shifted, became the circular central chamber of the training temple at the Ehlewer Enclave. A crisp fall day. The day Trayor had pulled him from the library. The day the scent of cuila breached his senses for the first time.

Let go and fall in. The advice was simple. But the doing of it, that was an experience so painful and dark, he could not have dreamed it in his most savage nightmares.

So many months had he spent, learning control, of body, of mind, of every stray thought, that to simply let go of all of that and let the cuila take him...where? The lack of knowledge shuttered his ability—no—his willingness—to open his mind to the possibilities the herb tried to awaken inside him.

Bitter-bright, it filtered through his sinuses, turned deep and pressed up behind his eyes. They burned in their sockets and watered. Sweet and hot and biting, the scent maneuvered into his lungs, coating them with a smoky hunger that rippled him inside and out.

Silvering spirals blazed within him, plunged through his gut, down his legs, out through the soles of his feet. His fingers tingled and the vision grew—of light braiding itself into spiked tendrils inside him and streaking outward, blazing through every bit of him and flaring into a light that bent the world around him...

He opened his eyes and it was real. Not imagined or conjured by the smoke wafting from the iron cauldron before him, what poured from him bent the air of the room around him, expanded the pulse of air and light within it. The dozen other heartbeats in the room pounded loud as his, each a unique pattern beating over the next and echoing within the chests of the Draigre seated before the fire ring...

He coughed, took a heaving breath.

The world tilted, exploded with color, collapsed like the debris carried by a spiral storm as it gave way and broke apart.

His body spasmed and he toppled, hot bile spilling past his lips and a thousand knives stabbed his head and spine. He fought to breathe, took the tingling cuila smoke deeper still into his lungs. It hurtled him again into an expanded awareness he had no foundation to understand. The pain followed him down, followed him out, as his body and mind fought for a balance shared on a plane in this new vision of the world.

His awareness erupted, and then he was falling, falling forever into a place some part of him knew had no true escape.

The memory collapsed. Cleod's knees buckled and he sat, the hard poit bench coming up to meet him. The small space rocked with churning light as his vision tilted.

A bar of sunshine crossed his wavering line of sight as the door opened, closed. Through waves of trembling light and sweltering air—how long had he been in the poit?—a face warped into view. Tray.

Cleod must have said the Draighil's name aloud, though he did not intend to speak. What else, that he had never intended, loomed now? Old needs and old desires swelled and overran his control. His lungs pushed rasping breath. His skin burned and he could sense his fingers shaking, though he could not focus his gaze to see the motion any more than he could clearly see Trayor's face.

"Where is the honor in this?" Cleod dragged the words from low in his belly.

"Honor? There's a time for that, and there is a time for actions of necessity. You taught me how to cheat, Cleod. You taught me that the road to victory is paved with whatever leads to it."

"Why?" The decisions he had thought made, twisted away, lost in the craving both generated and satisfied by the cuila. Longing roared through him. Need.

Cuila was not ercew. He gasped. It was everything he had wanted ercew to be. His gut twisted like a rope spun in the hands of a master trickster. Old gods, he had missed this feeling! He had never wanted to need it again. And yet...*and yet...*

He tipped his gaze to Trayor's face, and, slowly, the pale man's features swam into focus. "What do you want, Tray?" Cleod asked, his voice low and strange in his ears.

The Draighil leaned close, smiled the stiff, righteous smile Cleod once knew so well. "The Draigon sign is of a monster like none I have seen. But you have." One side of his lips curled upward. The other marred straight by the scar, did not respond in kind. "Only one man knows what it is to face Shaa and live. I want you to tell me about that fight. I want you to tell me how to kill Shaa."

Pressure and heat weighted Cleod's body and mind. Every breath pulled the cuila deeper into his pores, his thoughts. Cleod shuddered, tried to straighten and stand.

A hand on his shoulder pushed him back with no effort. That was wrong. To be handled so simply, before he could think or react—that should not be possible.

"Shaa?" he asked, the word an echo, half-caught in the sweat that rolled down his face. His belly churned.

"The Draigon." Trayor leaned close. His eyes dilated and brightened with the cuila's impact on his awareness. Like a wave crashing, the trance washed over Cleod's mind as well, backed by the power of Trayor's demand.

No! Cleod's perception hurtled outward. Pure instinct guided the response. As it had with Leiel, Gweld led his actions. Consumed, raging, it slammed through him, and he *pushed.*

Trayor lurched back, but not in startlement. He was laughing.

Cleod surged to his feet, staggered as he tried to take a step. With an effort, he held upright. The cuila. Gweld surged through him, stronger than it had been in years. If the herb had burned near him when Leiel stepped from the trees, his sword would not have missed its mark.

Breath hissed in his throat. Cuila. It seared every bit of him, inside and out, filled a need he had long thought impossible to sate. What a fool he had been, to think anything could match this feeling, this satisfaction.

Deep in his mind, a screaming began.

Trayor lowered his chin and the *shove* that backed the gesture slammed into Cleod's mind. He reeled, body rocking, as his awareness spun outward. The air fluoresced and control, long dormant, exerted its dangerous dominance over his trained skill. No sword was at hand, but his fists bore the earned strength of years on the trail and hard labor.

The first blow landed hard and Trayor cursed.

Cleod smiled. Not easy. Never easy. No matter how Trayor cheated, there would be no simple victory. "Not weak," Cleod said.

"No," Trayor agreed. "But I didn't expect you to be. If you were, I wouldn't bother with you." He struck, angled his body in the small space to carry the most power in a short strike.

Cleod blocked that blow, but not the one that followed. He stumbled, and his scarred hip brushed the stove. For the first time he was thankful for the scar tissue along his flank. The scent of seared flesh filled the space, but no pain lanced him. He stepped away, and his vision shifted again, at once heightened and blurred by the smoke filling the space and his lungs. His body was slick with sweat, his mind awash with cuila. Honor of the gods, it felt good! It felt *right*. Gods, he *did not want this.*

Gweld claimed him, driven on the hot vapor rising from the stove. A laugh, of half-expressed thrill and desperation, escaped him and he stepped into combat. The small, blazing space between the stove and the door became a battleground as hallowed as any he had tread in search of a Draigon's blood. So long it had been since he felt so fiercely capable. The strikes he landed sent rolls of energy up his arm and spilling into his gut. It was akin to joy, the response along his spine.

Each block, each blow, given and received, became part of a dance, pain and music rolling together in brutal harmony.

But Overlash had claimed too much of his strength. Trayor's fist cracked against Cleod's skull, turned him, dropped him to one knee, as his arms clutched for a hold on the bench seat behind him.

"It's not *me* you're meant to fight, Cleod. Not today." Trayor bent close, his voice heavy with strained breath. "I want Shaa. So you are going to help me kill Shaa. You've been telling yourself lies. You're not a trail hand. You're not a chaperone. You're a Draigon-damned beast-slayer. It's time you remembered who you are."

The next blow erupted fire through Cleod's skull and sent him plunging into darkness.

Chapter 38

Cleod

When had he last spent this much time on his knees? So much simpler, to have just done as Soibel asked all those years ago and returned to the Enclave. Cleod's body heaved and shuddered, fought the air around him, the darkness of the room, the heat and heaviness of the night. Which night was this? How many had he spent in this place? Where in the name of all the gods was he?

"I remember when you conquered Overlash like you swatted flies." Trayor couched before Cleod, his face seemed to flicker like the light of the candle burning on the table by the wall. The space was dark, unfamiliar. Not the Nest. Where? A fire burned in the stove. Hot. So hot. Not the comforting heat of the poit, but one more demanding. The air was powder-grey with smoke.

Trayor shifted closer. "You're not weak, but you've got a lot to remember. Breathe deep. You've only got a couple of days to make yourself useful, or I'll finish what Shaa started on the Spur."

Sweat ran down Cleod's face and into his eyes. He pressed them shut. Shaa. The Spur. Fire and damnation. What he would not give to have destroyed the monster in that moment... If he had not failed then, Leiel would still be herself. The scars that plagued him would have been worth the pain to earn them. He would not have wasted so many years furtively riding across Arnan, running from himself.

As though he had read Cleod's mind, Trayor said, "You've wasted enough of your time." He shoved Cleod onto his back on the floor. The impact rocked down his spine. Darkness amplified the candle's dancing light to warped trails that blurred into Gweld-light and swirled overhead like aurora. Cleod's stomach heaved again, but there was nothing in him to offer up in response.

"The two of us, Cleod. Draigon-damn me, but you and I made a formidable pair. I'm the greatest Draighil who's ever lived, but *still* the Draigre mumble your name under their breath. You're the monster under their bunks. I've yet to figure out if they *want* to be you, or are afraid they might end up like you."

Trayor shifted, settled back on his heels. "You know, Hoyd never got over the shame of having you as his mentor. The fool spent his whole life trying to prove he didn't carry the stink of your disgrace."

Cleod coughed smoke, and the hard planks of the floor pressed at his shoulder blades and the points of his hips, drove the ache through his entire body. He sucked breath. "And you?" The demand was hoarse and brittle.

"Draigon blood washes away all."

"He died."

"He died gloriously, finally rid of your taint."

"You. You killed Wynt." Cleod gathered strength, rolled a little and propped himself on one arm to meet Trayor's gaze. "The *two* of you."

Trayor smiled, half lit, half bent in the dim, dancing light.

Cleod stared, and smile tugged at his lips. "You *need* me." He shoved himself into a sitting position, through the nausea and shaking that accompanied the action. After all these years, he was needed. Would Trayor be here if that was not the case? Would the Enclaves have sanctioned the use of so much cuila to quell the trance-pangs of a worthless man? So many years. So much doubt...and guilt. If he allowed acknowledgment of the ever-present twist in his gut, that would be its name. Leiel's face skittered through his mind. What he knew now...

Trayor's scowl torqued his facial scars into gruesome lines, ridged like sticks piled to burn. "I need what you *know*. That it's attached to the rest of you is, at best, an unwelcome burden."

Cleod laughed, and the sound pushed back the pain and unease lurking in the darkness and in his body. Cuila smoldered, hot in his lungs, and his laughter carried it on his exhalation. To be needed for something more than guard duty and pandering to arrogant merchants... His heart beat heavy, a deep thudding that pressed into his gut and settled the roil of his belly. "My knowledge and my sword and...what else?" At the base of Cleod's skull, something beat furiously, sharp-clawed and panicked. He shook his head, rattled the frantic warning into silence. Duty. Loyalty. What did he owe anyone when so much loomed unfinished? The need that burned and flamed behind his eyes glazed the surface of all, permeated every sense. Purpose.

"You upright beside me, to explain to the Melbis Council we're both needed to defeat what's coming out of the sky for their girl."

Cleod grinned. "It must burn you, the idea of me standing with you."

Trayor pushed to his feet with a grunt, turned away. Something about that was wrong, that Tray found it so easy to turn his back, but why that would be...? The answer skirted the edge of Cleod's mind, refused to take shape.

Once again, Cleod pushed to his knees. For a moment he swayed. Why was he so off balance? Then he staggered upright.

Trayor turned to face him, looked him up and down. His smile was tense. "I'll stand wherever I need to to bring down Shaa."

Bring down Shaa. The words rang and bit, clattered through Cleod's mind. Yes. It was worth standing with anyone to see that goal achieved.

"You'll need these."

A folded bundle landed with a slap on the table between them. Cleod stared at the uniform.

He fought vertigo, stepped closer. A moment of hesitation, then he reached to caress the black leather. A turn of his wrist spread the jerkin open, and he sucked breath at the sight of the copper-scaled hide that formed patches across the back and side of the shirt. He pulled the pants free. The right hip had been almost completely replaced. The copper was starkly bright against the classic tone of the uniform.

Something rolled up from low in his belly. He named it pain. He named it relief. But the accompanying pulse pounding in his neck told him that what he was feeling was something else entirely. Choking a little, he looked at Trayor. "These are mine." Not newly his. But the very leathers in which he had battled Shaa on the Spur. The memory of his reflection in dawn-lit glass hovered, along with the pride he had felt in that moment. "The Ehlewer kept them? *You* kept them?" The thought staggered. All these years, had the Ehlewer still been waiting? Still held a place for him?

Trayor's face twisted again. "I had them repaired." He planted his palms on the table and leaned in and met Cleod's gaze.

Copper. Old knowledge arose, lifted from the depths of his mind on the memory of hours spent in the Ehlewer Enclave's library. "The Draigon, Wynt."

"Hoyd deserved a better death than he got. You can at least honor him."

Hoyd again. Something tugged at Cleod's mind and he frowned. "He was Draighil. How was he supposed to die if not fighting?"

Trayor straightened, turned away. "Don't speak of him again."

Understanding came, unwelcome. "He *didn't* die fighting." Why should that matter? And yet, somehow it did, because Trayor went stiff, neck rigid. His reply was clipped.

"He died. You've no right to care how." Trayor yanked open the door. "Get dressed. We meet the Council in an hour, and you need to at least look the part."

The slam of the door cracked through Cleod's head, and he swayed a little. His fingers curled, pressed into the once-familiar leather. The scent of cuila unfurled, and he blinked, raised the pants. Slick and shiny, they shown with the oil used to keep them supple, an oil that carried the odor of the vision plant. He frowned, lifted the fabric to his face and breathed deep. Sight bloomed, shifted, and he rocked a little as Gweld yanked at his senses. But his stomach rebelled again and he dropped the clothing, staggered back, pressed the heels of his hands against his eyes. Gweld dropped from his awareness like a hot stone too quickly clutched.

His knees found the floor again with a crack that disintegrated all muscle control, and he had to reach out his hands to break his fall. Bent like a dog on the dirty floor, he heaved for air as moisture streaked his face. Damn them all. Trayor. Hoyd. Leiel. And the Draigon. Especially the Draigon. It was long past time they paid for everything.

CHAPTER 39

Cleod

How had he ever tolerated politicking and mindless chatter? Cleod stared out the window at the dusty street and the equally dusty people moving through it. The old glass warped the scene, bent and turned it, and the voices behind him were a similarly unfocused blur of anger and worry.

Simple and clear, the proposal Trayor laid out before the Melbis Council had them pacing the room, spewing protests and counter arguments. Cleod turned to watch. Fingers pointed his way. Voices raised. A short man with the same pale Farlan look that marked Trayor cursed Cleod for his very existence.

Cleod smiled. He had missed this. The rush of power, the fear that signaled respect as they looked at him. Nowhere in all the years on the trail with Kilras had Cleod received this veneration, owed him through his value and training.

"It's unheard of!" the short man said, his voice crisp with declaration. "This could doom us. An unprecedented act in violation of the agreement—"

"Not unprecedented," Trayor said.

"Not?" An old man in the back of the room stepped forward as he spoke.

The smile that took over Trayor's face lacked only fangs to make it more vicious. The councilmen pulled back a little. "Hoyd is credited with the death of Wynt in Giddor. He earned, with his death, the right to claim the Draigon's."

Cleod straightened, his throat suddenly dry. For a moment, the scent of Cuila filled his nose, memory touched stronger than it had been in years by his recent reintroduction to the smoke. *The arrogant Farlan boy, pinch-faced and miserable on the infirmary cot, trying his best not to puke what little he had managed to consume in the wake of his first session of Gweld training.* What had it meant for Hoyd, that Cleod, his chosen mentor, had abandoned the Ehlewer? A tingle ran from the base of Cleod's skull along his scalp. His fingers curled into fists before he shook his head and forced himself to relax. Draighil died. That was the nature of their work, when they failed.

And yet he, Cleod, having failed, was alive. He pressed his lips together. A failure he would now redeem. He had been tricked, betrayed, by the Enclaves, by the monster Shaa, by Leiel. Her face flashed, unlined and vibrant against the canvas of his mind. For a moment his breath caught, then Trayor's voice cut the angry cacophony filling the room.

"The Draigon that calls for your Sacrifice is *Shaa*, you fools. I have killed more Draigon than any man who has ever lived. And only one living man has ever faced that monster and survived. He stands in this room with me. To kill the king of the Draigon, will take more than one Draighil. Tossing out tradition is a small price to pay."

Silence fell, hovered a long moment, then was thrown aside by a frustrated outburst from the short man. He flung an arm out toward Cleod. "*That man* is no Draighil! You come to us with promises that are half-threats and expect us to trust you and this—this—" Words failed him, and he simply glared between Trayor and Cleod. "The price you ask is more than tradition. You threaten us all with a slow death should you fail."

"You assume we will. We did not in Giddor."

"You lost one of your own! That's why you needed to bring in this half-drunk peasant."

Cleod dropped his chin and fixed his gaze on the man. "Would you do it, then?" he said, his voice a low sliver of malice thrown straight toward the short man. It pierced. The man stepped back.

"You are no Draighil," the short man said again, though his voice trembled.

That drew a smile. "You're braver than you seem," Cleod said. "But I have always been a Draighil. Before my first day of training, I was one." *A glimpse of silvered water, the scent of crushed oak leaves...*

Cleod felt the Gweld-backed flicker of Trayor's glance, smiled.

Trayor laughed. "Arrogant cefreid."

"That's long been my advantage," Cleod said. *The whispered sound of a page turning, old paper, carefully handled...* He blinked, drew himself straighter, rolled his shoulders back. "Never having to live up to Farlan expectations."

"Whatever your reckless goals, we will not condone them." This from a new voice that wavered with age. Cleod shifted his gaze, and Trayor turned to face a stooped man seated in the back corner of the chamber. "We've bent once already, these last days, to the will of that Draigon-sent witch. We'll not bend further, to satisfy your need for spectacle."

"Though the witch did say the bargain might be altered," the short man said.

"This was far from what she meant!" The man in the back snapped out the words.

"Witch?" Trayor demanded. "One of those haughty, Draigon-loving bitches sent to make your decisions for you?" He stepped forward, wove through the scattered council chairs until he stood before the old man. "One came here?"

"One often comes," the old man said as he looked up at the pale Draighil. "You should not be so surprised, Draighil. The Draigon always get what they want."

The Councilman's words went through Cleod like a hunting bolt. Leiel. They had met Leiel. The Draigon had wanted Leiel. "Who did they want this time?" he said.

"Teska Healer." A young voice this time. Cleod did not turn to acknowledge the speaker. Not one man in this room mattered. Not even Trayor. The only person that mattered at all was the woman they had selected—who had been selected for them—to be given to the Draigon. How had he ever thought that men such as these mattered at all?

"Teska Healer," Cleod repeated. "She must be special to rate the attention of Shaa."

Trayor swung around and glared at Cleod.

Cleod narrowed his gaze at the other man. The blink of an eye, and the Draighil's image shifted. *Kilras held out a steaming mug, his face opened into a grin, laughter crinkling his eyes. "I'll teach you to make the best coffee in Arnan, if you sober up long enough to pay attention."* Cleod's diaphragm drew taut and he forced a breath, his attention back to the council room. He was where he was supposed to be. Exactly where he should have been all these years. Too much time wasted, those years on the trail. What had been the purpose of any of that? A shake of his head and he broke his gaze from Trayor's.

The pale Draighil scoffed, swept his gaze from face to face among the Councilmen. "Get her," he said. "Go through whatever ceremony you require to satisfy your traditions. Whoever she is, Shaa is coming for her. You have two Draighil ready to face the monster. We have offered our service. Accept it, or face the consequences of me telling all of Melbis you refused to try to save this girl."

CHAPTER 40

Leiel

Leiel leaned against the wall of the trade office in the narrow passage between it and the bank. The heat was unrelieved even in the deepest shadows, and she spared a moment of pity for the people gathered and sweating on the town common.

For any other naming, she would be present in the crowd to confirm the choice she had demanded. Not that her presence was ever necessary. Never had a council dared oppose the will of the Draigon. Despite the terrible shift events had taken, it was unlikely such defiance would start with this choosing. But Cleod was in that crowd. And the dark turn in his behavior since Trayor's arrival in Melbis left too great a possibility of vicious reaction should he spot her among the onlookers. What had happened?

She frowned. What had Trayor possibly said to have turned Cleod so completely from the constancy and support of his work and friends in the caravan? For three days, she had witnessed Kilras's determined attempts to seek Cleod out, to talk with him. But it was as though he had never parted with the Enclave, never abandoned the values of the Draighil. He and Trayor were again settled in a united front, paired in purpose as they had been that long ago day in Adfen when they had laughed and chatted on the Tower balcony as her name was called.

Yet, when she had watched Kilras and Cleod return to Melbis, her sense of her old friend had held a calm she had not anticipated after his violent response to her presence and her truth.

She closed her eyes and shook her head. Draigon Weather. And, once again, she and Cleod were at the heart of the storm.

The ties spun between you and Cleod Draighil, they hold the potential to be the binding or unbinding of all Arnan. Gahree's strange words churned Leiel's gut. When she and Cleod were children, the stories they had told each other had been full of hope, dreams for a future that paired their lives and their adventures for as far as they could carry imagination. Then, thirty had seemed old, forty impossibly ancient. Now, Cleod approached that mortal mark, while she looked forward to a future in which that span of life was marked by a single day passing. Her story and Cleod's—she had thought it ended long ago, on the rocky spine of the Spur—until she had seen him at the Seebo, strong as she remembered, proud and yet strangely humbled, laughing, but still angry. Still a man half-driven by the destiny he had once forged for himself.

And she had known their tale was not yet over—not while he had within him the drive and strength to face Shaa again. He would do it. Not for the sake of the honor of the Draighil, or of the Enclaves, or even for his own pride. He would have done it for her, to correct what he thought was his failure to save her, and keep the promise he had made so long ago. The same Cleod she had adored as a child. The same Cleod whose determination to comfort her had nearly destroyed them both.

Now, the worst turn of his best aspects seemed once again to have claimed him. He and Trayor had been side-by-side for days. What had happened?

"Leiel Draigon."

Her eyes snapped open.

A man in a broad-brimmed, burgundy hat gazed at her across the narrow space. Old Gods! How had he gotten so close to her without any warning at all?

An arid breeze kicked up dust between them, but he did not break her gaze to protect his eyes. They had never met, but he was no stranger. Since the day she had delved into his first letter home, she had formed a heady respect for him, one backed by curiosity and an appreciation of his accomplishments. His silence alone—to have spent decades traveling Arnan with never a slip to indicate his true origin—was worthy of awe. And he had sought out Cleod in her friend's worst time of need. That had earned him, at the very least, her undying gratitude.

"Kilras," she said, her voice pitched low in the dry air. "I have wanted to meet you for many years."

A turn of his lips faded before it became a smile.

She straightened away from the wall. "I suppose the same cannot be said of you."

"I wished to never meet you."

She held his gaze. He was asking the same thing Gahree had asked: why she had not trusted him to know what was going on with Cleod and to intervene before it went too far. "Gahree and I expected you to take the southern route to Melbis. And Shaa—at the Seebo—what you found —" She shook her head. "Kilras—Cleod defied the entire class order of Arnan to become a Draighil. He did that for my sake. And he thought he failed. He's never forgotten. He's never resigned himself. But we have, all of us, always underestimated Cleod's need to finish what he starts."

The next words formed in her mind, but she hesitated. Giving herself credit for the motivations of others was pure arrogance. But that was old thinking, drawn from her youth when she had not allowed herself to recognize her true worth. Cleod had always been influenced by those around him, especially when being so had let him access the parts of himself that needed to seek a higher purpose. He had done it with her, with the Enclaves, even with Kilras. What had happened on the Spur—and failed to happen—would always matter to Cleod. She breathed deep, let it out. "And we have underestimated that need, especially, when it relates to *me.*"

Kilras took off his hat, ran his hand through his long hair. He held the hat a moment, then traced his fingers along the brim and put it back on, casting his face into shadow. "I know," he said. "But how was revealing yourself an answer to that?"

She took a stepped toward him. "In Adfen, in the Tower, I tried to speak to him—but I could not tell him the truth. He was lost in what he had spent a lifetime making of himself. But now—I have read your words, I know the man you have helped him become. That man, I thought I might be able to reach."

"But you didn't count on the strength of his training."

"I didn't count on him hating the Draigon more than he cared for me."

Kilras shook his head. "He hates them, now, because of more than his training. He hated Draigon because he thought he let them kill you. And now because he thinks they've corrupted you. Outside the influence of the Enclaves, even that hatred's manageable. That's not why he is standing beside Trayor today."

She studied him, the sun-wrought creases around his eyes, the casual strength of his stance. Yes. This man would always stand for Cleod, as Cleod had always stood for her. "What changed?"

He shook his head. "What's changed in Cyunant, Leiel, that the Draigon are showing their true selves to their potential killers?"

Of course. Everything she knew about the man demanded forthright clarity. "It's not what has changed in Cyunant. It's what has changed in Arnan."

"You mean Wynt's death."

She bowed her head a moment, nodded. How many years had it been since anyone not of Cyunant, not Draigon, had spoken with such knowledge of the true nature of the Sacrifice? "I am sorry," she said. "You were friends."

He gave a single, crisp nod. "What happened?"

The breeze kicked again, dislodged a few strands of hair from the tie holding it off her neck. She reached up to tuck it back, took the seconds to consider her words. "Two Draighil," she said. She opened herself as she spoke, to measure his reaction within the trembling colors of her Gweld-expanded senses. The cool, blue light around him did not so much as shimmer, though his gaze narrowed at her words. How had Cleod never noticed Kilras's ability to bend perception?

"Two?"

"Hoyd Draighil was given credit for her death, but we know Trayor was there."

"That's why both you and Gahree came to Melbis."

Leiel let out a short laugh. "I am not surprised by how much you know, Kilras, but it is disconcerting. How has Cleod not recognized what you can do?"

He offered her a half-smile. "There hasn't been a day since I met Cleod that I let myself seek the light in his presence." He glanced toward the Common, where the crowd was now singing. "As to why he is *there*—He was back in control when he left the caravan—a feat to be respected, given the shock you gave him. I expected him back by late meal."

"Trayor Draighil, then."

"Yes. He's always been as dangerous to Cleod as ercew. He's the only Ehlewer who could influence Cleod. And I think I know how."

Her stomach did a flip. "More than words," she said. "We both know how many of those it takes to move Cleod."

"Cuila."

"Cuila? The vision herb the Enclaves use to ease their entrance into Gweld?"

Kilras nodded his head. "After the battle on the Spur, do you think Cleod took so quickly to ercew out of self-pity? He *needed* it."

Leiel straightened. "You're saying his cravings began with the cuila?"

"The use of cuila isn't about assisting trance. Or easing its aftermath."

Bile rose in the back of Leiel's throat. She swallowed it back, pushed down the new flare in her belly that marked a flare of rage. She spoke low, straining to suppress the anger that threatened to overwhelm her tone. "Then the only reason Cleod was able to break with the Enclaves was because he became a drunk."

"Yes." Kilras sighed. "They let him go because they never dreamed the ercew would work. They thought if he didn't drink himself to death, he'd never be strong enough to survive without either ercew or the cuila. Dead, useless, or returned to their fold—those were the options they saw."

"But how would Trayor talk Cleod into burning—?" she began, but then raised a hand and shook her head to dismiss any answer he might offer. How did not matter. And the who was obvious. *Why* mattered more, and she almost asked that question as well. But again, a few seconds of consideration brought the answer. "Two Draighil. The two greatest who have ever lived," she said. "Set to kill the mightiest Draigon known."

Kilras turned away a little, gazed down the length of the alley toward the street as a roar of approval pulsed through the streets of Melbis. "It's done," he said. He looked over his shoulder at her.

Their eyes locked. She nodded. The more complicated truth remained unspoken between them.

"Two Draighil," he said. "And two Draigon."

The top of her mouth was dry, as the question he had not asked hung in the air between them. "I cannot kill him."

"Then he will kill Shaa," Kilras replied. "Or he will kill you."

CHAPTER 41

Leiel

From the edge of the tree line, the hill sloped away toward the plains. Browned grasses twisted in the dry breeze, which bent shifts of color over the undulating surfaces of their strands. In the distance, the rooftops of Melbis formed a ripple, like a log afloat in a wind-whipped lake. Beyond, a low rise billowed with smoke, pluming into the bright sky, a smoldering scar cut toward the sun.

Gahree bent her head as Leiel finished speaking and said nothing. No surprise graced her expression.

Leiel's throat went dry. "You knew," she said. "You knew about the cuila. What it does."

Gahree smiled, tipped her gaze to meet Leiel's. "Of course I knew. As you did, had you stopped to consider."

Leiel drew a breath, bit back hard words forming on her lips. How could she have known? What did she know of cuila? What had Cleod told her of Gweld training? The day at the farm when he had mentioned it so long ago...*the training makes you sick, but the elders have a plant they burn that counters it...* Maybe not those exact words, but something close. Gweld training made him sick. Gweld training. But that was not possible. She knew that now. Gweld was a natural state for those able to access it at all. Anyone capable of finding Gweld should find it as easy as breathing. The cuila. All along, it had been the cuila that caused the suffering. How could she not have made the connection? Only outside influence could chain Gweld to a pained response in the body—and train it so deep it would never go away.

"You once told me it was being forced to conform to a way of learning that made Gweld painful." Leiel paused, pressed her lips together. "That's exactly what they use the cuila to create. The plant is what molds them all." She shook her head, closed her eyes. "Even free of that drug all these years, Cleod still feels pain after touching Gweld." She looked over at the older woman.

A nod from Gahree. "The plant is powerful—from the first day he was exposed, it altered him, body and mind. He will never be free of its influence. We have sought a cure, through the centuries, but even our knowledge has fallen short." She tipped her head toward the fires burning in the distance. "And there awaits the cost of our failure."

Leiel stared at the smoke. "That day on the Spur—I never asked you—how did you let him live?"

"Distraction on a level he was unprepared for. I let him become aware that I could join him in his trance."

"You touched his mind."

Gahree offered a tip of her head. "What could ever have prepared him for that?"

What indeed? All their childhood, Draigon lore meant tales of monsters and raging beasts. "The Enclaves truly don't have any idea what the Draigon are?"

"Oh, they have some idea," Gahree corrected. "The way a dog knows heavy weather is coming. Those men have been around long enough to have acquired the knowledge they need. The Elders know we are not simply animals. But beyond that, how much have they ever been willing to let themselves suspect? Believing we are what we are— that would twist the tail of the world they have built and send it yipping all the way back across the Ardrows Dur."

Leiel laughed a little, but the lightness of the moment did not hold. In the distance, hatred and swords awaited the woman beside her. "I told Kilras I cannot kill Cleod. But there are two of them, Gahree. Two Draighil..."

"Yes."

"They could destroy you."

"They can."

Leiel drew a breath. "It's my fault. If I hadn't—"

"Do you think, wild daughter, that Trayor would not have sought out Cleod if you had not done so first? This was planned, long before either of us had a chance to influence events. Even had Kilras led his people on the southern route and Cleod never crossed my sign at the Seebo, Trayor would still have found Cleod, and they would still wait for me on that hill. But the world has turned in our favor. Now, Cleod knows what you are. And that is an advantage."

A jolt twitched Leiel's entire body. "How? He *knows*. How will he not use that against us? When he tells Trayor, tells them all—"

"You assume that he has already done so. But we have seen no sign of that. No armies march north to Cyunant. No farmers gather in fields with pitchforks and fire to burn witches. And they will, Leiel, once the truth is known."

"So he *will* tell."

"Of course. What man have you ever met who could resist proving how much knowledge he holds?"

Almost, Leiel laughed. There was more truth in that statement than she cared to contemplate in the moment. "Then *how* is any of this to our advantage? If they kill you today—"

"Then they will have used that knowledge to do so. Because Cleod has cared for you, Leiel. What threatens today is not his knowledge, but his fear. He has loved something he does not understand. And he is a man who *must* understand. The two of you have always had that in common. You are within him. Whatever happens today, he will carry your words and memory with him. You can shape his future, as much as the cuila."

"But how?"

"That, wild daughter, will depend much on what this days brings."

Leiel shuddered. "We've got a fight ahead. And not just today."

"Just so. But we are ready."

"Ready for the Enclaves, and the entire Farlan army, to march on Cyunant?"

"If it comes to that."

"We're too few."

"Are we?" The woman turned her green-gold eyes to meet Leiel's. "Truth and her tales are not the limited purview of the Draigon. We are as alone as we perceive ourselves to be. Were you alone on the farm, all those years?"

Leiel shook her head. "No. But Torrin and Elda—"

"Are what? Not strong?"

"They are not an army."

Gahree laughed. "What is an army?"

"Trained and paid." The Draigon were the former, and the latter did not matter among them, but something else did, something they did not have. "An army is numbers."

"No. An army is a gathering of those organized to fight for a purpose." Gahree looked out toward the rising smoke. "And purpose we have always had. And today, ours is Teska Healer. Today, she is what matters most. Do not forget that, Leiel. Teska holds a promise we cannot afford to let die, no matter any other cost."

"The cuila...what will it do to her?"

"Teska is half-Draigon by knowledge. She should be safe."

Leiel nodded, not quite understanding, but accepting. Prime worry reasserted itself, and prime solution. "Two Draighil. Two Draigon."

Gahree shook her head. "No. I will go alone to fight them. You must stay in reserve. If the worst happens, save Teska. She is what matters."

Leiel drew a hard breath, but Gahree spoke again into the space where Leiel might have offered argument. "You cannot kill Cleod, wild daughter. Even to save me or Teska. You do not have that in you. But turned as he is by the cuila, he would not hesitate to strike you down. If the choice comes to that, it is only I who can make it. Now, ready yourself. Even for a Draigfen, it's a long run across those plains."

Most of the rolling expanse of grasslands lay behind Leiel before she felt Shaa take flight from the hills beyond Melbis. Deep inside, the sense of anticipation, of *lifting,* flipped Leiel's belly, and the earth seemed to fall away beneath her feet. Into the darkness, black against black in a new-moon night sky, the great teacher pressed wings through mountain air and gained height over the curve of the earth.

Ahead on the low hill, the fires set to mark the place of Sacrifice flickered and flared in the dry breeze. Distance that had taken Leiel all day to cover on foot and with stealth, would be crossed in moments by Gahree in her Great Shape. The wind shifted and the acrid-sage scent of cuila filled Leiel's nose. She turned her head, closed her eyes, felt the burn of the drugged air in her throat. It was not the first time she had smelled it, but it was the first time since she had shared Kilras's knowledge of the terrible purpose of the plant. The herb pushed at her mind, and she blinked, refocused. This was the thing that had turned Cleod's mind in his youth, the thing that twisted and reclaimed him now. If not for the change wrought by the taking of the great shape, it would be working its violence within her as well.

The breeze changed again, carrying the smoke away to the east, and she looked again to the fires burning in an uneven ring around the girl chained to the post. Would the cuila touch her, or was she, as Gahree asserted, by nature immune to such influences? Oh, the waste and danger if that were not true!

Shadows moved in the flickering light, cast lean and erratic by the movement of the flames. Which was Cleod? The sense of him was so changed since just a few weeks ago, since she had followed him over the plains from the Seebo. Here, in the night, she could not distinguish the pulse of his mind from Trayor's. Two Draighil, then. Two men bent on murder and victory, and by pride. What had she done? What had she set in motion through her arrogant need to reconnect with a man she had long ago abandoned to his own life? Hope and caring. Not destiny, but the best of all dreams. Did any of that matter now? Or was it the only thing that still could? Her stomach clenched and she lengthened her stride.

Above, beyond her, the sky carried the flexed beat of ancient wisdom. A chill erupted along Leiel's shoulders. Suddenly, with all that she was, she wanted to cry *halt*. To Shaa. To Cleod. To the night itself. Even on the Spur, with all that she hoped for, and all that she loved, in danger, she had never once doubted the outcome, the rightness of what was about to happen. But something was different this night. Different from any Sacrifice she had stood witness to for the last decade. More than the fact that two warriors awaited Shaa—or that one was a man she wanted to protect more than she wanted her own life—something she could not define signaled *wrongness* in the core of her.

Then a shadow that was more than night passed above her and it was too late for any thought to matter. A cry rose from the hill ahead, and Leiel broke into a run. Ahead on the rise, shapes were moving again, blurs of changing angles, and her mind blazed with fire and the tumbling colors of Gweld. She ran, blurring into expanded awareness as she gained ground, broke over the top of the rise at the edge of a circle marked by fire.

CHAPTER 42

Cleod

The only indication of the creature's approach was the disappearance of stars as the giant body blocked their light with its flight. Dual-edged, now, the comforting bonfires set ablaze around the perimeter of scorched earth Trayor had designated as their battlefield. Though they marked a safe boundary, they had done damage to night vision. Smoke wafted on the wind and made it impossible to tell whether the air moved on its own, or as herald of the Draigon's arrival.

Cleod craned his neck back, side-stepped over the ashy ground as the beast swept overhead, banked hard, and disappeared downslope. Shadow and silence ruled. Then impact. The earth shuddered, rocked him on his feet. Beside him, Trayor staggered, too, a curse ripped from his lips as the ground heaved.

The shock of the landing seared up Cleod's spine, and the breath he had just drawn stuck in his lungs. Energy streamed from the creature across the entire range of his senses. The air rippled with ghostly flames and the earth trembled and he blew out hard as he caught his balance. Behind him, Teska Healer cried out—in fear, in warning— as Leiel had once done.

Beside him, Trayor drew his sword. The tremble of metal sliding along leather, the song of steel striking the air, pulled Cleod back into the night. Teska was not Leiel. Leiel was—Leiel was somewhere else. Leiel was *something* else.

Cleod stepped to the side, sliding into the shadows cast by the bonfires. He reached over his shoulder, found the crystal-topped hilt of his sword. The blade pealed as he pulled it free, and his senses rode the sound, flying into the night in search of the creature he had come to destroy.

Even as Gweld engulfed him, a shadow pulsed along the rise of the hill. The air vibrated with a great breath indrawn, and the movement of air as giant wings lifted somewhere in the darkness, flattening grasses in the generated wind.

Daylight had reigned during his previous encounters with Draigon, and so no experience prepared him. The night exploded with the true measure of the Draigon's brilliance and ferocity. Pulsed motion became a tinder-lit outline, indistinct, before it seared itself into a shape etched cleanly against the darkness, every scale rimmed in fire, a blazing line drawing, burning red and bringing each smoldering inch of the Draigon into perfect relief. Heat cast outward as the great wings arched against the bowl of the sky, impossibly wide, impossibly streaming light and fanning the bonfires into flaring mania. Shadow, cast aside, absorbed the pulse of heated exhale, and the dirt Cleod stood on caught the generated heat, pressed it upward through his boots, stripped moisture from every cavity of his body, and left him hot and hollowed to the core.

Shaa. More than he remembered. More than he had ever dared let himself recall.

As Gweld blossomed around and through him, he knew—it did not matter that there were two men on this hilltop. A hundred men, a thousand, could not face what stood before them, and survive. Any other Draigon, perhaps they could defeat. But Shaa…? What madness had ever led him to believe he could conquer such a creature? To think he was mightier than the thing before him? That a fight against such a Draigon could ever be fair?

Memory trembled, flared—a pulling back, a shout uttered in desperation—*Where was it written that any fight was ever meant to be fair?*

Across from him, Trayor let out a cry and charged the waiting monster. A heartbeat. Trayor's voice in the poit. *I learned to cheat from you.*

There *was* a way to triumph. Because something more important than victory graced the hilltop, and the value of that thing to the Draigon, Cleod suddenly knew. Understanding burst through him with the impact of a lightning strike.

Teska. Teska was why the Draigon was here, as Leiel had been the reason on the Spur. And if Teska was the thing the Draigon valued, she was also the thing he would use to break the beast.

Ignoring the sudden churning of his gut and the scream rising in his mind, Cleod pivoted and ran for the woman chained behind him.

Chapter 43

Leiel

Consciousness, multiplied and weighted with purpose, slammed through her—Cleod, Shaa, Teska, Trayor—the last ferocious with a rage that threatened to sunder all it touched. Burning through Gweld, Trayor's mind snapped like a chained beast at her senses. She focused thought, ignored the violence of his presence. Above, billowing air blasted with the sweep of mighty wings. Motion beyond sight marked the deadly dance engaged outside the ring of fires—Trayor and Shaa, speed and brutality and cruelty and blood, a half-recognized roil of chaotic violence masked by darkness and smoke.

A heartbeat, gasping smoke and air and cuila, and her gaze found Cleod across the embered earth. He was dressed as she remembered from the Spur, but the black of his fireleather was now patch-worked with ragged panels of copper scale. Her heart skipped, but she forced attention away from grief.

His gaze was fixed, wide and tense, on the sky. As she watched, a shudder ran through him, left him slack-jawed. Then he clamped his mouth shut, broke, and ran. For a moment, hope thudded her heart in her ribs, that he might choose escape, choose not to fight. But his sword was in his grasp, and too much purpose marked his action.

Out of the firelight, to the sounds of battle engaged among winds whipping over the land and a scream of rage from Trayor, Cleod bore down on Teska. Chained to the post, the healer had no recourse, and not even the space of a breath to dodge his approach. She dropped low, but he caught her arm and yanked her back upright, met her gaze as he leveled the blade of his sword against her throat.

Leiel froze in mid-step, her lips parted. Her thoughts tumbled as she tried to absorb what she was seeing. Air whipped her, and the sage-bitter odor of cuila filled her nose again. Her Draigfen body held the plant's influence at bay. But Cleod's gaze changed as the gust hit him, and she knew, with all she was, that his actions, if still chosen, rode the smoke on instinct born of pure desperation.

But who he was in the moment mattered less than the fact that too much distance separated them. Should he draw back on the blade, not even her Draigon-touched reflexes were enough to bridge the space in time to save Teska.

CHAPTER 44

Cleod

Light erupted in streams of green and gold, and heat blasted him, shook every particle of the air. But no fire backed it, only dry waves of wind and anger. Shaa raged, attention torn now between the battle she fought and the threat to the Healer. The beast's frustration battered Cleod's expanded senses, and he tipped the blade up a hair, snicked the thinnest line of blood from Teska Healer's throat. A hint of copper scent flicked through the air, and his stomach flipped again. Then, within Gweld, he heard Trayor laugh, dark lines ripping through the blaze of color. Spears of fire darted through the night as Shaa and the Draighil wove a dance of rising violence.

At the base of Cleod's skull, another presence pressed a scream though his awareness. For a moment he could not differentiate it from Shaa's. Then the contact came clear, and he understood—Leiel. Leiel in Gweld. Whatever hope he held that he had misunderstood what she now was shattered—exploded through his mind and slashed like knives. He shuddered, body and mind, and the woman in his grasp let out a cry of pure terror as the steel bit a fraction deeper into her flesh.

His mind flailed, and he snatched at the first memory that slipped through. Strong fingers gripped his shoulders, steadying, the touch accompanied by understanding words of assurance. A flash of an instant and his father's voice was more than recalled, it was present. *I know son. But you cannot help her now.* Leiel...? Then fire—only fire—filled the space in his mind where his father's words held sway, and Cleod planted his heel, spun on it, pulling the woman tight against him as he turned. Her hair tangled against his lips, whipped by the searing wind of Shaa's energy as the beast wove and dodged Trayor's motion-blurred strikes. Cleod grabbed Leiel's hair...no...Teska's hair and twisted, forced her head back to reveal the bloody line on her throat. "Leiel!" he shouted, the words shining bright in Gweld as they bent the air. "Leiel, you have a choice! Whatever they have made you, you can redeem tonight."

CHAPTER 45

Leiel

Gweld ringed his words in red light. Old gods how had it come to this? How had she let it? Tears packed the back of her throat, and she stepped forward into the circle of smoky light.

Light flared from him as he caught sight of her. He stiffened, eyes glazed and bright. "They took you from me. As they took your mother from you. I promised Shaa would pay for that. I promised you. I promised."

"You kept it, Cleod." She spoke the purest truth she knew. She pressed it into her words, her tone, into the Gweld that flowed between them. For an instant, the color sense of him changed, lightened and shifted, as he balanced on the edge of understanding the message she sent—his thoughts crossed hers—"*What in the name of all the old gods am I doing here*"—then the wind shifted, a gust from Shaa wings perhaps, and blasted smoke over him and her hope fled as color bled from his energy again. Teska went stiff in his grasp, her eyes wide, and Leiel's stomach dropped as though it were suddenly lined with stone.

"I *will* keep it," Cleod said.

She stepped closer, but it was still not enough. If he pulled back on the sword, there was nothing she could do. Words, again words, to try to reach him. "No one has to die here."

His gaze reflected the flames around them, his hair and Teska's whipped by the air. "Or maybe we all do," he said.

She froze, and watched his eyes go flat and deadly and she felt him as she never had, the expanded presence of him rushing across her mind, his words like brands stamped one after another through her consciousness. "*Who are you to make such a statement? You who played dead for years. You who left me for dead—or worse—on the Spur. This stranger matters more to you than I ever did.*"

Teska's eyes went wide, stark, her pupils blazing in an expanded sea of white. The smell of her fear pressed through the smoke, and Leiel watched as Cleod wrapped his senses around it, enveloped every drop of it, and pushed the emotion through tranced awareness. "*Shaa dies, or I will kill the girl. Shaa dies, or I will see that we all do.*" Leiel rocked back with the force of the thoughts, the pure emotion behind them. The fear was not only Teska's.

With all that she was, Leiel knew he meant it. Pressed beyond reason, his mind poisoned and tumbled, the anger in him so hot she could taste it rushing out of him with his breath—he would cut Teska's throat simply because that act was the only thing in his control.

"Idodben, Cleod!" she shouted, felt the word barely flick against his awareness. Too deep in Gweld, too caught up, too turned within, for even the ancient command to breach, he was bent to his course.

His demand pressed outward, and scraped the edges of the extra-conscious realm, and shook the expanded awareness of all it touched.

Shaa roared in response.

Beyond the ring of flames, battle raged, unseen, part of the cacophony of movement and sound ringing through Gweld and air and bones. The earth shook with striding impact. Steel rang with impact on scales like polished stone, vibration trembling all senses across layers of consciousness. Through it all, Cleod's message echoed.

Laughter skittered through those layers of consciousness, bending and warping planes of color and light. Trayor, lit by triumph as the moment tolled the reason he had sought Cleod out after all these years.

A shriek, unuttered, rose through Leiel's spirit, threatened to pierce her and rip her to pieces, as though the decision Shaa made claimed part of her soul.

Her eyes never left Cleod as Shaa's thoughts exploded across the shifting rainbow sparks that marked Leiel's attuned awareness.

"*Teska must live, Leiel! Her skill and knowledge cannot be lost!*"

"*And your knowledge?*" Leiel sent the thought backed by panic, a roiling that rose from her stomach and leached moisture from her throat. "*Centuries, Gahree!*"

"*All I know has been saved, Leiel Draigon, written down, passed on. There is nothing to be lost in me. Save her. It is our purpose here.*"

"Gahree!" Leiel's cry was lost in a thunderous whirl of wind.

"*I leave the Draighil nothing. Save Teska and go!*"

Chapter 46

Cleod

To Cleod's left, Trayor burst through the smoke pulling after him a lightning-filled explosion of color and noise.

Trayor halted with sword raised, facing a wall of flame that boiled like a pyroclastic plume rising from an erupting volcano. It rolled up to cover the stars, heat pouring from it like liquid over stone.

But it was no Draigon that emerged from the smoke. Small and dark, with hair like black water in moonlight, a naked woman stepped from the roil. Her skin unmarked by soot or flames, she stepped and the earth trembled and the ground smoldered beneath her bare feet. Intention ran through every line of her body, and her arms extended straight down at her sides, hands open and empty, palms toward the Draighil. Her eyes flashed green-gold, the color vivid and strange in the light of dancing flames.

A jolt shot through Cleod. He knew those eyes, bright and consuming. He had faced them in the heat of battle, wide and gleaming in a face that was anything but human. They fixed now on Trayor as she came to meet him. Draigon. Woman. This creature before them, which was she? Leiel—Leiel was also this. His heart pounded up into his throat, and his vision pinholed, then exploded with churning light. Muscles locked around bones that suddenly seemed brittle as twigs within him, as he shook so hard he feared his limbs would snap from the tension.

His chest heaved as he watched Trayor step back, faltering, as the Draighil lowered his sword a fraction.

"No," Cleod choked out, the word barely a whisper. Cleod stepped back, shoved Teska to her knees, and sprinted to join Trayor.

"No!" More powerful than the word was the thought behind it, the scream arcing through Cleod's brain. He punched it through Gweld like a thrown pike, a preternatural bolt, straight into Trayor's back. "*Not a woman! Not a woman!*"

The message carried like the point of a spear, and Trayor gasped, recovered and stepped forward with his sword in motion. The monster in human form died before the blade completed its arc.

Leiel

With a scream rising inside her, Leiel lunged, caught the healer before she fell. But beyond the fires, heat erupted, violent and consuming, and the roar that accompanied it marked a collision of defiance and destiny. Inside, Leiel, too, raged, her eyes tearing and tight, her skin taut over her body as she let go of all she was and hoped and feared, and spiraled into a self greater than she had ever dreamed to be. She changed, body dissolving, unfurling, becoming. And a great limb broke the post holding Teska to the earth as Leiel struck, seeking something that might be vengeance, heart breaking within her at the sound of steel slashing flesh tore through her. *Save Teska and go!* Leiel bent and cradled the girl in her grasp, felt a rip of shock through Gweld that rent a hole through every connection that linked Arnan.

Like debris whipped in a funnel cloud, emotions boiled through the trance state, tore thought from consciousness— individual awarenesses sundered, blended into a swell of chaos that tangled rage and triumph and grief.

Her mind. Trayor's. Screaming. And Cleod. His response stripped past them all. Raging, marked by a shift that was only half-sane. Cleod. He was still Cleod—she saw it in the pain bleeding through Gweld between them—his—hers—so much sadness. So much loss. It changed the light. It burned. It broke...

She snapped her body upward, took wing, and fled before she killed. Or died of grief.

Cleod

Everything became roaring, as though Cleod stood beside a rushing river that plunged over a cliff with impossible purpose. Smoke still rolled into the sky, filled his lungs and nose, as though the air itself cried out, torn, brutalized, and dying in the night.

He braced himself, sucked for breath. The air was still dry and tight. But a new scent burned as well, coppery and stark. At Trayor's feet, the split-open corpse of the dark-haired creature sprawled sightless and limp among blackened grasses. Her blood leaked over her torn flesh, soaking dark into the ground like an offering spilled to revive the drought-blighted landscape. Just the Sacrifice demanded on this day, but turned and molded into a new and startling form. A woman had been meant to die—and one had. Or a creature enough like one that bile rose in Cleod's throat, and he would have turned away had he been able lift his gaze from the body on the ground.

As it was, the world tilted, and he staggered, backed away from the corpse. At the edge of his hearing came the sound of tearing, shrieks of rage and brittle violence barely contained. His body heaved. A great wind pressed down upon him, rocked him, tossed smoke and fire across his vision as a Draigon took flight. As *Leiel* took flight—

Night engulfed him, endless, the darkness stretched so thick and deep in all directions that he doubted the dawn would ever break it. Or perhaps it was only the darkness weighting his lungs and his heart that might never again be lifted to the light. Leiel... The sound and wind of wings carrying a great body into the air. A Draigon that was not Shaa. Leiel, drawing away now, farther into the great black pit that had somehow engulfed them both—

Trayor screamed, a roar of triumph and rage blended in one ferocious sound.

Cleod jerked, then braced as the pale Draighil turned, his face a twisted mask, and lunged with one hand outstretched and a bloodied blade swinging. Instinct took over. Though action was slowed by the thousand emotions feuding within him, Cleod bent and countered, blade rising to meet metal with singing metal.

The swords hummed with impact, and shock ran up Cleod's arms.

"How long? How long have you known?" The demand left Trayor's voice rough and ravaged. "A woman! These monsters are human? How long have you known?" He pulled free, swung again.

Cleod moved back, blocking, dragging in great gulps of hot air and dancing on his feet to keep from stumbling on the uneven ground. Every strike rang deep in his bones and into his skull, and his thoughts tangled and snagged. For an instant Leiel's face wavered in his vision, then fire rolled through his thoughts, and the next blow tore away awareness of everything but survival.

"I asked you how to kill Shaa and all along it was as simple as this? Hoyd died, you gutless cefreid! Bonniri and dozens of others, and all along the monster was only a woman? How long have you known?" Trayor's words were hammer strikes, more brutal than the bashing impact of the sword.

Like a whip crack, a wave of pressure snapped up the length of Cleod's spine, and he snarled out a breath, then twisted and left Trayor staggering. In that delayed instant, Cleod shifted the pattern combat from defense to attack. Three hard blows, steel on steel, sent Trayor down to one knee in the blood-spattered dirt. Cleod glared, blade poised at ready. "And how long have *you* known, Elder of the Ehlewer that the Draigon were more than just beasts? How many have died—or been maimed like me, because the Elders had too much pride to share the truth?"

Trayor stared an instant more, then shoved to his feet and away, put enough distance between them to make further attack inadvisable for either of them.

Cleod lowered his sword, glared back. "*I* have known only since I arrived in Melbis," he said. "You've had how many years?"

"Since I gained the title of Elder," Trayor said. He pointed his sword at the body on the dirt, firelight cast by dancing shadows over the corpse. "What *is* that?"

"What we have always fought." The words came hard. "Why we've never been able to win."

"A *woman?* The Draigon are *women?*"

Cleod could not even swallow. His lips were hot, pressed together in a rigid line that wanted to mar his face like a scar. The old injuries along his hips and shoulder shot needles into his spine and down through his knees. His legs trembled. What was he doing here? The question was wrong. As wrong as Trayor's. As wrong as the answer to either. He tried to shake his head, managed only a twitch that angled his chin down, and left him staring all-too- directly at the dark hair of the woman on the ground. It waved in the sooty dirt like water pushed by a current. Leiel's face drifted through his mind again. The edges of his thoughts echoed with her words, the sound of her wings... He sucked in a breath. "Not women," he said, throat bitter with smoke. "Not *only* women."

"What in damnation does that mean?"

Cleod raised his gaze and met Trayor's in the flickering light of the dying fires. Cleod's hand shook as he slid his sword back into the harness across his shoulders with a snap. "It means you can't kill me yet."

CHAPTER 47

Leiel

The ground fell away beneath her, but the horror spread across it could never be left far enough behind. No tears were possible. Only the pounding of her heart and the dying of light in her vision spoke of the grief flooding her mind. Across every spectrum she could fathom, the world was rendered in darkness, the echo of Gahree's dying became charcoal ripples flaring across the earth and sky.

Crouched between her scaled shoulders, the woman, Teska, shuddered and sobbed. Did she even understand what she had witnessed, the truth of the loss sprawled smoking and bloodied on the plains below? Leiel sought to make sense of it through an awareness blended and expanded within her Great Shape. She formed no understanding herself. Every part of her knew the truth of what had happened, but she could not accept it, nor speak the truth of it even within her own mind.

What had she done? What had she set in motion? The greatest Draigon in a thousand years lay broken and lifeless on the smoldering plains, and the men who had slain her would soon gather themselves to continue the fight.

Teska is what matters. As though Gahree were there speaking the words herself, they pushed, weighty, through grey grief.

Leiel forced focus, sent her thoughts to the sobbing Sacrifice she carried. "*Rest, Teska. I have you. You are safe. Hold tight.*" What else could be done? For this, Gahree had died.

Leiel could not now address the hot rage and pain that tore through each motion of her body and muddied every thought. She must complete her duty here, then get to Cyunant. The other Draigon must already know. The shock of life torn from Arnan had ripped through the air and the land and all aspects of Gweld-touched awareness—but she must carry the word, she and no other. She must bear the tale not only of Gahree's dying, but of her own complicity in it. But first—first she must act as teacher, as mentor. All the things Gahree had once been for her, she must now be for Teska. Teska was who mattered now.

Leiel stretched tension into her wings, banked through the darkness, blocking starlight and sky. She caught the rise of air coming off the line of hills and let its blast carry her on a glide into the shallow valley between rolling ridge lines. One hard beat, another, as leathery skin, stretched taut between great arches of bone, caught thick wind and pressed it into the ground. She slowed, chest lifting, and dropped to earth. Soil and grasses crumbled beneath her, as though impacted by more than just the weight of her body, as though the momentous horror of the grief she carried bore as much mass as the Great Shape she inhabited.

Curled between her wings, Teska shook and swayed with the landing. Leiel bent her neck and craned her head around to look at the woman crouched between her shoulder blades. For a moment, something boiled in Leiel's belly, heavy, and sharp, as though a vertebra had broken loose from somewhere along her spine and stabbed straight through her gut. Not her fault. Not Teska's fault. The sound of a steel striking through flesh, hard and wet and terrible rang through Leiel's mind. But no scream, not a ragged gasp of pain or regret—unless it was her own. Not Teska's fault at all. Only Leiel's. Shaa's death—Gahree's death—

Leiel shuddered. The Great Shape transmitted the tremor through the air and the ground until the trees rocked, pushed by moving air and flexing earth. Teska cried out, staring up into Leiel's eyes.

Dark and tear-filled, the gaze speared Leiel, pulled her back from the brink over which grief had balanced her. She gathered frayed emotions and bent a mighty forelimb, stretched her neck out and away from the woman in an invitation for her to dismount and find what comfort she could in the camp at the edge of a copse of oaks. A camp that, had the night not read them a story of loss, would soon have been filled with wonder-touched laughter and steam rising from brewing tea.

With an effort she hardly knew how to calculate, Leiel pressed a thought into the space where her mind touched Teska's. *"Find what rest you can here. Eat. Wash. Sleep. I will stand guard until I am certain we are not followed this night."*

The healer shook. The rhythm of her sobs vibrated through Leiel's body, but her reply held strength and clarity, as though the pain and fear she expressed through her actions was separate, somehow, from the strength of her will. "Will they try to follow us tonight? They have so much attention to give to the celebration of their victory."

Leiel drew a breath that rocked her massive body. She blinked her great eyes closed, as though doing so could shut out the images conjured by Teska's words. *"I do not think they will follow. But it is best I be certain before I abandon this form. Climb down, Teska. Find what comfort you can. I will join you soon."*

With trembling limbs and a grasp made weak by the witnessed horrors of the night, Teska twisted her body around and lowered herself along Leiel's forelimb to the ground. Silence reigned a moment; no sound or motion filled Leiel's mind. In Gweld, she could see Teska's still shape, immobile in the night, rimmed with the sheeting colors that outlined everything in Leiel's trance vision. Waiting.

Leiel opened her eyes, and Teska's slender, shadow-in-shadow shape came into focus.

"Why are we here?" the healer asked. "You say you will join me...but we cannot fly from here if you—if you are human like me."

Sane questions. Something that might have been relief swept through Leiel. Neither cuila nor witnessed horror had bent the healer's mind.

Though the expression did not translate in the form she now inhabited, the flicker of a smile swept through Leiel's mind, bright enough to flash light across the darkness clouding her thoughts and spirit. Teska was, thank all the old gods, as perceptive as Leiel had been told. She could only hope the rest of the stories of the healer's skills and value had not been exaggerated, that the price all Arnan had paid this night, for this one woman's survival, had been worth it.

No more than smiles or laughter, were tears possible in the Great Shape, but they fell heavy in Leiel's thoughts. The churning pain in her belly did not diminish. *"There are things here, left by Gahree, that I dare not leave for others to find. We must camp here tonight as people, and make our way north in the morning, as people. No one, for a while at least, will be looking for us as we are. In a few weeks, if all goes well, I will take this form again and take you North to your new home."* Even as she sent the thought, doubt filled her like smoke drawn into her lungs. Was anywhere safe now that the Draighil knew the truth? For how long would any of the Draigon continue to have a place to call home?

In the darkness, Teska stood a few seconds, as though she had heard the unspoken thoughts beyond those Leiel had shared. Perhaps she had, Leiel reminded herself. Gweld, for the healer, was not a state entered, but the very place she dwelled. Who was to say if private thoughts, especially powerful thoughts of pain and worry, even existed in her presence?

"Build a fire, Teska Healer. You will find clean clothes and food in the bag hung from the tree beyond the fire pit." Leiel did not wait for a response, just straightened, wings flared, neck crested, and moved away, her steps cracking over the dry earth and spiking thick dust and particles of broken flora into the air. A few strides brought her clear of Teska and the fragile camp, and she leaped, unbent her wings and thrust into the sky with a rush of air that bowed branches and churned water in the stream winding through the narrow vale. The small valley fell away, and for a moment she considered simple, continued flight. Away. Just get away. Leave the bottomless, dark ache that carved its way though her chest the way she left the ground, let the stars guide her through the night to somewhere she could find a way to forget what had unfolded tonight in the wake of her terrible choices... The idea held for a single heartbeat—forget—before the horror of that idea surged through her with all the power of the grief she bore into the sky. Forget Shaa? Forget Gahree? With her cryptic stories and her ringing laugh? Forget the dreams she had passed on and the hope she had engendered? Forget all she had striven and died for? Never. Never. Leiel might, as wildly, wish to forget how to breathe.

She flew south, swept low over the trees dotting the hills. Once she shifted to her natural state, it would be days before she could again gather the strength to take the Great Shape and carry Teska to Cyunant. So, tonight, she would lay Draigon sign away from the camp. That they must travel north was no secret, but she could distract any followers, mislead them about the exact route she and Teska must take toward safety and escape—set false sign and hope it was enough.

CHAPTER 48

Cleod

How can this be a Draigon?" Trayor's voice was raw with strain.

Cleod stared, taking in the whole scene again. Small. Small and dark and bloodied. Shaa. He shook his head. This was the creature that had nearly killed him so long ago? How was that possible?

"They won't believe us." Trayor knelt beside the corpse, stared into its face. "Shaa—this is Shaa? A Draigon took flight with the girl—" He looked over his shoulder at Cleod. "How do I know it's true? This could be anyone."

This could as easily be Leiel. Leiel was also a monster now capable of setting the night aflame, a being of mayhem and death. "There were two. As there are two of us. This is Shaa," Cleod said. "The eyes."

A breeze cleared the smoke for an instant, and he pulled fresh air into his lungs. Mayhem and death—was that what he had once again become? A pounding began above his sinuses, and a tremor begged to claim his limbs.

Trayor bent and shoved dark hair from the woman's face. Her eyes were open, staring into the inky sky, and their color was undimmed, unfaded by death. Green-gold, they caught the dance of fire and reflected it, flashed like gems. With a curse, Trayor jerked back. Cleod's stomach heaved and he turned away, disgorged the hot contents of his stomach into the smoldering sand.

"Draigon-damned witchcraft." Trayor's words were accompanied by the snick of his knife being pulled from its sheath. "Eyes it will be."

A chill raised Cleod's skin. Mouth bitter with bile, he looked up in time to see Trayor grasp the corpse's dark hair and jerk her head back in the sand. Cleod's gut flipped and he lunged, caught the Draighil's wrist, stayed the hand that held the blade. "No."

Trayor jerked free with a snarl. "How dare you—"

"If you cut her, they might fade. She's not really human—who knows how this works? We have to take her whole, to the Council." He released the Draighil's arm. A few seconds passed, then Trayor nodded and sheathed his blade. The shudder that wrung Cleod's body as the knife slid home was pure relief. Those eyes... "Why?" he whispered.

"What?" Trayor gained his feet and faced Cleod.

The headache erupted, and Cleod slid a foot back in the sooty dirt, caught his balance. "Why? Why did she... change?" Why would a creature as powerful as Shaa choose this manner of death, instead of going out in a fight? From the depths of his mind words echoed *I leave them nothing. Take Teska and go.* The healer. The woman—the *creature*—on the ground, had died to save Teska Healer's life. Cleod shook off the thought. "Fireleather. There is nothing of her we can use. Nothing for armor, or weapons. Like this—what use is she?"

Trayor shook his head, and the motion blurred Cleod's sight. Overlash was building. Trayor showed no sign of it. Cleod closed his eyes. Had the years away from Enclave training made him really that much weaker? Or had something else changed? The small muscles at the back of his neck tightened, pulled at his shoulders and jaw. He frowned. *Kilras*...would that his old friend was here...

Cleod shook himself. No.

Kilras had no part in what needed doing by Draighil. For the years of work and comfort the Dorn had offered, Cleod would always be grateful. But such a life could never have been his final destiny. How had he ever considered that it could?

He looked at Trayor, paler than ever in the fading flickers of firelight. What good was friendship in the face of a destiny chosen long ago? His path had been marked years before he and the Dorn met. And, if Shaa's death this day had not brought the resolution and comfort he had dreamed of for so many years, it had opened the door to something even more powerful. The final destruction of *all* the Draigon. Even, and perhaps most especially, the thing that had been Leiel Sower.

Hollow, the wind kicked up and blasted the thickening smoke of the smoldering fires over him, shrouded him in swirling darkness so dense he could hardly see. Overlash hovered, kept at bay by the cuila—and even that would not hold much longer. He pulled himself straight, though the muscles in his hips and and back burned, and locked down pure will as his weapon to stave off collapse. In Melbis, the Council waited, and what a victory they were about to witness.

The room rumbled with raised voices and milling bodies. Through a haze of pain that left him nearly sightless, Cleod squinted at the Councilmen as they circled the cloth-draped body sprawled in the middle of the floor. Overlash wrung him. His throat, ravaged by smoke and heat, burned raw as he tried to swallow. He lifted a cup in an unsteady hand, but it shook so badly he could not take a drink. Forced to remain upright by pure necessity, he braced his stance and let the Council's chatter sweep over him.

"A Draigon was seen in flight, leaving the hill of fire, and you ask us to believe Shaa is dead?" The old man of the group stepped forward. "You expect us to accept that you have succeeded in doing what generations of Draighil could not? Where is the proof that you have done what you say?"

"The proof is here before you," Trayor said. He reached down and whipped back the blanket. The woman's watery-dark hair flipped with the motion, settled back in a ragged fall across her torn torso. Her bright eyes, still undimmed and staring, gleamed through the dark strands.

The image pierced Cleod's faded vision, lodged in the back of his mind and spun there. A whistling ripped his hearing, and his breath shortened in his chest. He bowed his head and closed his eyes, need circling his gut like rats on a meal. Would this interminable jammering never end? Cuila. A bed. A drink. Those things he had earned this day.

"What is this?" The demand rose from the small short man who had questioned Cleod's status at the previous meeting. "We're to believe this corpse of a woman is a Draigon? Is *Shaa*? What kind of foolery is this? You expect us to pay your tribute, but you've nothing to show for your supposed battle but this...corpse? What are we supposed to do with this? How are we supposed to convince the people you have succeeded in killing Shaa, when Draigon Weather has not lifted in the least?"

Cleod raised his head, forced focus through swimming sight. The heat had not eased? Overlash had buried his senses deep enough that he had not noticed. He turned his head to stare out the window. Light played over the city, yet the dawn had brought none of the relief that usually marked the completion of Sacrifice.

Trayor took a step back, puzzlement on his face as he glanced toward the window, at the dust-blown street still baking in the sun. "It should have changed." He turned back to the Council, pointed at the body. "Her eyes. This is Shaa. What other creature has eyes like that? Tell me!"

Councilmen gathered around the body, but the old man shook his head.

"Witchery. What proof is this, when Draigon Weather still reigns?"

I leave them nothing. Of course. Cleod choked on a laugh, loud enough that the angry gathering turned to face him. "The *weather* is your proof." He raised a shaking arm and pointed out the window, at a whirl of dust raising itself in the street. "Shaa died in *human form*. Her death, like that —" He tipped his head to indicate the corpse. "Dying like that, would not change the weather. The drought was tied to her monster form. We're stuck with it, until we can find a way to make the Draigon change it again."

"Or Shaa died not at all!"

Cleod pulled himself around to face the cluster of men in their red tunics. Here, as everywhere in Arnan, the color of blood marked power. Arrayed before him, in his swimming sight, the crimson-clad figures bled into each other. "I faced Shaa on the Spur. I stared into its—*her*—eyes. *These same eyes.* Do you think, if we had failed last night, that either Trayor Draighil or I would be alive to stand before you? Test me, councilmen, and see how easy it is to accuse me of lies."

"So you say." The protest rose from the youngest of the Council, a thin man with thinner hair. "You who abandoned your profession after facing Shaa! Why should we trust any word you utter?"

Light streaked across Cleod's sight and, for a moment, what lay before him was not a room filled with men and anger, but a well-beaten trail and open sky and a row of wagons rolling into the distance... Abandoned. Cleod swayed. What had he done? Kilras could not rescue him from this. And what could not be salvaged, could only be completed.

Trayor's voice cut the air, burst the vision like a water bladder cast to the ground. "It was my sword that struck this creature down. This —" He pointed to the body, sprawled on the floor. "This stepped from the smoke where Shaa had stood. It shook the ground with its steps, and smoldered the air." He reached back, drew his sword and dropped it next to the corpse. The metal, stained and pitted, rang hollow against the floor. Streaks of corrosion marred, wavering over the blade. "That sword has cut through Draigon scale for decades and never suffered a mark. But last night, after killing *this*, it is as you see it now. What human has blood more corrosive than Draigon hide?"

The words were spears tossed through Cleod's thoughts. How had he not noticed the damage to Trayor's blade? What had Leiel become? Could her blood, too, scorch metal? Which was truly more dangerous, the Draigon, or the woman? His belly cramped, and he choked on bile as he forced himself not to curl around the pain. How badly did it show, the need turning his gut? The Overlash battering him? Longing rose up, tightened his chest, but this time for a firm hand on his shoulder and a voice in his ear that was not laced with rancor.

And it came to him, the true reason Draigon Weather remained unchanged. Why are there two Draigon in Melbis? Shaa had fallen, but Shaa had not wrought this drought. "The Draigon seen in flight...what color was it?"

Stillness as the men stopped their milling. "What?" the old man asked.

"*What color?*"

"Bronze. It was...bronze..."

Cleod heard the realization dawn in that reply. He trembled, but took a step forward, forcing steadiness into his legs. "Draigon are women. All the women you have sent to Sacrifice. All the women *ever sent anywhere.*"

Silence.

Then Trayor laughed. "Women," he said. "Every woman you have ever considered for Sacrifice. That's how we turn Draigon Weather. If these women are worth the Draigon killing and dying for, then they'll be what we use to make the Draigon lift the drought. Round them up. Everyone you've ever wanted to. We'll put them to good use."

CHAPTER 49

Leiel

The air lay dry and strange on her human flesh. She moved through the forest on a fall of pine needles so thick even the sticks layered among them were too cushioned to crack with her weight. Ahead, the glimmer of light from the campfire Teska had lit flickered a welcome. From fire to fire this night—one framing loss, the other an attempt at comfort, despite the fact that heat still reigned and would for as long as she decided it would. Tears slid over Leiel's cheeks. Her head was dense with them, caught behind her eyes and in her throat.

She stopped and tried a breath that stuck only half-inhaled. Then bent her head and let the sobs she had no wish to hold back shake her naked body from ragged hair to toes. For a moment, she thought she was simply melting in grief, as though her blood had turned molten and slagged her bones to liquid. The feeling was so like transition that for a moment she feared a shift. But the sensation rolled deeper even than that called up from the part of her that filtered knowledge and story into change. Only once had she felt the like, on a lonely, too-bright morning after flames lit the Spur and, she thought, carried away what was left of her mother. A simple prick of a pin was the horror of that morning, compared to this liquefying burn that now threatened to pull her into the earth. Age, experience, scale...what made Gahree's loss so brutal that nothing she had ever known could begin to compare? Did it matter? Did Gahree's death mean, any less than Ilora's had, that Leiel *must* go on? If there was no understanding to be found, this time, she must discover something that mattered in the wake of this terrible night.

Leiel heaved, sucked breath, trembled until shaking to pieces seemed a true possibility. Faces in her mind, smiles and laughter—Gahree, Cleod... Screams took over and flooded her with their flailing weight. Then a voice slipped through her mind. *Oh wild daughter, you have done well tonight. The healer is safe, and change is upon Arnan. Guide it with your hope and the aspects of your grief based in love, not rage or guilt. What is the point of the worst of you going forward? The story unfolds, and the end is yet to be spoken...* All music, all laughter, all welcome—the voice, real or imagined—cooled the fire in her bones, and drew air into her lungs. Gahree—Gahree—how do I tell the others what I have done? How do I tell them what we have yet to face because of me?

No answer came. How could one? Gahree was dead and lost, and whatever wisdom she wished upon Leiel in this moment, lived only in Leiel's idea of what the Draigon would have told her. And that existed as the most hopeful part of her need. Hope. Always, that had been Gahree's message. Could it still be called upon? Once, Gahree had infused it into Leiel's life so deeply that she had trusted that a death sentence was actually the best of all things— that Sacrifice was life and staying safe was death.

That Sacrifice was life... Leiel raised her head and blinked back tears. She found herself on her hands and knees in the pine needles and moss.

Sacrifice.

Once, it had stood for mayhem and loss and death. Then it had simply become ritual bringing new women and girls to Cyunant. But it had been, all along, a true giving up, a true surrender. It was giving over of the old for the new, the known for the mysterious, the feared for even more feared.

Sacrifice.

It was the thing Gahree and all the Draigon had always prepared for—much as they had prepared Leiel and so many others—as Leiel had learned to prepare others.

Sacrifice had been, perhaps, Gahree's plan all along. Maybe not today, but... With a jolt that set Leiel heaving, the truth of the inevitable settled deep into her bones. Gahree had known that, at some point, the Sacrifice would be *herself.*

Leiel shivered, sat back on her heels and wiped at her eyes. Gahree, why could you never speak without that rolling, cryptic humor? Outrageous things you said and meant and asked me to dream. Outrageous things you made me believe that I, too, was capable of. How I love you for all of that, and how I wish I had understood sooner that you would never name a thing Sacrifice without it truly being just that. I always understand, it seems, a bit too late.

That brought a laugh she could not even feel was inappropriate. Gahree loved to laugh. And nothing was more alive or more dangerous than a woman laughing when all the world seemed lost.

Leiel swallowed down the last of her sobs and pushed herself to her feet. Distant, through the trees, Teska Healer and a crackling fire beckoned. The questions also waiting there were as unavoidable as the sunrise.

The fine-woven wool trapped heat soft against her skin. She ran her hands over her arms and sighed. Over the fire, a pot of water steamed, the herby scent of tea rising to fill the glade. A ladle hung along one leg of the tripod supporting the pot. For an instant of twisted familiarity, Leiel let herself believe the woman seated cross-legged on the far side of the fire was Gahree. Then the woman turned, and Teska's dark eyes shoved aside the memory of a timeless, green-gold gaze.

Leiel blinked, and broke contact. The empty space her ring had occupied for so many years pulled a separate ache through her senses. She flexed her fingers, shook her head. With a frown, she reached up to twist back her hair as she looked back at Teska. The healer nodded, hands folded in her lap.

"I found tea, in one of the bags."

"Thank you." Leiel knotted a bit of twine around her plait. What to say? Her body was too light, brittle—a breath too deeply drawn could shatter her. And yet, Teska was her responsibility, and not one that could be abdicated or handled with the carelessness that had marked her latest efforts. Damn the over-confidence that had led to this day. She shut down further thought. No time, now, for self-pity or recriminations. Those would come later, if she and the woman across from her survived the next few days. The other Draigon would judge her before she had time to judge herself.

Leiel got to her feet, picked up a battered metal cup from the huddle of dishes beside the fire, and dipped tea. She passed the cup to Teska and chose another for herself. "I'm sorry," she said. "I am not the companion I would prefer to be this day."

Teska shook her head. "How could you be?" Her words caught a little, and Leiel looked over in time to see a single tear fall before Teska bowed her head.

Leiel went still, for a moment, unable to respond. Then she straightened her shoulders, gripped her steaming cup tight, and went around the fire to sit beside the other woman. "How could anyone be?" she said in agreement. "I never imagined—" She stopped. She could have, if she had thought through the consequences of her actions. Far too late, now, to dwell on that. Far too late to change anything. Only a single shocked truth could Leiel think to voice, and the words slipped out before she could contain them. "I did not believe that he was capable of such actions."

"He?" Teska raised her head.

Leiel pressed her lips together and met Teska's gaze. "The man who cut you." Leiel raised her hand and brushed fingers against her own throat. "I grew up with him, long ago. Once, before I became what I am now, we were friends."

"The tall man?" Teska asked. Her hand twitched, but she did not touch the red line across her neck. "He tried—I thought he was going to let me go. For a moment, he seemed to want to. But the other man, the Farlan man, the smoke he made—the Tall man's Enai changed when the smoke got thick and strange."

Leiel paused, lowered her cup from her lips. "Enai?"

"His...radiance." Teska spoke hesitantly, as though the concept she tried to impart was too strange to voice with clarity.

Leiel nodded. Long since familiar was the splendor of luminosity of the world seen through Gweld-touched eyes. "What of it?" Leiel asked, her head suddenly so hot she thought her hair might start to smolder. Teska had seen energy from Cleod? Of course. The very reason the Draigon had come here. Teska's world was lit by Gweld. For her, no shift, no change in focus, no act of will was required to see the vibrant plane of existence. Teska would have read Cleod's spirit the way Leiel read her favorite book.

"What did you see?" Leiel asked. Who was Cleod now? The violent man who had threatened murder? Was there anything left of the man she had watched on the trail, anything at all after the turmoil she and Trayor had injected into Cleod's life?

Teska drew a breath, let it out. "Grandmother told me the Draigon understand Gweld, but that it is different for you."

Leiel nodded. "I think it is different for most of us, each from the other. My mother and I see within it in a similar way, but we are family."

"What is it like for you?"

"Color," Leiel said. "Everything shines with different colors. And they change all the time. I have learned to understand what is happening in the world around me by watching them shift."

A nod from Teska acknowledged the explanation. "For me, it is about...density. I see Enai—from people, from animals, even from stones and trees and flowers. When all is as it should be, the Enai is clear. When things are wrong, or there is pain, or struggle, it becomes translucent, or even opaque.

"That Draighil, your friend, his Enai was battling itself. It was muddy at first, when he chained me to the pole..."

Leiel suppressed a flinch at the thought of Cleod fastening the bindings. He had done as much with her, but, somehow, him chaining Teska was harder to think about. She forced her attention back to the healer.

"But it changed throughout the day. I think there may be a bright edge to his being, when he is clear. Once, he stood straighter. He looked at me like he might really see me, and I could see through to him for a moment. But the other man, the Farlan man, he noticed. The fires they lit around me, he added something to the flames. It was bitter and smelled of pain, if such a thing can be. It filled the air and the tall man's Enai grew dense again."

"Cleod," Leiel said. "His name is Cleod."

"Cleod..." Teska repeated. She shook her head. "Cleod carries a terrible struggle inside himself."

"He was only there because of me." Leiel made the admission with a steady voice. That she could speak at all without her voice shaking might have surprised her, if she had been able to feel such after this night.

Teska shook her head. "He was there because he wanted to be."

Leiel frowned. "But you said he—"

"Struggle does not mean he did not choose to be where he was," Teska said. "I think he wanted to be there—but for his own reasons. Not for the reasons the other man forced upon him. Without the other Draighil, the tall man— Cleod—I think he still would have been there. But he might not have been there to kill."

Leiel sat back. Cleod was not, by nature, a killer. She had always known that. He was capable of killing, yes. Who wasn't, if circumstances bent enough? Yes, he had attacked her, but that had been a reaction annealed to the core of him by the Enclaves and their insidious teachings. She had not known, until he drew his sword against her, how deeply they had engraved their marks into his soul. The depth of their ongoing manipulations might as well be etched directly into his bones. Had anyone, even Kilras, suspected that?

No one except Trayor.

That man had known. And known Cleod well enough to turn that control to victory over not only Cleod, but over the strongest of the Draigon. Shaa had died for all their ignorance.

Leiel closed her eyes as rage pushed bile into the back of her throat. She choked it down, breathed deep, and made herself take a sip of tea. The smoke and heat of it slid through her, taking the anger, not away, but deep into her belly where it turned circles and knotted into a hard lump that she could hold tight and claim the weight of, and use to still her trembling soul.

"Cleod is strong." The words came quiet but firm. "But the Enclaves laid claim to him long ago, and I did not understand, until far too late, just how strongly they had done so." A log settled in the fire and she glanced at the new waft of sparks that rose in the aftermath.

"Two Draighil," Teska said. "How was that allowed?"

Leiel blinked, frowned. "Two Draigon as well." She shook her head. "No good that did."

"I'm sorry," Teska said. "You came for my sake."

"No," Leiel shook her head. "Neither of us can afford to let guilt take us over. This has happened. Now we must go on. We must get you north, and we must prepare for what is to come."

"To come?" Teska's words were soft and carried a tremor.

"Cleod knows about me. He knows the truth of what the Draigon are. And now, so does Trayor. Soon, all the Draighil will know. All of Arnan."

Teska swore a low-breathed oath so vile that Leiel sat back a fraction. Then Leiel laughed. "Yes!" she said. "I hope you know more phrases like that. I think I am going to use up all mine before we make it north."

The healer offered a small smile. "Another thing my grandmother taught me well. She used them often, to describe the leadership of Melbis—and most fools in general."

Again a laugh burst forth, and Leiel let it roll free.

Teska stared.

Leiel shook her head. "If I can laugh, we'll be all right, Teska Healer." Had Gahree been seated there with them, Leiel could not have heard the words more clearly. *Where there is laughter, there is hope, daughter of wings. Never doubt it. Never doubt yourself as long as you can still find humor within.* Leiel sent her own thought into the night. *I will hold true, my friend, my teacher, my courage. I will hold true because you believed I can, and I believed in you.*

She nodded to Teska. "Gahree always appreciated fierce laughter."

That roused a slightly stronger smile from the younger woman. "Very well. I shall try to laugh." She held silent a moment. "How long will it take us to get north?"

"I have no easy answer for you. You would be half-way there by now, if I had not had to come back and retrieve Gahree's things."

Truthfully, she could have asked the healer to pack up the camp, and then just flown them north, and waited for the comfort of Cyunant to look through Gahree's possessions. But the thought of someone else's hands on the embroidered pack... Not yet. Whatever Teska might become to her or among the Draigon, right now she was too much a stranger. Leiel swallowed. Or perhaps it was just a purely human need to touch that which had been her friend's.

Leiel got to her feet and crossed to the far side of the fire, lifted Gahree's pack from where it leaned against her own. She held it against her chest.

When she turned it to see the embroidered, dancing tree, would she find it changed? Or perhaps vanished altogether? She breathed through a tight throat. "Gahree would have carried you north, as I carried you here. But I cannot risk her secrets, even for a short time, to the hands of the Draighil and the Enclaves. They know from where we flew. They will be searching, since they know now, that we are only human at heart. That we, any of us, can die as easily as they." She stared down at the canvas bag in her hands. She had to look. She had to look and with all that she was, she did not want to see the damage the day had wrought upon that shining, glorious tree.

She swallowed, forced action, and turned the pack.

The tree was still there. And the leaves—the golden, shimmering leaves remained. Only the trunk had changed, darkened, thickened. And the tangled roots that snaked from its base seemed more abundant somehow.

Leiel's lips parted and she drew a slow, soft breath, as though to move quickly or with too much purpose, would disrupt the delicate threads. Then she laughed at herself. This bag was Gahree's. And Gahree would never carry anything that could not endure.

"Beautiful tree," Leiel said. "I am so glad to see you whole." She looked closer. More than whole. "I wish I knew your secrets, but those will have to wait." She tugged at the pack straps, folded back the top flap, hesitated. Never had she gone through Gahree's possessions, beyond fetching the occasional dented cup or bundle of maps. Leiel bent her head, and made herself open the drawstrings, and reach into the bag.

Two pairs of neatly folded pants, and three shirts, a bundle of warm, wool socks...the idea that a Draigon might have cold toes brought a smile. The maps came next, tightly tied in neat piles, marked with notes and organized by region and city. Beneath, a medicine wrap packed with herbs, a few hair sticks, and a comb. A half-dozen books... Simple things. What had she expected? A spirit as open as Gahree's needed only so much to sustain it.

Leiel set the pack down, hefted the books, and went back to sit beside Teska. "What languages do you read?"

The healer pulled her head back a little, and Leiel smiled. "Arnani, then." Not so long ago, she too had not considered that more languages might exist than the one she knew. The books piled in her lap covered half a dozen, but one with a soft green cover drew her eye. Leafing through it, she nodded at the appropriateness of Gahree's planning. "Gahree loved learning. She loved stories. She would be glad if you found use in this."

The healer said nothing as Leiel offered her the volume on rare plants, just accepted the book into a gentle grasp.

Leiel shifted through the small pile. She stopped when she spotted a familiar, leather bound volume barely the size of her hand. The Fenar translation book that had taught her so much, freed the stories that had given her the courage to reach for the liberty she now enjoyed.

Tears gathered in the back of her throat, but she swallowed them down before they reached her eyes. With hands far steadier than they should be, she opened the book. Familiar words. Familiar tales. From this she had learned how to read the true story of the witch in the woods... She turned another page, and reached quickly to catch the folded sheets of paper that fell from between the leaves.

Teska glanced up at the sudden motion. Leiel shrugged, set aside the book to unfold the paper. Gahree's wild scrawl greeted her.

Greetings Daughter of Wings—

Leiel, I write this knowing you will find it in a time of great pain and need. I could wish I was there to tell you this last story, but why waste a perfectly fine wish when I can simply write down what I need to share?

In this land of Arnan, there are some few who can become Draigon. Many have the strength and many have the spirit, but more is required than either of these things—something born deep in the bones which allows the taking of the Great Shape of Draigon. Thus, there are souls throughout the world who knowledge can carry only so far, and who courage can sustain, but not carry forth.

Your friend Elda is one such, as is the smith, Torrin, and so many others. And there are also those who could be Draigon, but have chosen to live in their born forms, for love or comfort, or a dozen other reasons I might name.

So many, Leiel, who value what the Farlan and their followers do not. So many who have been helped by us and who help us in return. And many more who know of us, as legend or whisper or fact.

We Draigon are few these days, strong on our mountain and our secret places, secure in our knowledge, but weak in the world. It could be that we have failed, all these years, by hiding and seeking only to protect what we have, rather than stepping forward and trusting that our value will be recognized once again. Or it could be that we are wise in our fears and worries, and have only done what was truly needed to keep our histories and our wisdom safe.

But the pattern we have so carefully nourished is not the one that has always existed, nor is it one that should exist, ongoing, as though it alone has value. You asked me about prophecy and I told you nothing so simple guided your fate. But you and Cleod have, from the moment I first watched you together, offered possibility that could render change across Arnan. Now that change has begun, and, as you are reading this, I am not with you to witness it unfold.

But others are, for we have readied them for years, and the list I have written on the following pages will tell you how to find them. Their skills and knowledge will be needed. Their voices, soft-spoken for so long, can perhaps, be raised at last. Some, you might approach gently, for they may not know how much they matter or the difference they can make. Others have been readying for years to step forward and stand for themselves and what matters most.

We are not unprepared for the coming change, though we might wish it would hold off a little longer, and leave us more time to laugh and dream and pretend we do not have greater work to do. My story ends in the middle of yours, but the tales you have yet to write are many and powerful.

Take care of Teska Healer. I leave in your care her value and her future. May your life be at least as long as mine has been, and only half as eventful.

With love and hope—

Gahree

Leiel stared at the ragged signature, smiled a little. Even writing a last message, Gahree had not bothered with something as irrelevant as neatness.

A swipe of a finger over Leiel's cheeks cleared tears. Change. She had learned from Gahree not to fear it, to seek within it only the things that would move toward a better future. With pain arrayed before her and turmoil building all around, the twisting luminous lines that marked the path to bright potential seemed thin and fragile. They glowed in her mind like gold thread woven though dark cloth, visible only if held at just the right angle.

She had to keep her grasp on that cloth, carry it home, see how many threads the others saw that she could not. Enough threads could weave a future worth creating. Leiel looked at Teska. Gahree's death had been to ensure this woman's life would continue, that her potential, *her* thread, would be part of the texture of the world. What Teska saw in all this would be as vital as anything Leiel could imagine.

Leiel handed the letter to the healer. "Read it," she said. "She believed in you. She believed in all of us."

Teska took the paper with a simple nod. "Thank you."

Leiel breathed deep and returned her attention to the rest of the pages. Gahree's list. More bright strands to be sought out and drawn into the light. Names, cities, occupations, short notes of telling information. A code, an unlinked army of strangers whose only commonality was their secret knowledge of, or friendship with, the Draigon.

She read, turned the page, smiled when she saw Torrin's name. Then her lips parted when she saw what was written after it. She borrowed Teska's oath, and the other woman started and turned a questioning gaze to the pages.

Leiel shook her head. "Surprise after surprise." She lifted the sheets. "An old friend who has always been more than he seems." She sighed. "What do you see when you look at me, Teska Healer?"

"I can't answer such a question. I see only when things are right or wrong for someone. For you, everything at this time is wrong. I cannot see what you might be, what you usually are, when you are calm and your Enai is not burning."

"Burning?" Leiel asked. But she knew what Teska saw. Every part of her was lit with urgency and longing—to get up and act, to go back and correct, to make *something, anything* happen to shake them free of the moment they were in. But this moment was more than an instant long, it would linger and follow them both, spread over all of Arnan in a wave of staggering knowledge—that Shaa, the mighty, terrible, blazing Shaa, was dead—and change, brutal and horrible, was poised to be loosed over all the land.

Chapter 50

Cleod

Women's faces woke him. Shaking, he stared up at the ceiling, the sweat slicking his body pooled against the small of his back, the sheet beneath him soaked and clammy. The ceiling above flapped and shifted. Outside, wind howled, sending dust whirling under shaking walls. Not a room. A tent. Not a bed. A cot. Hazy recollections. Doors slamming. Locks turning. Sobs echoing in dry air. Smoke and heat and blood.

He gasped, raised trembling hands to his head and pressed the heels of his hands to his eyes. His face was wet. Heaving a breath, he tasted tears. "Kil..." The Dorn's name slipped past his lips. The past days crashed over him, along with a rage that gagged him. He rolled onto his side, body heaving. A scream spiraled through his mind as he shook, the remains of whatever he had last eaten splattering into the dirt bedside the cot.

Pain erupted behind his eyes and he choked again, body convulsing. Fingers wrapped around the splintery cot frame as memory pulled at him, snatches of clarity between bursts of pain. Screams. Tear-filled eyes. Blows of resistance. His eyes snapped open and he stared at the scratches that covered his forearms. Old gods what had he done?

Faces. Women young and old dragged from their homes, through the streets. His hand turned a key in a lock.

His fingers uncurled their brutal grip, and he spread them wide as they shook. Other faces. Other eyes. Men, other women, shopkeepers, traders—faces twisted with anger or fear or glee—so much emotion, yet none backed by action. A chill pierced his shoulders. That would change. A shiver chased over his scalp and down his arms. The question ricocheted through his mind again. What had he done?

A gust of silt-charged air whipped into the room. "All your old gods be damned—can you go nowhere without leaving a stench?"

Cleod raised his head. Trayor stood in the tent doorway, its flaps whipping behind him in the grey light. "What is it now, Tray? It's barely dawn."

The Draighil knelt and added wood to the little stove in the middle of the space. A quarter turn of the flue backed sweet smoke into the air and Trayor coughed, looked at Cleod with bright eyes. "We're needed. The Council sent word—someone released the women we locked up. It will take Gweld to find them in this dust storm."

Cleod stared, a curse caught in his throat. His thoughts jumbled, twisted. Gweld...Overlash...Leiel's face flushed and tense with horror as she watched him pull the blade against Teska Healer's throat.

His stomach flipped again. No worse, that memory, than that of walking through Melbis backed by a gang of the Council's guards, knocking on door after door and dragging mothers and sisters and daughters from their home. Some fought, slapped and punched and slashed at him. Had he hurt anyone? Killed anyone? The night was a blur...

"Who died?" he whispered.

"What?"

"Did we kill anyone?" The words came louder, jerked from his throat.

Trayor laughed. "Useless. You can't remember your name from moment to moment like this. We killed Shaa. *I* killed *Shaa*."

"Who else?" Cleod demanded.

Trayor glared. "No one, *yet*. But don't think you get to live through this, cefreid. When the Draigon are wiped from Arnan, I'm going to take your head off. Now get up. We've a hunt ahead of us."

When the Draigon are wiped from Arnan. When they were dead. When Leiel was dead… Cleod choked on the thought, but…it was not entirely unwelcome. Leiel. The cause of all this. Blame…he was laying blame? On Leiel? Pressure built behind his eyes and he shook his head, though the action relieved nothing. What could relieve anything now? He swallowed back bile and reached for his boots. "How did they get loose?"

"They had help."

"You're surprised?"

"These people will learn to accept the unprecedented—"

"Or what? You'll kill them all?" Cleod stood, yanked his shirt over his head. "Whatever you think we're starting here, there are exactly two of us, against whatever elements of this town can rally against us."

"You're afraid of *these people*? If they had any strength, they wouldn't need us to fight the Draigon for them. We'll tear this town down if we need to."

Cleod shook his head, dizzy now, the heat and the smoke and Trayor's voice echoing in his skull. He lifted his sword harness, fastened it across his shoulders. "Have you said enough?"

Trayor snarled a curse of reply and shoved out of the tent into the faint light and blowing dust. It blasted over Cleod's face as he stepped outside, and he bent his head, reached for his brekko—realized a heartbeat later that he had neither the protective scarf nor his hat. His vision tipped, swirled with the sand, and need rose in his gut, but for the first time since the poit, it was for nothing consumable. Beyond hunger or pain, the urgency that welled in him escaped naming before he could identify it, and the snap of his name on Trayor's lips yanked him back into the moment.

Overhead, a patch of brighter sky flashed for a moment, and he glanced up into a streak of sunlight before blowing dirt smothered it.

"Move," Trayor said and led the way into the storm.

He was close. The wind had not completely wiped away their footprints where they wove and dodged between buildings. Damn the Council. They should be taking care of their own Draigon-damned messes. But they had only panicked at finding the cell doors open, and none among them had clear enough minds to take action. Only the fact that he and Trayor were camped nearby gave them any chance to recover the prisoners. Eight women on the run in a city now so clogged with soot and airborne dust that only senses trained beyond the normal human range could trace them.

Where did they think they had to go? Shadows blurred by blowing silt moved at the edge of the alley ahead. Cleod lengthened his stride, rounded the building to block the far end. Footsteps and harried breath told him his quarry drew near, but the figure that greeted him was not any of the scared girls he sought.

Kilras stepped out of the yellow haze.

Cleod jerked back, not just a motion through his shoulders, but an actual step he could not control. Then he straightened and met his old friend's gaze. "I'm not looking for you."

Kilras tipped his head to catch a gust of wind and dust with the brim of his hat. "Yes, you are."

At Kilras's shoulder, Sehina appeared, her hair tangled in fly-away strands. Cleod looked at her, then past her, as several wind-etched faces appeared over her shoulder. They looked back at him, steady and bold, no fear in their expressions. Just the way they had looked at him when he first turned the key in the lock of their cell. Here with Kilras. Here with Sehina.

The shattered locks...

"No," he said, as a knot twisted at the base of his spine. He shifted his gaze to Kilras, met the Dorn's eyes.

Kilras gave a single nod and stepped forward. "You *are* looking for us. Now you have to decide whether you've found us or not." The Dorn's hand dropped to the hilt of his sword, and his fingers wrapped the hilt with firm surety.

Cleod's throat went dry. He shook his head, slowly. "Don't, Kil."

"I don't want to." Kilras's gaze did not waver.

"Shaa is dead."

"And the Councils think that negates the agreement with the Draigon?" Kilras flicked his gaze at the sky, grey-gold with silt and blowing dust and ash. "This is the Draigon's response to that thinking. There will be no lift in the Weather as long as the terms of the agreement are ignored."

"The Draigon are liars. The Draigon are *human.*"

Kilras shook his head. "The Draigon are what they have always been."

Cleod reached back and drew his blade, the steel singing out of its scabbard.

"Kil—" Sehina's voice trembled like the swirling dust, but it was rage, not fear, that Cleod heard in her voice.

"Take them and go, Sehina," Kilras said. He stepped sideways, narrowing the angle between Cleod and the women.

A tremor burned Cleod's muscles. He moved to go around the Dorn. But Kilras blocked him again.

Cleod froze. "Draigon damn you, Kil, what are you *doing?*"

The Dorn flashed a grin far larger than made any sense at all given the situation. Damn him for being ever the optimist. "What I have always done. I'm taking in strays."

Cleod's jaw dropped open a fraction and he stared. In that instant of hesitation, Sehina grabbed the hand of the first woman and bolted down the lee side of the nearest building. Before Cleod could move, the others followed, disappeared in the swirling dust.

"It's not like you to be slow, old friend," Kilras said. "I can only assume you don't want to catch them, any more than you want to harm me. You're being used, Cleod, by the Councils and the Enclaves—just like you were before."

A laugh barked free, torn from the deepest well of Cleod's gut. "I know that." His very blood burned, and the taste of cuila lingered in the back of his throat so that every swallow washed it straight through him.

"Come back," Kilras stepped toward him. "You know I can help."

Cleod shook his head, belly tight. Trembling he could not control crawled over him, feet to shoulders, until the sword jerked so hard in his hand that he forced himself to return it to its sheath before he dropped it. "Not this time," he said. He straightened, stepped away, his chest so tight that he had to think about each breath. "It's gone too far. This is what I am meant to be."

"No one is meant to be anything," Kilras said. "You have choices."

"I chose long ago."

"You don't have to go with Trayor."

He stared at Kilras for a hard, bitter moment, then shook his head. "Yes, I do." The words tore through him, shearing his throat like splintered metal. Air heaved in his chest, half choking him, and his eyes burned as he blinked back the moisture trying to gather there. Even when he blinked, the back of his eyelids held the image of the Draigon woman sprawled in the ashes and blood and dirt of her death. And Leiel's screams, mingled with the ones trapped inside him.

But he had *wanted* it.

He ached to his bones, from the tragedy unfolding, and for the cuila that assuaged both longing and guilt. "There's only one thing to do now. Finish it. Finish and be damned."

"You're not damned." Kilras took another step closer. Once the confidence behind those words would have been a lifeline. Now, it was simply an echo lost in a storm spiraling out of control.

Another shudder rocked Cleod. With a sound that was half animal snarl, he turned away, put his back to anything that might be salvation and walked away though the rising wind.

"Cleod!" Kilras called—and everything was in that simple cry—friendship and shelter and forgiveness and the last of anything Cleod might call hope. Everything he no longer deserved, if ever he had.

"Cleod...stay!"

He kept walking, the sanctuary implied in the Dorn's words abandoned behind a wall of blowing dust.

About Paige L. Christie

She Writes Stuff

JordanCon 2024

Paige L. Christie is originally from Maine and now lives in the North Carolina mountains. She is best known for the Legacies of Arnan fantasy series: Draigon Weather (2017), Wing Wind (2018), Long Light (2019), Storm Forged (2022.) Her work can be found in several collections, including Galactic Stew, Witches Warriors & Wise Women, and several More Tales of Valdemar anthologies.

As a believer in the power of words, Paige tells stories that are both entertaining and thoughtful. Especially of interest are tales that speak to women and open a space where adventure and fantasy are not all about happy endings. When she isn't writing, Paige runs a non-profit soup kitchen and food pantry, herds SO MANY cats, and dreams of cheese. She is a proud, founding member of the Blazing Lioness Writers. Sign Up for Her Newsletter at PaigeLChristie.net!

facebook.com/paigelchristie

instagram.com/paigelchristie

Also by the Author

More Words to Savor

Novel Series

The Legacies of Arnan

Draigon Weather – The Legacies of Arnan: Book One
Wing Wind – The Legacies of Arnan: Book Two
Long Light – The Legacies of Arnan: Book Three
Storm Forge – The Legacies of Arnan: Book Four

Stand Alone

Shorts in Anthologies

"Blue" in *Galactic Stew* from Zombies Need Brains
"A Devil to Help" in *Witches, Warriors, & Wise Women* from Prospective Press
"Green Dreams" in *Become Legend: The 2020/2021 JordanCon Anthology*
"The Mercy of the Lorn" in *Neither Beginnings Nor Endings: The 2022 JordanCon Anthology*
"And They Lived" in *The Leaf Does No Harm: The JordanCon 2023 Anthology*
The Tieg Stories in *More Tales of Valdemar #s 14-18 from DAW Books*

Acknowledgements

Thanks are given to the following amazing people:

Brett Lester Christie: My little brother, who chooses courage and compassion every day. For being smart, and funny, and kind, and a critter lover, and a brilliant artist. I'm so proud you're my brother! (And I'm still bigger than you.)

Ellen Morrissey & Rebecca Sanchez Hefner: My fellow Blazing Lionesses—For providing endless inspiration and encouragement, destroying plot holes, asking the hard questions, scratching out all the bad words, and never telling me it was good when it wasn't. This book, like the first, would not exist without the two of you. Endless love to you both!

Jennifer "Clyde" Webster, Supreme Benevolent Dictator of the Universe: For storming the capital with me, and always encouraging me to fight the good fight, both on the streets and with these words in print. More adventures! More chocolate!

Patti K. Christie, World's Greatest Mama: For keeping me laughing and hoping even when times are tough, and always having the courage of your heart.

Julie Thorner, Traveler of the world and the Spirit Roads: For taking me places I would never otherwise have gone. For believing in me when I could not believe in myself. For your time, and your trust, and your support. Words will never be thanks enough.

Michelle, Ohia, & Keith at Liquid Spark Marketing: For answering Julie's call and building me the most gorgeous website on the planet. You are all amazing!

Sue, Rose, Cheryl, & Molly, the Goddesses of Land's Creek Log Cabins: For making the hardest work fun and offering support in my time of need. Your hearts are as open as your hands are hardworking and I love you all!

Debra Mills, Basket Goddess and Art Supporter: For space, and time, and patience, and laughter, and hugs when things got rough.

Tsering Tso, Arè, Dromla, all the women of Maigong Village, and the Ani's of Damo Nunnery: Your strength and spirit, your love and generosity, are an inspiration. Thank you for sharing the Holy Land with me.

Ffion Wyn Morris, Wordsmith of Wales: For the fabulous translation of "Stones, Offered Freely."

All the folks who bought Draigon Weather and made this second book possible—You keep me writing!

LONG LIGHT CHAPTER 1 (PREVIEW) THE LEGACIES OF ARNAN: BOOK 3

Kilras - 47 years

Night held Melbis in dusty silence as moonlight silvered the stone-laid yard behind the Nest. Kilras made his way toward the tiny building in the center of the desiccated garden. The muscles of his arms and back hummed with tension, and the hand resting on the sword hilt at his hip tingled in too-warm anticipation of potential necessity. He stood, gaze scanning the night for a threat undetermined but present enough to vibrate long-untapped senses.

Only the dry whisk of breeze over dead plants and the creak of the Nest's weathervane sounded in the night air. No noise at all came from the poit building. A few steps from the door, Kilras stopped, waited. The innkeeper's words had carried stark warning — a man of the Enclaves had met Cleod when he returned to the Nest.

Kilras listened, worry twisting through him. No motion. No sound. He reached for the poit door. The wooden handle was smooth, and the door swung open with silent ease. Warm air, thick with a bitter permeation of burnt sage and seared blood, rolled out to greet him. Kilras pulled back, opened the door wider, and the brutally concentrated weight of the narcotic-laced air spilled around him, dissipating into the night. Undernotes of other odors touched his nose. Sweat and anger and the thick desperation of fear. Kilras's throat burned and he gagged, his heart pounding. Gweld awareness flashed and he stepped back, let the air clear. *Cleod*. By all the trails they had traveled together, what had happened here?

A brittle breeze kicked through the dusty air, thinning the toxic waft from the poit, and Kilras inhaled deeply of the clean air in which he stood, held his breath, then stepped inside.

On a narrow shelf above the small wood stove, a small lamp burned, its pale glow flickering into the close space, offering enough light to clearly display the marks of struggle that marred the wooden benches and walls. Dark streaks of blood, splintered wood, and a finger-width smear of charred material that might be flesh along the hot edge of the stove.

Cuila. Pungent and powerful. Almost, Kilras *reached*, but long-trained effort stopped instinctive response. He backed out of the space and let the door swing closed. It quivered as it contacted the frame, vibrating like the tension lacing his body. He pushed air out through his mouth.

Cleod. Poit. *Cuila.* The scent answered the question of why, and of how, but not who. But who else? Draigon Weather. Two Draigon in Melbis. The Enclaves. Trayor.

A series of curses rolled through Kilras's thoughts. He scanned the ground in the faint light offered by the moon, but nothing marked a direction he might follow. Again, old knowledge demanded action, but he held back. Always, the possibility existed that a time would come when the true depth of his skill would be required, and several times through the years he had thought that moment had arrived. Each time, as now, he resisted. Because any way was better than the danger that could arise from exposing the full range of his competence, or the danger of it slipping his control.

He crouched, touched a finger to a dark drop on the flagstones. Whatever had left the stain had long-since dried. Blood? He rose and looked around, slowly taking in the shadowed details of the garden. One way in from the building. One way out through the back gate. Lorrel, the innkeeper, had seen nothing. Kilras walked toward the fence, lifted the latch on the gate and pulled it open.

In the street behind, he stood for a long time. From here, Trayor could have taken Cleod anywhere. A waiting horse. A cart. Enough people passed this way it was impossible to discern which tracks to follow.

But Trayor had not acted without purpose. The back of Kilras's skull tingled and an old memory surged forth, backed by the pure unease that had flooded him four years before when he raised a glass to drink to an old friend's passing. As then, the hot urge to *act* lit the edges of his senses. He forced it back. Draighil never acted without purpose. Two Draigon in Melbis.

And two Draighil.

This time, the curse that rose in his mind slipped forth unrestrained. Sweat slid down his spine, and he shook his head. Only five years had passed since the last Sacrifice in Melbis. Why were the Draigon back? Who mattered so much? Mattered enough to draw Shaa off the mountain? To draw Leiel with her? But Trayor — Kilras swore again.

How long had this been planned?

Kilras bent his head. No safe way existed to track Cleod until the sun rose, not when he had to consider Sehina and Rimm and Nae — and those in their care.

How much did Trayor know? How much did he suspect?

Did it matter?

Whatever was in play, the roots of it had been planted years before. And it had been set in motion so quietly that none of Kilras's contracts had enough warning to say a word. The danger posed by whatever had been initiated tonight was incalculable.

Heart tight, breath an ache, Kilras turned and made his way back through the dark streets toward the caravan camp. Preparations needed to be made. And decisions. If he could not find Cleod, reach him before the Sacrifice was named, any weakness in planning could have irrevocable consequences.

Definitions

Places & Terms of Arnan

Adfen (AD-fen): The capital city of The Spur region; former educational center of Arnan.

Anyaluft Rayyat (anya-LOOFT Ray-YAT): The Great Desert in the Southwest of Arnan. Desert bordering the trade roads and down toward the southwest coast toward Bajor.

Bajor (BAY-jor): The major trading port on the west coast of Arnan. Southwestern point of the main trade roads.

Blayth Hound: Wild dogs not native to Spur region, trained for guard dogs/attack dogs

Brekko: Face cover made by the desert traders designed to keep out dust and debris in desert wind

Bynkrol (BIN-krol): Another Enclave located in Oryok

Cefreid (KEH-freed): Farlan term for someone not of Farlan descent

Cuila (CUE-la): Vision Mint, used to poison awareness to change brain chemistry for permanent changes allowing Gweld state to be maintained. Used early in Draighil training.

Dorn: The Trail lead of a merchant caravan

Draigfen: Draigon Woman - Draigon Touched Woman: one who has been influenced by a Draigon

Draighil: Draigon Slayer trained by the Enclaves

Draigon: Gigantic flying creature to which the Farlan sacrifice women to counteract Draigon Weather

Draigon Weather: Extreme drought conditions caused by the presence of Draigon

Draigre (DRAIG-ray): Candidate for the position of Draighil

Draigdyn: Draigon Man – Draigon Touched Man

Drearloc: Carnivorous insects that travel in large groups underground, and emerge to devours any animals above ground. Travel in large groups.

Ehlewer (EH-lewer): Located in The Spur - One of the Enclaves in charge of training Draighil

Enclave: Farlan organizations in charge of training Draighil

Eroganke (ER-oh-GANK-ay): One of the two gods worshiped by the Sanctuary priests - "The God of Belief"

Ercew (ER-kew): Strong alcoholic beverage that is highly addictive

Farlan (FAR-lann): Descendant of the Far Landers

Fen: Fennar word for woman

Fennar: The language of the old people of Arnan and of the Draigon - Woman's Words

Giddor (GIHH-door): Smaller port on the South-Southeast Coast

Gweld: Trance state allowing expansion of senses, and hyper-natural physical and mental response. Also allows limited connection of multiple consciousnesses, and projection of illusions.

Hlewlion: Mountain cat, cunning and very dangerous

Ilris (ILL-ris): Southern Central, North of the Trade Roads where Spur country fades to the plains.

Kittown: Town located two days ride east of Bajor on the edge of the Anyaluft Rayyat. Known for its glass artisans

Oryok (OR-yok): North East port city. The major east cost trade port on the East coast of Arnan. Eastern point of the Trade Roads.

Overlash: The physical and psychological backlash that comes as the aftermath of using the Gweld state.

Poit: Steambased bathing chamber similar to a wood-fired dry sauna

Ruhelrn (RUhellern): The Lead Sword of a Caravan

Sibora (Seh-BORRA): Capital of the Land of Arnan. Location of the Palace of the King. Central City known for arts and wine and fine food and drink. The largest city in Arnan. Known also for fine Inns, spas and Memorial Garden.

Trachwant (TRAYK-want): One of the two gods worshiped by the Sanctuary priests - "The God of Desires"

For Jack

Made in the USA
Columbia, SC
13 February 2025

53744514R00159